By the same author:

THE G-STRING MURDERS

MOTHER FINDS A BODY

GYP

S Y

A Memoir by Gypsy Rose Lee

With an Introduction by Whoopi Goldberg and an Afterword by Erik Lee Preminger

A Fireside Book Published by Simon & Schuster, Inc. New York

Library of Congress Cataloging-in-Publication Data

Lee, Gypsy Rose, 1914–1970.
  Gypsy : a memoir.

  Reprint. Originally published: New York : Harper,
1957.
  "A Fireside book."
  1. Lee, Gypsy Rose, 1914–1970.   2. Entertainers—
United States—Biography.   I. Preminger, Erik Lee.
II. Title.
PN2287.L29A3   1986   792.7'028'0924 [B]   86-6482
ISBN 0-671-62286-2 Pbk.

To ERIK, my son,
So he'll stop asking so many questions

INTRODUCTION

I discovered Gypsy Rose Lee one Saturday afternoon when the film *Gypsy* played on the *Million Dollar Movie* on Channel 9. For me, she quickly became an inspirational figure, someone I could follow in my imagination as she floated from world to world, and who eventually showed me how to do the same. She was a highly ethical woman, an elegant maverick who single-handedly transformed a low-brow entertainment into high art with her intelligence, wit, playfulness, and unerring sense of self-preservation.

There were many things I admired about her: the way her poise and brains showed through whether she was peeling off her garters in front of a packed burlesque house or entertaining the luminaries of her day at home, against the equally dramatic backdrop of her extensive personal art collection. Then there was the mischievous and inventive sense of humor that used everyone from Nietzsche to Lee herself as fodder. And then there was the way that she slipped from persona to persona like a chameleon. This was a woman who played with and enjoyed her image as deftly as she made her art, keeping both her public and her friends continually fascinated and entertained. One day she invited the columnist Walter Winchell to see her show and surprised him with a special routine based on his piece of that morning. Then, there was the surprise of her murder mysteries, which had a stripper named Gypsy Rose Lee as their protagonist (a device that ingeniously—and characteristically—drew even more attention to the author by way of both sheer gall and charm, not to mention talent). Finally, came this book, *Gypsy*, as classy and witty and brazen as everything that had come before. It became a musical, and then a film, which I eventually saw on the *Million Dollar Movie*, and you know the rest.

Underneath it all, I think, was a very realistic woman with a very accurate assessment of herself, her work, and the times she lived in. Gypsy Rose Lee was a true artist who combined unrelated traditions of entertainment into a totally new and unique form that—ever so gracefully—forced her audiences to reexamine their assumptions about high-brow and low-brow; and the relationship between brains, money, and sex. Yes, Gypsy Rose Lee was a woman way ahead of her time, a stripper and the most eloquent woman of her day—received by kings, queens, and presidents. Which proves that no matter what you do, as long as you do it with class and style, it's acceptable in a tight-ass world.

Ladies and gentlemen, I give you *Gypsy*.

—Whoopi Goldberg

P R O L O G U E

1

THIS WAS MY LAST farewell tour. I've made six, more or less, but Las Vegas would be the end. Less determined minds than mine might have been influenced by the crowd that gathered around me at the station. People were poking their heads into the car, trying to get a better look, scratching up the fenders with their scuffling, and shoving pieces of paper at me for my autograph. Twenty years ago I would have accepted all this as a tribute. I know better now.

Unlike most Rolls Royces, which are sedate black, mine, made to order when I was playing the London Palladium, is maroon and gray with my initials on the door in gold. Twenty-seven pieces of luggage, including five Siamese cats, in two plastic dome-type carriers, a guinea pig, and two turtles in a fish bowl were being unloaded from the car by a redcap. Erik, my eleven-year-old son, supervised the job, while I posed, showing a bit of leg, for a picture. The press photographer had thoughtfully brought along a toy-sized suitcase which I held in one hand. The other hand held my skirt, lifted to the garter line. The caption of the picture was to read, "Gypsy Rose Lee and Her Las Vegas Costumes."

I didn't need a crystal ball to see why a crowd had gathered.

Erik, with a practiced eye, counted the luggage. Besides the seventeen Vuitton suitcases, hatboxes and shoebags, there were the scenery, make-up box, music, typewriter, a portable television set,

Erik's stamp album and school books, a wicker lunch basket and a net shopping bag filled with oranges, jelly beans, cat food, dried bugs for the turtles, graham crackers and magazines. The trunks had gone on ahead.

Tattered hotel stickers covered the suitcases. Where they hadn't peeled off you could almost follow our route: The Ritz, Paris; Savoy, London; Oriental, Bangkok; Moumounia, Marrakech. There were others from Rome, Oslo, India and Australia. Some of the stickers were faded now. It had been a year since my last long tour. During that time I had been playing night clubs in Vancouver, San Francisco, Buffalo and wherever I could. There had been seven weeks in summer theatres, too, and a few television shows. Las Vegas would wind up the season. A season like so many others I have almost lost count. There have been seasons in a carnival, vaudeville, night clubs, Hollywood, but since 1931 the act has stayed pretty much the same. H. L. Mencken called me an ecdysiast. I have also been described as deciduous. The French call me a déshabilleuse. In less-refined circles I'm known as a strip teaser.

Erik and I have a house on East Sixty-third Street in New York. It has twenty-six rooms, a marble floor in the drawing room, a pool in the patio, an elevator and seven baths scattered about, but we don't spend much time there. We're usually on the road. I try to arrange my bookings in such a way that we can be home for Christmas, but this isn't always possible. This year, for instance, we would be in Las Vegas. One Christmas we were in Spain; I was making a film there. Another Christmas we were in Paris while my costumes were being made. One awful Christmas we spent driving through a blizzard to Miami where I was booked in a night club. Erik opened his presents that night under a tinseled tree in a hotel lobby in Richmond, Virginia. He was four then and it had been difficult explaining to him how Santa Claus knew we were going to check into that particular hotel when we hadn't known it ourselves.

Erik's belief in Santa Claus was shattered the following year in Dayton, when we ran into Tiny Pierson, a comic I had worked with in Michael Todd's *Star and Garter*. Tiny was doubling, between shows, as Santa Claus for the local orphanages. With his round pink

face and big fat stomach he was most convincing, but when Erik
was sitting on his lap he noticed that Santa's beard was coming
loose. Leaning closer, he smelled the glue. "That's spirit gum!"
Erik exclaimed. "Like Mommy uses to glue on her brassière with."

Later, when he had thought it over, Erik was glad to know Santa
Claus was an actor. "It's nice," he said, "having him in our business."

This year we had celebrated our Christmas before we left for
Las Vegas. We get more presents that way. It's too easy for people
to forget you if you're on the road all the time.

We had arrived in Chicago at two thirty the following day. The
prospect of a three-hour stopover wasn't too pleasant. A misty rain
clouded the skyline. People walked about with their heads pulled
down into their coat collars. They looked cold and miserable.

The cab driver opened the door invitingly. "Where to, lady?"

"Henrici's," I replied, almost from force of habit. They serve
good coffee, it is right down town, but most important, they have
no objections to pets. Erik's face lighted up at the name. "Isn't that
where you had your birthday party when you were in the Ziegfeld
Follies?"

I tried to remember.

"It was when you hurt your foot and had to do the act sitting
down." Erik said. My son has a memory like mine, sharp and clear
for the trivia; but unlike me, he remembers names and dates. Next
to Jules Verne, his favorite literature is my scrapbooks. The family
history is very important to him.

"That was about 1937, wasn't it?" he asked. "Were you married
to your first husband then?"

"No dear. That wasn't until later—I think."

"It couldn't have been *much* later," he insisted. "You married my
father in 1942 and you'd been divorced from—"

"We'll talk about it some other time," I said.

After lunch we left the cats and the turtles in the check room at
the restaurant. Erik put his guinea pig in his pocket and we started
out for a walk. The mist had lifted and a wintry sun made everything yellow hued. Erik and I walked on silently, stopping from
time to time to glance into a window; then suddenly the street
seemed to change. I looked around expecting to see the Oriental

Theatre, which I had played in vaudeville; or the Shubert; where
I'd appeared for weeks in the Follies; or the Frolics Night Club, or
even the Rialto Burlesque House. I didn't see any of these land-
marks, but I knew the street. It was as familiar to me as home is to
some people.

There was an old sign, hanging a bit crooked. The electric lights
had burned out here and there, but I could make out the lettering
HOTEL GRANT. Below, in smaller letters, was ROOMS $2.00 AND UP.
I looked up at a window overlooking the letter H and saw the dingy
net curtains, the green shade that used to roll up suddenly and flap
against the pane; the same noisy El roared by, and I remembered
how it used to shake the bed when my sister and I shared the room
with Mother and the six little boys in the act slept in the room next
to ours. I almost expected to see Mother leaning out the window,
yelling at me to be careful when I crossed the street.

"I used to live in that hotel," I said to Erik. "A long time ago,
when I was a little girl."

Walking closer Erik and I passed the all-night movie theatre that
used to run features like *The Road to Ruin,* and *What Every Young
Girl Should Know.* The current attraction was *Striporama,* starring
Georgia Sothern and Lily St. Cyr. Erik slowed down to gaze at the
rather startling photographs out front. An odor of stale beer wafted
through the ventilator of a bar-and-grill next to the theatre. It had
been a chili parlor when I was a child; now great slabs of corned
beef and pastrami were piled high in the steamy window. "What
has happened," I thought idly, "to all the chili parlors?"

In front of the hotel I held my hands to the sides of my face so I
could see into the dimly lighted lobby. There were the same old
brown leather chairs, and the elevator, like a bird cage, with the
piece of wood used to keep the door open between trips. The reception desk was where it used to be, but the board with the keys
hanging from it had been replaced with more modern mail slots.

Erik held his hands to the side of his face, the way I did, and
peered into the lobby. "You lived here?" he asked, a note of sympathy and disbelief in his voice.

"It was nicer in those days," I said, but as I said it I wondered.
I saw again the washbasin in the corner of the room, the bare elec-

tric light bulb hanging from the ceiling and the big spot on the carpet the chambermaid had tried to blame on Mother's dogs.

"Is this the hotel where you met that man with the suitcase filled with pickled babies?"

"No dear. That was the Brevoort in St. Louis. This is where my pet monkey burned his hand on the Christmas-tree candle—"

"And where Aunt June broke her front tooth kissing her doll? And where your mother booked the act at an Elk's smoker by mistake?"

Was it by mistake? I remember we had taken a streetcar to the lodge hall. Mother had carried the music, the boys carried our costumes divided between them, and June and I had the gilded guns and make-up. It had been a long ride on the streetcar and when we finally got there the head Elk wouldn't let us go on. "I had no idea it was a kid act," he kept saying. "This is a smoker. A stag party. This is no place for kids!"

"I don't care what it is," Mother had said. "I have a contract, and you either play us or pay us!" Then when she saw the man was adamant, she told June and the boys and me to wait in the dressing room, and pushing open the door to the stage she faced the audience and almost spoiled their entire evening by making a speech. It must have been a good one, because after it one of the less important Elks had passed a hat and when Mother came back to the dressing room to get us she had more money than we would have earned had we played the date. Ushering us past the head Elk Mother sailed out of the lodge hall. "He'll think twice," she said, "before he tries to cheat another helpless woman." I wasn't sure it had been by mistake. Mother didn't make many of them.

"I wish I'd been in the act with you and Aunt June and the boys," Erik said. "But I guess your mother couldn't have found a place for me. I can't sing or dance or do anything."

"I couldn't sing or dance, either," I said, "but she found a place for me."

"Your mother," Erik said, "must have been a very nice woman."

I couldn't help smiling at the word. Mother had been many things, but she had never been "nice." Not exactly. Charming, perhaps, and courageous, resourceful and ambitious, but not nice. Mother, in a feminine way, was ruthless. She was, in her own words, a jungle mother, and she knew too well that in a jungle it doesn't pay to be nice. "God will protect us" she often said to June and me. "But to make sure," she would add, "carry a heavy club."

ACT ONE

2

MY SISTER, JUNE, was two and a half years old when Mother and Father were divorced. I was four. We had been going to dancing school for six months. June could dance on her toes, like a ballet dancer, even before we went to dancing school. Father, who was a reporter on the Seattle *Times,* didn't approve of dancing lessons, perhaps because of the expense, but Mother believed in starting things early. After the divorce we went to live with Grandpa. He had built a little house in West Seattle and there was an extra room for just such an emergency. The house was near a dancing school, but Grandpa was sorry about that. Like Father, he didn't approve of theatricals, as he put it. Piano lessons, yes. And singing lessons. Those were accomplishments a young lady could display in her own parlor. But not toe dancing. "It's a waste of good money," he would say to Mother. "Wait until the girls are a little older, then have them trained for a decent livelihood. Like schoolteaching or—"

"But, Papa," Mother would tell him impatiently, "Professor Ballard says June is a natural-born dancer. Why, she's double-jointed in every bone in her body."

"He's a natural-born liar," Grandpa would say. "Always has been. All he wants is that fifty cents an hour. Double-jointed! Poppycock! And what if she is? Is that any reason to capitalize on the child's deformity?"

My sister wasn't deformed. She wasn't even double-jointed, although in those days any child who could do the splits or stand on her toes was thought to be.

June looked as though she belonged in the theatre. Her eyes were large and very blue, with deep circles under them. Even before Mother touched up June's hair with peroxide, it was bright yellow. Her legs were long and wiry, with bumpy knees. Mother massaged the bumps every night with cold cream, but they never went away. Even had this been serious it wouldn't have mattered because Mother's mind was made up. Her daughters were going to have a theatrical career.

We made our debut, with Grandpa's half-hearted permission and his money for costumes, at one of his lodges. It was a Knights of Pythias celebration following the installation of officers, and Grandpa played piano for us. He played for the installation of officers, too; it was because of his connection with the lodge that Mother managed to book our act. I sang "I'm a Hard-boiled Rose" in a tough costume—a sweater and skirt, a feathered hat and striped stockings—but the evening belonged to my sister. From the moment she stepped on the stage in her pink tarlatan ballet dress with a butterfly in her hair, the audience was hers.

Mother stood in the wings and prompted June as she danced. "The rose step," Mother would say, her voice carrying to the back of the lodge hall. "Smile, dear, smile. That's right. Now, arabesque, arabesque."

June smiled and did the arabesque. Grandpa played the piano by ear so he didn't have to keep his eyes on the score, but he never once glanced up at June. It was the only way he had left to express his disapproval. The audience applauded wildly and June took bow after bow and said, "Fank you," in a clear high-pitched voice. "Fank all of you."

The next day my sister's picture appeared in the papers, under the caption KNIGHT'S GRANDDAUGHTER DANCED. Grandpa bought ten copies of the paper and clipped the notice from each of them. He pasted one in his scrapbook, next to a clipping on the perils of drink, and sent the others to friends and relatives including Big Lady, my grandmother.

Big Lady traveled a lot. Sometimes months would go by before she would get home to Seattle. Grandpa didn't approve of Big Lady's jaunts but there wasn't much he could do about them. She would pack a trunk with expensive-looking hats and travel to Juneau, or Tonopah or any place where ladies went who could afford the elaborate hats Big Lady made and who were flashy enough to appreciate them. Once Big Lady packed a trunk with corsets, some of them embroidered with real gold threads, and others trimmed with beads and lace, and went to Goldstream, Nevada. My earliest recollection of Big Lady is when she returned home from that trip. We were still playing the lodge halls and my Grandma Dottie was alive. When Grandpa told me the tall elegant woman was my grandmother I couldn't believe it. I already had one grandmother so I named the new one who wore such lovely clothes and smelled so good the Big Lady.

When Big Lady was home, between jaunts, she would exhibit her needlework at fairs and expositions and often she would win. Grandpa's letters to us during those times were happy and hopeful. He was always sure that this time Big Lady was home to stay. Then a few weeks later he would write us that she was on her way to a lumber camp near Spokane with a trunkful of handmade nightgowns, or off to Bisbee, Arizona with a load of embroidered shimmies. The fairs and expositions were nice, but the flashy ladies paid better. No one knew this as well as Big Lady.

The day after our debut Grandpa looked over at me, then at June, who was practicing her "rose step." "You may be right at that about June," he said to Mother. "She might do pretty well in theatricals. I still don't think it's the life for Plug though."

Plug was my nickname, and I lived up to it. I was big for my age and more than just chubby. My hair was cut short in a Dutch bob, with bangs, and my teeth came to a peculiar point in front. They were going to be straightened when I was nine years old. That was the plan and Grandpa put away a little money each month to pay the dentist. But by the time I was nine, we had been in show business, off and on, for five years and there was no longer any time for teeth straightening. Besides, Mother had spent the dentist money. "Shoes are more important at the moment," she said when she drew the money from the bank. "We'll fix the teeth later." Then, because Mother liked to justify everything twice, she added, "The braces would show from the audience, anyway."

The braces might have shown, but I don't think the audiences we played to would have cared. All I did in the act was sing "I'm a Hard-boiled Rose" and for that I didn't need teeth and Mother knew it.

June's talent carried the act. June's talent and Mother's courage. Mother wasn't surprised to find show business competitive. She had expected that and was prepared for it. From the first, Grandpa's lodges were a great help. Besides the Knight of Pythias, Grandpa belonged to seven others. He played the piano free for all of them and Mother thought that when they had an entertainment the very least they could do was to engage his granddaughters. We played all eight lodges many, many times.

When we played on the same bill with another kiddie act, things always seemed to go wrong for them. Pieces of their wardrobe would be missing. A toe shoe would get burned. A blond wig would disappear. The act's music would be lost. Mother was always very sympathetic on these occasions and would join in the search for the missing articles, and sometimes she was the one to find them— always too late. Later Mother would say to us, "They shouldn't have left the things lying around so carelessly."

Mother was not above teaching June a routine she had seen another child perform. She would elaborate on the original and in time convince herself that it had been her idea in the first place. If anybody criticized her for doing this, she would shrug her shoulders and say, "That's show business." In her more dramatic moods she would add, "I'm a woman alone in the world with two babies to support." She said this years after June and I were out of the baby stage, and even after there were three ex-husbands contributing to our support, but that was a detail Mother always chose to forget until the alimony checks were past due. Mother didn't call it alimony. If it was mentioned at all, it was "a financial settlement."

Besides our real father, who lived in Los Angeles, we had two other fathers. June and I never got to know them very well. They weren't around long enough. One was a chiropodist. I know that because I heard Mother and a friend of hers talking about him one day. The friend called him a corn doctor, and Mother was always sensitive about things like that. "Corn doctor," she repeated slowly and thoughtfully. Within a month she had left him and we were back in show business again.

Whenever Mother was married we didn't work; we trouped only between marriages. One of our fathers was a wholesale grocery salesman whom we called Bubs. He used to bring home samples to June and me, and I think we liked him very much, but I'm not sure. Mother divorced him because he was cruel, cruel and inhuman she charged in her complaint. He wanted to send us to school—not dancing school but public school. He also tried to make us go to Sunday school. Mother explained to him that June was too high strung for Sunday school, but he insisted and so we went. My sister became hysterical when they told us the story about Moses in the bulrushes and had to be carried out of the room. She cried all the way home and cried for three days whenever she thought about the sad story. "He might have got dwowned," she kept saying between spasms.

Bubs said she was a spoiled brat and that we were both heathens. He accused Mother of not raising us properly. Mother cried and held both of us close and defied Bubs to lay a hand on us. "If the story of Moses does *this* to the child," she said, "can you imagine what would happen if she heard about the Crucifixion?" We never had to go to Sunday school again until years later when we were playing Omaha and then we went because we wanted to.

As soon as Mother divorced Bubs we went back on the stage, this time for good. Mother decided she would never marry again. "It isn't fair to the children's career," she said.

Whenever we trouped, Mother carried several lodge buttons with her. She had a right to eight because of Grandpa, but with the exception of the Shriners and the Knights of Pythias, Grandpa's lodges were fairly unimportant organizations. It was all right to play them in Seattle, where we could live with Grandpa, but on the road their halls were too small to make an appearance profitable. Of all the lodge insignia, Mother's favorite was an elk's tooth. Every town has an Elks' Club, but aside from that she really liked

the tooth. She wasn't exactly an Eastern Star, but she carried that
pin, too. Bubs had been a Mason.

Mother called the pins her money in the bank. She also called
them her nest egg and her railroad fare home. They were very
useful. Once, I remember, we ran out of money in Bend, Oregon.
Mother looked over the town carefully. The largest lodge hall
settled the question of which pin she would wear for the day. The
largest hall in Bend was discouragingly small and needed paint and
the green shades hanging on the dusty windows were torn and
shabby. Mother wasn't discouraged. She dressed carefully and
pinned the button suiting the occasion to the collar of her knitted
dress. There was a trace of dead-white powder on her face. With
June on one arm and me on the other, Mother called on the head
man of the lodge.

The Mogul was very polite to Mother—they always were—and
nervous, too. "Sit down, sit down," he said, and pulled up a leather
chair. "And what," he said, expansively, "can I do for a charming
lady and her two lovely little girls?"

Mother smiled at the Mogul, a wan, sad little smile with a hint
of bravery underneath. She held June and me close. "My babies!"
she said.

June dipped into her little curtsy. I was too frightened to do
anything but grin at the man, and he frightened me more by
grinning back.

"They are little show kiddies," Mother said. "I thought we were
supposed to play your lovely little town, but it seems I got my engagements mixed up again. I'm not much of a businesswoman and
I—we were really due in Prineville but I bought the wrong tickets.
I used our last cent in the world to get to the wrong town." She
laughed bravely, but her eyes were filled with tears, and she reached
into her purse for a handkerchief. She looked quite faint. The
Mogul was alarmed. He jumped to his feet to assist her, but Mother
begged him not to bother.

"Please," she said, "I'll be all right. Really I will. As soon as I
have a little hot soup."

June snuggled closer and began to whimper. "I'm hungry, too,
Mommie."

"Don't cry, Angel," Mother said softly. "Mother knows."

I was supposed to cry, too, on such occasions, but I never could. That day it was worse. I had just eaten three hot dogs and I was afraid that somehow the man would find it out.

"We aren't asking for charity," Mother went on. "All we ask is a chance to earn a little money, just enough to get us back to Seattle."

The sympathetic Mogul's eyes strayed to Mother's left hand. She was fingering the lodge button, not too obviously but just in case it had been overlooked.

"What about your husband?" The Mogul asked.

"He deserted us a year ago," Mother whispered.

The expression on the Mogul's face hardened. "A lodge brother!" he said. "To think a lodge brother would do a thing like this! Let his wife and two babies go out into the world alone!"

Mother stared at her lap. She swallowed painfully, but when she faced the Mogul her eyes were dry. "Please don't blame him too much," she said. "He—he tried."

The Mogul was a man who made his decisions quickly. He reached for the telephone and asked for a number. "I'm calling a lodge brother," he said to Mother as he waited for the connection. "He manages the local theatre. Our lodge hall is too small for an act like this, but I know Mr. Willis will be happy to let you perform in his theatre after the movie." The Mogul cupped his hand around the mouthpiece as he talked to Mr. Willis, but even so I could hear every word. So could Mother. She waited until the Mogul mentioned money, then she interrupted. "Perhaps I should see Mr. Willis personally," she said. "He'll want to know about publicity and music—you know, all the little details."

Mr. Willis wasn't as sympathetic as the Mogul. He didn't like Mother's proposition of playing the house on a fifty-fifty basis, and agreed to it reluctantly only after Mother had reminded him that she was a lodge brother's wife and alone in the world with two babies to support and that the Mogul was our friend. "And naturally," Mother added, "you pay for the exploitation—the window cards and throwaways."

That night we played to a full house, mostly lodge brothers and their families. Mother accompanied us on the piano and prompted June from the orchestra pit. "Smile, dear smile. Now the rose step." We took eight bows and three encores. As Mother later said, there wasn't a dry eye in the house.

After the show the Mogul brought our share of the proceeds backstage to the dressing room, and he and his wife drove us to the station. They gave June and me a bag of oranges and a box of gum drops. As the train pulled out, Mother nudged June, "Wave to the nice man and lady," she said. "Wave and throw them a big kiss."

June kept waving and throwing kisses until the Mogul and his wife were out of sight; then we began to divide the oranges while Mother counted the money. "Seventy-one, seventy-two, seventy-three . . ." When she had finished, she put the money in a chamois bag and pinned it to her underwear; then she leaned back comfortably in the plush seat.

"Not bad," she said. "Not bad at all—considering the size of the town."

Grandpa met us at the train in Seattle. We took a streetcar to his little house, and on the way Mother told him what a hit we had been in Bend, Oregon.

Mother didn't mention the $78.90. "This is our secret nest egg," she told June and me, patting her chest to make sure the chamois bag was safe. "We mustn't let anyone know we have it."

3

IT'S HERE, PAPA, IT'S
here! Girls, the letter is here!" Mother closed the front door and
stood with her back pressed against it. She let the other letters fall
to the floor, holding the important one to her chest. "Oh, please,"
she murmured, "please, God, make it good news."

June and I held our breath while Mother tore open the long white
envelope with the name Alexander Pantages printed on the upper
left corner. We had waited almost two weeks for the letter; ever
since the day of the audition. Grandpa hadn't wanted us to do the
act that day. Grandpa had never been to the Pantages Theatre in
Seattle, he was too busy with his lodge meetings, but he had heard
disturbing stories about the owner. A lodge brother once told him
that Alexander Pantages made his money cleaning spittoons in a
saloon in Alaska. Grandpa doubted that a job in a saloon would
pay enough to build twenty-five theatres all over the country, but
he thought there was something shady in Pantages' background.
Where there's smoke, Grandpa said, there's fire.

"Why don't you have the girls do the act for Mr. Orpheum?"
Grandpa had asked Mother. "He runs a pretty nice theatre."

"There is no Mr. Orpheum," Mother had replied impatiently.
"Besides we aren't ready for the Orpheum Circuit yet."

Grandpa didn't play the piano for our audition that day. Mother
played for us instead. When the audition was over, the man

sitting in the audience said, "You'll hear from us, one way or the other. Next act please."

For two weeks Mother had waited eagerly for the mail each day, and was disappointed when the letter didn't come. Now as she read it, her mouth formed each word, "submitted act to Mr. Pantages who offers you the following weeks and terms . . ."

Grandpa shifted his wad of chewing tobacco from one jowl to the other, then aiming carefully through the window, he spat the juice on the clematis vine. "You're not going, Rose," he said. "You're not taking those girls away on another wild-goose chase and that's final."

He picked up his hat and his lunch box and started for the door. Grandpa worked in the baggage room at the King Street station, but he still kept his old railroad schedules. After almost thirty years with the Great Northern Railroad the company wasn't too insistent that Grandpa report for work at eight on the dot, but Grandpa hadn't been late since the day he married my grandmother and if he could help it he wasn't going to be late now.

Mother, clutching the letter, stood between him and the door. "Papa," she cried with a note of desperation in her voice, "read the letter! This is no wild-goose chase. He's offering us one hundred dollars a week for twenty-five weeks consecutive. Don't you realize what this means? This is *real* show business. This is what I've worked so hard for. It's June's big chance. Look at her, Papa. Just look at her. Almost six years old and still playing lodge halls."

Grandpa looked, instead, at his round silver watch with the huge black numerals on it, "It's seven forty-seven, Rose, and I've heard this same story from you every time you left Seattle. I'm still paying off the two hundred dollars I borrowed on the house to send you off to that harum-scarum Hollywood."

Mother stepped back as though she had been struck. "That isn't fair, Papa," she said. "Not after what I went through in Hollywood. Not after what my babies went through."

Grandpa was sorry he had mentioned Hollywood. He had promised Mother he would never speak of it again, not after the stories Mother told him. The stories made him so angry he had pounded his fist on the kitchen table and said the law should step in and close up the whole place.

Mother had told him how June cried real tears for Cecil B. De Mille and how another child who couldn't cry at all got the job. It was the same way with the director of Mary Pickford's picture, *Daddy Long Legs*. June read for a part in the dream sequence and another child, who wasn't half the actress my sister was, got the part.

Mother dropped the letter from Alexander Pantages and buried her face in her hands. "You promised me you'd never mention Hollywood again," she sobbed. "You've broken your word to me, Papa."

I didn't care if we went on the Pantages Circuit or not, but June was crying and Mother started crying again, so I cried too, louder than both of them. Mother held June close to her and I clung to her legs and cried harder.

Grandpa walked slowly back into the room. With a deep sigh he sat down in the big leather rocking chair, his lunch box hanging loosely from his hand. "You win, Rose," he said. "How much money do you think you'll need?"

With a surprised, happy cry Mother threw herself on Grandpa's lap. She snuggled down in his arms like a little girl. Grandpa patted her head and rocked her back and forth in the rocking chair.

"I have the most wonderful Papa in the whole world," Mother murmured. Grandpa rocked her and petted her head and after a while Mother said, "We won't need much money, Papa. We have to have a wardrobe trunk, but we'll get a cheap one, a few photographs for in front of the theatres, warm coats for the girls, new costumes—"

Grandpa brought the rocking chair to a sudden stop. "Costumes?" he said. "You just got those new dresses for the act!"

Mother kissed him on the ear, and mussed his white hair playfully. "Now, Papa," she said, "you wouldn't want the granddaughters of C. J. Thompson to wear those old rags . . . not on the Pantages Circuit."

Mother didn't have to know much about show business to learn

the Pantages Circuit wasn't the Big Time. She heard it over and
over again from every act on the bill, from the stagehands and the
musicians. All of them, it seemed, had either played the Big Time,
or were going to play it. There were no Small Timers on the
Small Time. They were all Big Timers who just happened to be
playing the Small Time.

"There's something about the Big Time I can't explain," one
of the Glencoe Sisters said to Mother between shows. "When you
walk in the stage door it sort of hits you. You *feel* important. You
know you wouldn't *be* there if you weren't good."

The Glencoe Sisters' act was named "Musical Oddities." Dressed
in Scottish kilts, they played accordions and harmonicas and a big
bass drum all at the same time. They were billed over us on the
Pantages Circuit, but every act, besides the Medinis who opened
the show, was billed over us. We were second on a five-act bill.
Our dressing room was always on the very top floor. Mother hadn't
learned about contracts yet, and ours wasn't a very good one.

The Glencoe Sisters had really played the Big Time. Mother
knew this because she had seen their scrapbook. She would have
known it anyway, though, because the sisters talked a lot about the
Big Time and how different it was from the Pantages Time. Mother
asked one of them why they weren't on the Orpheum Circuit that
season. "You're doing the same act," Mother said. "If you were
good enough for the Big Time last season why aren't you on it this
season?"

"It's that agent of ours," the Glencoe Sisters said, adjusting the
contraption that held the harmonica to the accordion.

"Agent?" Mother said thoughtfully. "We don't have an agent—
do they cost much money?"

"Ten per cent, right off the top," the Glencoe Sister replied.
"But you just got to have an agent. And if you're smart, you'll slip
him a little extra, as an incentive, you know."

Mother didn't know, but she made a mental note of it. She made
a lot of mental notes that season. The following year when we went
back on the Pantages Circuit, there were six little boys in the act
besides June and me. Mother had found them in dancing schools
and amateur contests. We had scenery too, blue velvet curtains

that looked almost new, and we had an agent. We were making three hundred dollars a week, and Mother managed to put aside a little each week for our nest egg.

Mother and June and I slept together in one hotel room, mostly in one bed with Mother's dogs at the foot. The six little boys slept three in a bed in an adjoining room. Mother cooked our breakfasts and night lunches over a Sterno stove. We could have afforded separate rooms but we *wanted* to be together. When Gordon joined our act he changed all that, and I held it against him.

Gordon, from the first time I saw him, seemed mysterious to me. During the years he trouped with us as manager, nothing happened to change that first impression. He told Mother he was thirty-two years old, but he looked ageless. He mentioned a family —his mother and father. We never saw them. He had, apparently, no friends. No one ever came backstage to visit him, and aside from the little he told Mother, we knew nothing about his past. He was selling soda pop for a small company in Detroit when we met him. He hadn't been working for the soda-pop company long. Mother thought he might once have been a broker or a banker. She was certain that at one time he had been rich. "You can tell that by his clothes alone," she said.

Gordon's ties, shoes, and even the leather-covered bottles for his mouth wash and bay rum were imported. His traveling bag was covered with stickers from all over the world. It had gold initials stamped on it, but they weren't Gordon's. His black overcoat was soft and expensive feeling with a fur collar. Mother said the fur was sable. Mother didn't worry about Gordon's being poor. She said he wasn't the type to stay poor for long.

Even the way we met Gordon seemed strange to me. Mother was playing hide-and-seek with my sister and me backstage at the Regent Theatre in Detroit. It was our favorite game, especially when we played it backstage. There were so many places to hide, so many musty smells of scenery and dampness. The rumbling sound of the organ accompanying the silent movie was exciting, and the darkness of the theatre added a ghostlike enchantment.

That day, June was hiding in her favorite place, the prop room. Mother was hiding behind the scenery and I was "it." I had just counted up to ten and was getting my breath to say, "Ready or not, you will be caught," when I heard my sister scream. At the same moment a crash of glass seemed to shake the stage. June screamed again. Mother flew past me and ran toward the prop room. "June!" she shrieked. "June! Where are you?" My sister didn't answer. She was yelling too loudly to hear.

When Mother reached the doorway of the prop room, she stopped so suddenly I bumped into her. She was breathing heavily and I was afraid she was going to have an attack of asthma—Mother always had asthma attacks when she was frightened or angry. Then I saw a man holding my sister in his arms. His black overcoat frightened me. Everything about him seemed black—his hair, his eyes, even the small tufts of hair on his finger joints, which looked as though they were glued on. "A big girl like you crying over nothing," he was saying. "You're not hurt."

Mother grabbed June from the man's arms and set her on a trunk near the door. June's nose was skinned a little. "Tell Mother what happened," Mother said.

June pointed to the floor, which was strewn with empty soda-pop bottles, most of them broken, then she cried louder.

"She took a tumble, that's all," the man said. "She tried to climb up on the soda cases and when they fell over, she went with them. A little skin off her nose is nothing."

"Nothing!" Mother shrieked at him. "Just look at that child's nose. How can she do a matinee in that condition?"

The man smiled. He dampened his handkerchief under the water cooler and began cleaning away the grime from the bruise. June stopped crying. Mother calmed down too. She even smiled. "June is a very excitable child," she said.

The man smiled at Mother again. After a moment he said, "May I buy the girls an ice-cream soda?"

Mother didn't answer right away. I wanted very much for her to say no. I didn't want an ice-cream soda; not with him. Mother lifted June down from the trunk, then she took my hand. "Yes," she said, "I think they'd like it very much."

On the way to the ice-cream parlor the man walked with Mother and June. I trailed along behind them. I heard my sister ask,

"What's your name?" the man said, "Gordon—Sam Gordon. What's your name?"

June carefully recited what Mother had taught her: "I'm Baby June and I'm going on four and a half." June really wasn't four and a half; she was almost seven. Mother had taught her to say that when we were on trains.

While we drank our sodas, Mother talked to Gordon. Her voice was low and she spoke slowly. "I lost their father when the baby was two and a half," she said. "June could dance on her toes almost before she could walk, so naturally when I was faced with having to earn a living, I thought of show business . . ."

I couldn't listen to her any longer. I couldn't look at her, either; her eyes were too blue, her cheeks too flushed. I'd seen her like that twice before and each time she had married the man. I pushed away my ice-cream soda, ran back to the theatre and slammed the stage door behind me.

The next day Gordon was at the theatre again, and between shows he and Mother talked for hours. After the last show, Mother told June and me that we needed a man to look out for our interests, that show business wasn't for a woman. She asked us if we liked Gordon, and then, without waiting for our answer, she said, "Gordon is going to be our manager. He's never been in show business but he's a salesman and he's sure he can sell our little act. He has some wonderful plans for us and we're going to make a lot of money." Her eyes didn't look as blue as they had in the ice-cream parlor and her cheeks weren't flushed. She looked as she did when she talked money and billing with theatre managers.

"I'm going to call him Uncle Gordon," June said. I didn't say anything.

When we left Detroit the following night, Gordon went with us. On the train to Chicago, he and Mother sat together. June and I sat at the back of the car, too far away to hear what Mother was saying, but we could hear her laugh. She laughed a lot.

"I hate him," I said.

My sister looked at me sharply, then she settled back on the straw upholstered seat, "*I* don't," she said. "He said he's going to buy me the biggest doll in the whole world and I fink he's nice."

In another three weeks Gordon had changed everything about our way of living. We didn't play hide-and-seek any more. Gordon said it was too tiring, that we had shows to do and we couldn't waste all that energy playing. At dinner June and I sat silently while Gordon and Mother talked. We never cooked our breakfasts in Mother's room because we had to have oatmeal and fruit and things.

"It's a wonder their stomachs aren't ruined." Gordon said one morning when he was ordering for us. "Coffee and rolls for breakfast!"

Mother didn't say anything, but she sneaked us a cup of coffee after Gordon had left. What we didn't drink was divided between Mother's two dogs.

Soon our act was different too. The boys were sent back to their homes and six new ones took their places. The new ones weren't as nice as the others, but they had more talent. One of them was from Shenandoah, Pennsylvania. He had a long Italian name that Mother changed to Johnny de Bell. He sang "O Sole Mio" in the act and Mother had to hold on to the back of his shirt through the curtain when he was on stage because the audience frightened him. Sometimes the audience frightened him so much that when he hit a high note he'd wet his pants. He was almost sixteen, but he was very little, not as big as the other boys, who were ten and eleven. He called his pajamas a kimono and had never used a toothbrush until he joined the act. Mother had to put the toothpaste on the brush for him, because if she left it in the bathroom, Johnny used to eat it.

Two of the other boys, Bubsy and Sonny, were brothers. They were from Avenue A in New York City. Mother and Gordon had heard them singing and dancing for pennies in the apartment court where we lived. Bubsy had been run over twice, and when Sonny was a year old he fell off a fire-escape where he had been sleeping. He called June his princess and his spending money went to buy malted milks for her. Because the brothers had lice when they joined the act June wouldn't play with them. Mother soaked their heads in Larkspur lotion, but it was too late. For a while we all had lice. Danny was from Philadelphia, and Tommy was from

Chicago. Although Tommy had never been run over he boasted that he had ten stiches in his scalp from a wallop his father once gave him. Jack was June's favorite of all the boys. He had long thick eyelashes and wavy hair. He didn't say "dem" for "them" and he was very polite.

I was dressed as a boy, too, because Gordon said another girl in the act would detract from June. We had new scenery and costumes, all very expensive-looking. Gordon knew a wholesale house in Chicago and he fixed it so that Mother could buy the materials at cost.

It was Gordon's idea that the boys in the act should receive no salary. "The experience they'll get is worth more than money," Gordon told their parents. Sometimes, if the parents insisted on a contract, Mother would compose one herself. Mother was very good at making legal-looking documents. Danny, for instance, had a contract. In it Mother promised that at the end of the year, should circumstances warrant it, he would receive a salary to the satisfaction of both parties. As Mother told Gordon it sounded good but said nothing. The name of the new act was "Dainty June and Her Newsboy Songsters" (reg. U.S. pat. office). None of the children's names was mentioned in the billing, but Mother's was. "Madam Rose presents" preceded the title. I don't know whether that was Gordon's idea or Mother's.

One feature of the act was my sister's finale gown. It was entirely covered with rhinestones and was so heavy it cut into her shoulders. Gordon said it looked like real money from out front, though, so Mother sewed velvet padding in the straps and then it didn't hurt June so much. On the program, it was stated that the dress cost one thousand dollars, and that there were a million stones on the skirt alone. Mother wanted to add that three women went blind working on it.

"We've said enough," Gordon told her. "You can overconvince people."

In addition to the stage wardrobe all the children had new street clothes. The boys and I dressed alike in knicker suits with leather coats and tweed caps. June had two fur coats: an opossum for every day, and for opening days and publicity days she had a white-rabbit fur coat with a big fur tam o'shanter to match.

Mother had a new beaver coat. It was cut long and full with a finger-tip-length cape of beaver over it. She wore a beaver hat pulled down over her ears to keep them warm and woolen hose with a diamond pattern in the weave. Mother often said there wasn't another beaver coat in the country like hers. She and Gordon had designed it, selected the skins and supervised the making, bringing just a few skins at a time to the furrier. The others were stacked high in the clothes closet of our hotel room. As a further guarantee that the furrier wouldn't switch skins each one had Mother's name written on it in indelible pencil.

The dogs were both dressed up, too, in bright red and green sweaters. When it snowed, Mumshay, Mother's favorite, wore red leather shoes which laced up the legs. Gordon said it was good publicity when people stared at us as we walked down the street. "You have to put a front in any business," he added. "Especially show business. I've been in it long enough now to know that if you let the managers think you have money in the bank they won't insult you by offering a small salary."

Gordon must have been right. The act was booked for the Lafayette Theater in Buffalo at $750 a week. Mother had never dreamed of so much money. When she saw the contract, she sat in our dressing room and cried for a long time.

"It's so wonderful I can't believe it," she said.

Gordon put his arm around her. "This is nothing, Rose," he said. "Just wait until I learn the angles. Then you'll see some real money."

Mother stopped crying. She walked away from Gordon, sat down in front of the make-up shelf and suddenly was very businesslike. "Gordon," she said, "we have to come to an agreement about this. It's only fair that you receive twenty-five per cent. After the expenses have been deducted, of course. After all, it's through your efforts that the act is making so much money. The little I invested will be paid back in a few weeks." She began estimating expenses with a pencil and paper. After a while she turned to Gordon. "There isn't a reason in the world why you shouldn't make a lot of money this season," she said.

But somehow, with all the economy, the expenses were higher than Gordon and Mother expected. They were so high, in fact, that there was practically nothing left over for Gorden when we closed in Buffalo. Mother couldn't account for it even though she handled the money. It was pretty much the same in Albany and Utica.

"There's that item for Grandpa," she said at one of the accountings. "After all, he did finance us long before we met you, Gordon. It's a legitimate theatre expense."

Mother's beaver coat was also a legitimate theatre expense. "You know I wouldn't pay that much money for a coat unless it was to put up a front," she said. It was the same with the diamond rings she bought for June. Mother wore them on one finger, and, as she told Gordon, they were rich-looking and if we ever needed the money, the rings could be pawned. Mother didn't like diamonds. She even thought they were a little vulgar. "But," she said, "they do impress the managers."

Then mother took to wearing a money belt. It was a large gray suède belt with many pockets. Mother wore it strapped to her waist and it made her bulge out strangely in front, but we were given to understand that there wasn't much money in the belt. Mother always said there wasn't enough—"We'd be in a fine fix if one of the children, God forbid, should break a leg."

4

 HEN GORDON
wasn't looking, Mother would fill a saucer with coffee and put it
under the table for the dogs. Gordon didn't object to the dogs sleeping in bed with us, but he didn't want them fed at the table. He
said it made him uncomfortable.

The dogs, their whiskers dripping coffee, would look from
Mother to Gordon during these arguments. Bootsie, the untidy
poodle, with her red-ringed watery eyes would peek up at them
through the matted dirty-white hair. "Look at that pathetic little
face," Mother would say. "Just look at it!"

Once Gordon got angry and threw his napkin on the table.
"Damnit all, Rose, I don't want to look at it. It ruins my appetite!"

Mumshay, Mother's other dog, was a sort of spaniel. She had
been given to my sister by Toto, the clown, when we trying to get
into the movies in Hollywood. Toto had named her M'cherie, but
the pronunciation had changed with the years. Mumshay's teeth
had all fallen out with the years too, and Mother had to chew her
food for her. That made Gordon even more uncomfortable. He
often said he liked animals as much as we did, but he liked them
in their place. Besides the hotel, the only other place we had was
the dressing room. June and I wondered sometimes just which place
Gordon meant.

We had many other animals from time to time besides the dogs.

We had a monkey, guinea pigs, rabbits, chameleons, white mice, turtles and even a horned toad that Mother refused to believe was poisonous. Horny caught cold and died before we found out if he was poisonous or not. Most of our animals died tragically. Their little graves, damp with our tears, were scattered all over the Pantages Circuit.

The most spectacular death was Sambo's. Sambo was June's guinea pig. He lived in a house made from a Log Cabin syrup can. A door had been cut in the can for him and holes punched in it for air. He was a big guinea pig and had to squeeze in and out the door. June and I both felt that Sambo was lonely so Mother bought a rabbit to keep him company. Sambo immediately chewed all the hair off the rear quarters of the rabbit and we had to give her away before she was chewed bald.

Then Mother bought us a white rat, named Molly, but Sambo didn't like her either and we couldn't blame him for that. Molly would snatch the food right out of Sambo's mouth, then she would plant herself in the door of Sambo's Log Cabin house and grind her teeth at him when he tried to get in. Molly was with us for only a few days when Gordon discovered she wasn't a lady rat at all. We changed her name to Solly and tried to find a nice home for him. No one, it seemed, wanted a white rat until we worked on the bill with Lady Alice and Her Pets.

June and I watched the act from the wings opening matinee. Lady Alice used a black-velvet-covered platform and on this dozens of trained white rats and guinea pigs performed. They wore ballet skirts and balanced poles on their noses and did all kinds of tricks. Two of them pulled a tiny glittering wagon, others rode on a Ferris wheel and climbed up and down ladders. They balanced on teeter boards and juggled balls in the air. Lady Alice stood behind the platform, wearing a blue taffeta evening gown and a band of flowers around her forehead and prodded them gently with a gilded stick as she called them all by name. "Hold the ball, Daisy, hold the ball," she would say. "Come on Jimmy, now it's your turn."

For a finale one of the guinea pigs played "The Stars and Stripes Forever" on a tin whistle while the others, balancing on Lady Alice's shoulders and arms, waved American flags in their teeth.

June and I thought it was the most wonderful act we'd ever seen. Between shows we followed Lady Alice around worshipfully as she fed the animals and cleaned their cages. We helped her set up the props for the act and discovered that even Sambo could play "The Stars and Stripes Forever" if he had the right kind of a whistle and was hungry enough.

The whistle had to be very sensitive so it would produce the notes as the guinea pig breathed into it nibbling at the food that was placed there. Actually the guinea pig blew only the first few notes of the number, the orchestra drowned out the rest.

June and I were certain that Lady Alice would take Solly and make an acting rat out of him, but we hoped to make a trade. Because this was my idea June made me do the talking.

I took Solly out of my pocket and held him up so Lady Alice could see what a healthy, handsome rat he was. My pocket was wet and soggy. We always carried our rats and guinea pigs in our pockets, and most times our pockets were wet.

"We'd like to make a business deal with you," I said to Lady Alice. "We have this very fine white rat who is already partly trained and we'd like to trade him for a lady guinea pig." Lady Alice looked closely at Solly. "I don't know," she said doubtfully. "My guinea pigs are all very precious to me."

June was so sure the deal was falling through that tears began to well up in her eyes. "But Sambo just has to have a wife," she said. "It isn't fair to make him live alone. It's—it's cruel."

Lady Alice hesitated for a moment, then she took Solly and put him in a cage with all the other white acting rats; then she told June and me we could take our choice of the lady guinea pigs, not the trained ones, of course, but their understudies.

The lady guinea pigs were all so beautiful that June and I took a long time making up our minds. When we had eliminated all but three Lady Alice said, "Why not keep the three of them for a few days? Put them in a box with Sambo and let him take his pick."

June and I found just the box we needed in the stage alley and, lining it with newspaper, we put Sambo and his Log Cabin house in it along with the three lady guinea pigs. Sambo had as much trouble as we had in making his choice. First he would sniff one of the lady guinea pigs, then another. By the time the show was over that night Sambo was dizzy from running around the box sniffing the lady guinea pigs. But it was quite obvious that he still hadn't made up his mind.

Mother said that often happened with people too. "We'll just have to leave them alone. We'll know by morning which one he has decided on." We put four carrots in the box and some lettuce leaves left over from our dinner plate. Then, leaving the dressing-room light on so Sambo wouldn't be confused in the dark, we left him alone with the three lady guinea pigs.

The next morning June and I hurried into our clothes and rushed through our breakfast, saving a sweet roll for the guinea pigs. We were so anxious to get to the theatre we buttoned up our coats as we ran. There was no one backstage that early besides the watchman, and we had to wait a long time before he opened the stage door. He was an old man and he walked slowly.

"Could you please open our dressing-room door for us?" June asked breathlessly. "Our guinea pig got married last night and we want to see which one he married."

Leading the way with his flashlight the watchman walked slowly across the stage and down the winding iron stairs to our dressing room. The leather-covered clock that hung around his neck bobbed from side to side as he went down the steps. After trying one key, then another, he finally unlocked our dressing-room door, and turned on the lights. When they heard us the guinea pigs began squealing. June and I leaned down over the box and looked in at them. The three lady guinea pigs stretched their necks way up at us and waited greedily for the food they knew we had. But Sambo, lying on a lettuce leaf, was rigid in death. His mouth was drawn up in a horrible grin, showing his long, sharp teeth, a piece of carrot stuck between them.

We couldn't believe he was dead. June picked him up in her hands and held his stiff little body close to her face. "Wake up, Sambo," she said, "wake up." The lady guinea pigs squealed until I dropped the sweet roll into the box. Then they were quiet and the only sound in the room was June sobbing. She rocked Sambo back and forth in her arms. "Wake up, Sambo," she said, "wake up."

The night watchman must have called the hotel because in a little while Gordon and Mother were both in the dressing room. Gordon took the guinea pig from June and Mother held my sister close in her arms and cried softly with her. "We'll get another guinea pig just like Sambo," Mother said. "Sambo is in heaven now and you mustn't cry any more."

Gordon looked down at the little dead guinea pig in his hands; at the stiff little body and the mouth pulled back from the teeth in that hideous grin. "Poor old boy," Gordon said. "We should have known better." Then he looked at Mother and smiled a strange kind of smile, "But do you know, Rose, I can't think of a better way to die."

"Gordon," Mother said sharply, "what a thing to say in front of the children!"

Breakfast, the day after Sambo's funeral, was going to be a dismal affair. I just knew it was. Mother was still sleeping when I lighted the Sterno stove under the coffeepot. I measured out the water and put the coffee in the metal top, then I opened the bag of doughnuts and asked June to call Gordon and the boys.

June had cried all night over Sambo's death and her face was white and drawn; the deep circles under her eyes looked like splotches of make-up. She broke off a piece of coconut-covered doughnut and dropped it into the box with our two new guinea pigs. She had named her new guinea pig Sambo Molasses C. J. Thompson. Mine, because it was a lady guinea pig, was named Samba. Neither of them was one of the three that had been responsible for Sambo's death. Mother had bought these in a pet store.

Gordon, smelling of toothpaste and bay rum, picked up June and held her high in the air when he came in. "And how's my girl, today?" he asked, bouncing her up and down. Then he went to the connecting door leading to Mother's room and tapped softly. He opened the door just a bit so the smell of coffee would greet her when she woke up.

"Time to get up, Rose," he said cheerfully. "Breakfast is ready." Gordon was always cheerful in the morning. He still didn't approve of our breakfasts of rolls or doughnuts and coffee but he had given up making us eat oatmeal and things like that. We were all dunking our doughnuts vigorously when Mother emerged from her room. She wore a padded robe over her outing-flannel nightgown and red crocheted bed slippers. "I've just had the most amazing dream," she said. She gulped her first cup of coffee without even waiting for it to cool; Mother believed that if you told your dreams before breakfast they wouldn't come true. She put down her coffee cup and we all sat quietly to hear her dream.

"In this dream," Mother said, "I saw June doing her 'Rube' number. She was wearing the same little gingham dress she always wears, with the starched bloomers hanging down from it, and the little hat with the pigtails sewn in it, but she was singing a *new* song. I could hear her as plain as I hear those guinea pigs!"

As Mother pointed to the guinea-pig box, our heads followed her hand. Mother's dreams were always graphic. Sometimes they were exciting. We listened carefully to every word. "When June finished her song," Mother went on, "a *cow* came out on the stage!"

Gordon whistled softly. "A COW?" he said. "Freud would call that a pretty sexy dream." Mother shushed him with a glance. I'm sure she didn't know who Freud was, but she did know the word "sexy" and she didn't approve of it at all.

"It wasn't a real cow," she said. "It was a sort of stuffed cow. It had great long horns, a big smiling face and a long pink tongue."

I tried to imagine what kind of a cow it could have been. I had seen cows many times, but only when we passed by them quickly on trains. None of them had looked like Mother's dream cow.

"It was an omen," Mother said suddenly and dramatically. "That cow leaned right over my bed and spoke to me."

We were all very quiet. It was frightening. Mother's omen dreams always were. Most times in these dreams Mother saw ghosts, usually the ghost of our dead great grandmother Dottie, but she had never seen a cow before. Especially a cow that talked.

June's eyes were wide and eager. "What did the cow say?" she asked in a tight little voice.

"That cow," Mother said, "looked me right in the eye and said, 'Do as I tell you, Rose, and you'll be on the Orpheum Circuit within a year.'"

"What did the cow want you to do?" Gordon asked without a trace of a smile. When he first joined the act he used to laugh at Mother's omen dreams but he knew better now.

"Well," Mother said, "he walked around the room so I could get a good look at him—her, I mean—and said, '*Put me in your act*.' " Mother paused.

"Do you know what I'm going to do?" she said. "I'm going to take that cow's advice."

That same day Gordon and Mother ordered the cow to be made. It would have a papier mâché head and a body made of brown-and-white fuzzy material with trousers for legs, and leather spats for hoofs. Two of the boys would be inside the body; one boy would be the front end of the cow, and the other the rear. Mother and Gordon had a song written for June like the song in Mother's dream. It went:

I've got a cow and her name is Sue
And she'll do most anything I ask her to.
I took her to the Fair one day
And she won each prize that came her way. . . .
O gee, O gosh, we took first prize
But nobody saw it took.

New scenery was made to back up the number. It was a farm-yard scene with animals painted on it and part of a barn showing. We rehearsed the number that week in Chicago and broke it in at the Kedzie Theatre. It was the hit of the act. The audience loved June's song, and they screamed at the cow that danced about and sat down and scratched its ear and collapsed in the middle. At the end when the boys pulled off the cow head and took their bows with June it was a solid show stop.

The following week Gordon gave Mother our contracts for the Orpheum Circuit. We were booked for forty-two consecutive weeks at $1,250 a week. "It was the cow that did it," Gordon said, grinning proudly.

"And your salesmanship," Mother told him.

We celebrated after the show that night with a Chinese dinner. Instead of yakamein, the cheapest thing on the menu, we all had sub gum chow chop suey that cost a dollar and ten cents. For dessert besides fortune cookies we had lichee nuts. Mother wept a bit over her second pot of tea. "The Orpheum Circuit," she kept saying over and over. "I just can't believe it, Gordon. My life ambition—"

The boys and June and I amused ourselves while Mother and Gordon talked by picking out bits of the shells inlaid in the teak-wood table. When we tired of that we had a contest to see which one could eat the most hot Chinese mustard without crying.

"The Orpheum Circuit," Mother said. "Headlining on the Orpheum Circuit—" Gordon reached over under the table and took her hand in his. "Now that I've done what I promised to do," he said, "when are you going to keep your promise to me?"

Mother pulled her hand away. "Not in front of the children," she said.

Gordon lighted a cigarette and took angry puffs on it. "We can't keep going on like this, Rose. Hiding and lying and being so damned careful all the time—"

Mother felt around under the table for her fleece-lined shoes. While Gordon laced them up for her she scooped the leftovers of the sub gum into a cardboard container; then, making sure we hadn't forgotten anything, she wrapped herself in the beaver coat. "I've made three ghastly mistakes in my life," she said to Gordon. "I want to be sure before I make another one."

Besides getting us on the Orpheum Circuit, the best thing about the cow number was that it gave us an excuse to troupe all sorts of animals. Not just turtles and chameleons and guinea pigs but big farmyard animals. A baby lamb was the first. We bought him from a farmer during a train stopover, and because it was Mother's birthday we named the lamb Waupie, after Wahpeton, North Dakota, where Mother had been born.

Waupie had long wobbly legs that bent at the knees and spread out awkwardly. We thought he was white, but it was hard to tell because he was so dirty. The first thing Mother did when we checked into the hotel was give him a bath. The tub was slippery and Waupie kept splashing around so that Mother couldn't get a grip on him. She finally took off her clothes and got into the bathtub with him. Then Waupie was calm and quiet. He let Mother rub the soap into his matted wool and snuggled up close

to her as she held him on her lap and scrubbed away at one black
spot that looked like grease. When Mother separated the wool she
found more black spots just like it.

"This poor little thing is covered with these ugly clumps," she
said, scratching at one of them with her finger. "Just look at this!
They're all over him."

Suddenly the black clump began to move. It crawled away from
the lamb's skin and up into the wool, and then we saw the legs. It
wasn't a grease spot at all. It was a horrible hard-shelled bug with
dozens of squirmy legs. Mother let out a shriek that shook the walls
of the bathroom. She pushed the baby lamp from her lap, and
knocking June and me off the the edge of the bathtub she ran naked
and soaking wet into the bedroom.

"Get them off me!" she screamed as she clawed at her body.
"Louise, June—quick—get them off me!"

June and I sprawled around on the slippery wet floor trying to
get to our feet. The baby lamb, slipping back and forth in the tub,
was splashing dirty soapy water all over us. He was making baby
lamb noises, "Baa—baa—baa—" Then he went, "Baa—gurgle—
gurgle—" Leaning over the side of the tub I pulled his head out
of the water just in time and bracing myself against the side I lifted
him out of the bathtub. June ran in to pick the bugs off Mother
while I held Waupie upside down to let the water run out of him.
When I was sure he was all right I wrapped him in a bath towel and
carried him into the bedroom. There were no bugs on Mother at
all. June and I both looked and looked, and after a while she
finally believed us.

Mother planned on training Waupie to paper. When it was time
for Waupie to make water, Mother would hold him over a newspaper, but no matter how much paper she put down Waupie would
soak through it. Mother couldn't understand how such a little lamb
could hold so much water, and how he could manage to "go" so
often.

Waupie wore the little comedy hat and followed June in the
cow number just the way Mother wanted him to, but too often he
had accidents while on stage. The audience thought the accidents

were very funny, but the stagehands, who had to clean up after him, didn't. Besides, it embarrassed June. Mother decided there was only one answer; Waupie had to wear rubber pants. The rubber pants got a bigger laugh than the accidents had and the stagehands and June were happier, too. From then on Waupie wore his rubber pants even when he went out walking with us.

As Waupie grew, and he grew very fast, we found it more and more difficult to get him into hotels. Mother could hide the dogs under her coat and the guinea pigs were tucked away in our pockets, but there was no way to hide Waupie. Mother had to argue it out with the desk clerks. In Racine, Wisconsin, we were asked to leave the hotel because of the lamb. Mother stood at the desk in the lobby, holding Waupie on his leash while she argued with the desk clerk.

"But he's a trained lamb," Mother was saying. "He's perfectly housebroken. Why, he's as clean as *people*. Cleaner than some."

The desk clerk was adamant. He said it wasn't up to him; if it were, he wouldn't object to the lamb at all. But he had his orders. The lamb had to go. Just as he said that I glanced down at Waupie and I realized that the desk clerk was absolutely right. I crossed my fingers and hoped the rubber pants would hold.

"We can't leave him at the theatre," Mother was saying as the pants got fuller and fuller. "They have rat poison all over backstage. Why, you'd never forgive yourself if that little lamb got rat poisoning and died."

Mother hated being interrupted when she was talking, especially when she was trying to put something over, but I knew the pants were almost at the breaking point. They were hanging down so far they almost touched the floor. I tugged at her sleeve and motioned frantically toward Waupie. Mother pulled her arm away without even looking at me.

"—It would just about kill the children if anything happened to that baby lamb," Mother said and just then with a loud pop the rubber pants burst. It was like a dam bursting. First the plopping noise then the rush of water.

The desk clerk was speechless. He was too surprised, too shocked to be angry. Mother glanced around at the puddle she was standing in, then taking my hand and leading the lamb on his leash she stepped daintily out of the wet.

"Have it your way," she said to the open-mouthed desk clerk, as though nothing at all had happened. "We'll be packed and out in an hour. We know when we're not wanted."

Gordon found a very nice home for Waupie the following week when we were playing in La Crosse, Wisconsin. He told the man who owned the Athens #2 Restaurant that Waupie had been blessed in a Greek Orthodox Church ceremony. Gordon made the story so convincing that the man had a special house built for the lamb in the back yard of his restaurant and even laid a strip of carpeting leading from the kitchen to the house so Waupie wouldn't get his feet wet.

Rochester, our next stop, was a sleeper jump from La Crosse and in a way I was glad Waupie wasn't coming with us. It was bad enough, I thought, to sleep three in an upper, without having Waupie along.

5

GORDON'S BLACK overcoat flared out behind him like the wings of a bat as he raced past the roaring, chugging locomotive and ran down the ramp alongside the train.

"Hold the train!" he shouted, throwing his suitcase into the first open Pullman door. Startled passengers watched him through the windows. "Hold the train! We're a show troupe! We've got to make Rochester in the morning!"

Gordon snatched the red lantern from the brakeman's hand before he could wave it again. "I told you to hold this train!" Gordon shouted in the man's face.

Mother, carrying the two dogs, wrapped like babies in their blankets, swung herself up the high step into the train, dragging June behind her. The boys, loaded down with luggage, climbed all over each other as they crawled up the step to the other door. Mother shoved the two dogs into June's arms.

"Come on, Louise!" Mother screamed, leaning way out of the train door. "The train's moving! Run!"

I was running as fast as I could, but I had the Christmas tree in one hand, my suitcase in the other and my guinea pig in my pocket. Besides, my shoelace was undone.

"Stop the train!" Mother screamed. "Stop the train!" She reached down and grabbed my arm. "Jump, Louise," she yelled. "You can make it if you jump." I felt myself being pulled through the door, and I landed flat on my face, Christmas tree and all, on the platform on the train. Mother rolled me out of the way and reached down to help Gordon get on board. But Gordon was too busy struggling with the brakeman.

"Show troupe, or no show troupe," the brakeman gasped as he ran beside Gordon, tugging on the lantern, "this train leaves on time."

Gordon let go of the lantern suddenly and the startled brakeman staggered against the side of the train. Mother and Gordon both grabbed out and pulled him up onto the platform.

"I told you to stop the train," Gordon said. "You could have been hurt."

The brakeman, clutching his lantern, leaned out the door, "A-board," he yelled, "A-board!" Then he slammed the door shut and dropped the iron bolt in place.

"Goddamned show people," he muttered, stomping past us to the next car.

"Nice language to use in front of children," Mother called out after him indignantly. She glanced around to make sure we were all there. Then with a satisfied sigh she said, "See? I told you we'd make it."

Mother led the way through the gloomy, green-draped sleeping car. She whispered as she gave us our instructions. June, she said, was to go in lower nine. Gordon was to take Sonny with him in lower ten. The three older boys, Johnny, Georgie and Danny were in upper ten. I waited, with the Christmas tree in my arms, for Mother to go on. I knew what was coming, and I dreaded her words.

"Louise?"

"Yes, Mother."

"You're in upper nine with Jack and Bubsy."

The porter was standing beside me. I looked at him from the corner of my eye to see if he heard. He didn't smile, as they usually did, but he *must* have heard. He couldn't have helped it. I turned my head away from him and climbed up the ladder. If only Mother wouldn't say my name so loud. Maybe if they didn't hear my name they'd think I was a boy.

I put my guinea pig in my tweed cap and placed her in the mesh hammock, then I put the Christmas tree in the hammock beside her. It was an old skeleton of a tree that hadn't been handsome even before the needles had dried up and fallen off. The ornaments, wrapped in newspapers, were packed in the dog bag. When we arrived in Rochester we would retrim the tree for my birthday; my tenth birthday party. That was our excuse for trouping the tree. We used the same excuse each year.

I pulled off my heavy rubber boots and hung up my leather coat and leaned back on the hard cold pillow.

The boys were giggling and whispering as they rummaged through the community overnight bag for their pajamas and tooth-brushes. I should have asked them to get mine too, but I couldn't trust myself to speak, I knew if I opened my mouth I'd cry.

Looking up at the shiny mahogany ceiling above the berth I could see the outline of my tweed knickers tucked into the tops of my heavy woolen stockings. I could even see the buttons on my shirt and my cheeks, red and flushed. Maybe the porter really thought I was a boy, I thought.

I heard my sister whimper fretfully and I opened the green draperies and peeked down at her. "My curler's too tight," she said. Mother was rolling her blond hair up in paper curlers. The finished ones hung down like little pork sausages. "There," Mother said, as she loosened one of them, "is that better?"

Mother pinned a small cotton bag with a cube of camphor in it to my sister's underwear, then she rubbed June's chest and neck with Vick's and tied a stocking around her neck. The year before, in Fredonia, New York, June had mumps and the act laid off a whole week. (It wasn't really mumps, it was swollen glands, but Mother thought mumps sounded more baby like.) Since then, Mother hadn't taken any chances on June getting sick again.

"Louise?" Mother said loudly. I pulled my head through the draperies and lay back on the pillow. I didn't answer.

"—bundle up good and warm. And no reading until all hours. We're getting in very early."

Above the noise of the train I could hear Mother's labored breathing. The dampness and the rushing for the train had brought on an asthma attack. Then I heard the boys whispering as they came back from the men's room. I grabbed my guinea pig from the mesh hammock, and swinging my legs over the side of the berth I lowered myself to the floor.

"You can both sleep at the head," I said. "That is, if you want to."

Jack and Bubsy stared at me. I always fought for the head of the bed. Being a girl, I thought it was my right. There was never a question of all three sleeping in a row. There was more room with two at the foot and one at the head. Besides, I didn't like having anyone breathe on me. Especially boys.

"Where are you going?" Bubsy said.

"If you must know," I replied, "I happen to be thirsty."

The ladies' room was cold and the chair was hard and scratchy. There was a draft along the floor and my feet were cold without my boots. I put Samba on the shelf and covered her with a Pullman towel. Then, reaching into my pocket, I pulled out my bag of marbles. Holding the green-and-yellow aggie to the light, I looked at it for a long time, then I thumbed it into the hair receiver.

"Oh, Samba, I just can't stand it any longer," I cried. "Not if I never sleep again. I can't. I can't." The guinea pig blinked her beady little eyes at me, and I threw myself down on the shelf and cried harder than I had ever cried in all my life. I was crying so loudly I didn't hear Mother when she came in.

"Louise!" she said, holding my shoulders and pulling me up from the shelf. "What's happened? Why are you crying?"

I looked up at her, and tried to tell her, but I couldn't. I couldn't say anything. I was crying too hard. Mother held me and began shaking me. I felt something press into my arm; it was Mother's container of asthma powder. I could see the label on the side of the container, LIFE EVERLASTING, then I heard Mother's breathing. She was gasping for air; little beads of sweat stood out on her forehead. She gave me a box of matches and pressed the container in my hand. Then she sank down into the chair next to mine.

"Help me, Louise—" she gasped. "Hurry—the asthma powder."

My hands were trembling as I opened the container of powder and tried to shake some out into the metal lid. It sprinkled over my hand and I pushed it into a mound with my finger. Then I lighted a match and held it to the powder. In a moment the flame died down and a ribbon of black, sweetish-smelling smoke curled up and was lost in the air. Mother put her face close to the mound of smoking powder and gasped it into her lungs. I pulled the towel off Samba and put it over her head so the smoke wouldn't escape. Mother's feet were sticking out from under her woolly nightgown and they looked blue and cold. Sympathy welled up in me and made me ashamed. Then in a moment I heard her breathe deeply and I could hear the rattling noise as the smoke went deep down into her chest.

"Ah, that's the first real breath I've taken since we got on the train." Her voice was muffled by the towel. "Why were you crying, Louise?" she asked.

I fished my aggie out of the hair receiver and picked up my guinea pig. "Answer me," Mother said from under the towel. "Why were you crying?"

"Nothing," I said. "It was—I—" I forgot all about Mother's asthma attack, all about my feelings of sympathy for her cold, blue feet and everything. All I could think of was the upper berth and the two boys waiting up there in the darkness for me to join them.

"It's the boys," I said. "I can't sleep with them any more. I just can't. I'm almost ten years old, Mother. I'm too old to be sleeping with boys!"

Mother's shoulders began to move up and down and I was afraid she was having another attack; then I heard her laugh softly.

"It isn't funny to me," I said, red-faced with anger. "You don't know how the porters laugh at me, how the other people laugh in the morning. They all know I'm a girl sleeping with boys!"

Mother took the towel off her head and pulled me over to her. "I'm not laughing, Louise," she said. "Gordon and I were talking about this very thing just a few days ago. He thinks because of my asthma and the dogs and all that I should have a sleeper alone. From now on, you and your sister will have an upper to yourselves."

Mother got up and emptied the ashes of the powder into the wastebasket, then she took my hand and we walked back through the green-draped car together. At lower nine, Mother stopped and opened the draperies. She rolled my sister over closer to the window, then she took my guinea pig from me and put her in the hammock alongside June's guinea pig. I wasn't *sure,* but I hoped as hard as I could. Mother got into the berth and told me to take off my knickers; then she held up the covers for me.

"Come on, Louise," she said in a whisper so she wouldn't wake up June. "Hurry, dear, so the bed doesn't get cold."

"Mother?" I whispered. "I really don't care if I don't get another single thing for my birthday."

❀

Birthdays were wonderful days, and my tenth birthday was the best of all. From the moment I woke up that morning I felt it was *my* day. Everyone sang "Happy Birthday" to me and the breakfast coffee cake had ten red candles on it. My presents were stacked up under the scraggly Christmas tree and I could hardly wait to open them. First I had to make a wish and blow out the candles. I wished very hard, and drawing in as much air as I could I blew out all ten of them.

Then I began to open my presents. Bubsy and Sonny gave me a secondhand Oz book; Georgie gave me his best aggie; Danny gave me a quarter, his week's allowance, wrapped in a piece of newspaper; Jack gave me a horoscope magazine and Johnny just kept shoving the coffee cake in his mouth as fast as he could, candle and all. He still couldn't understand why people got presents on their birthdays. June gave me a set of modeling clay which she wanted to take back because she liked it herself, and Gordon gave me a book with over a hundred illustrations in it entitled, *Dreams, What They Mean.* I was very good at telling fortunes. Mother said that was because I had been born with two veils, or cowls, as she sometimes called them. One of the veils had covered my face, the other, my body. I never saw them, but Grandma Dottie was supposed to have kept them pressed in her Bible until they dried up and blew away like dust. Even Grandma Dottie, who didn't believe in superstitions, had to admit that people born with a veil had unusual occult powers.

Besides horoscopes and palms, I could also read fortunes in tea leaves and playing cards, and now with my new book I would be able to interpret dreams. Gordon was pleased that I liked my present. "You can charge a nickle a dream," he said and Mother shushed him. "Don't go putting ideas into her head," she said.

Then Mother gave me her present. It was a real live monkey, named Gigolo. He was a white-faced, ringtail monkey and I loved him with all my heart the moment Mother put him in my arms. Even when he bit me I loved him.

It was a glorious, wonderful day, and it would have been perfect if after the matinee we hadn't been arrested. We had been arrested before, but each time Gordon had been able to talk the child-labor authorities into letting us finish the week. Not in Rochester. They took all of us away from Gordon and Mother and put us in a car and drove us downtown to the children's shelter. Mother and Gordon followed in a taxicab. Through the windows I could see Mother gesturing to the taxi driver to stay close to the police car and weeping on Gordon's shoulder.

A policewoman sat in the front seat of our car with the driver. The boys and June and I crowded together in the back. Bubsy, eying the policewoman, whispered so she couldn't hear: "They'll throw us in jail. Wait'll you see, they're taking us to jail right now." Bubsy knew all about jails because his father had been arrested many times. "First they'll grill us," he whispered authoritatively, "then they'll fingerprint us and before they're finished we'll talk all right."

"They won't make me talk," Sonny, his baby brother, said. "My fadder talked onct and the gang busted two of his ribs and almost poked his eye out."

The policewoman in the front seat squared her shoulders and looked straight ahead. "I'm not talkin'," Sonny said loudly.

They didn't put us in jail, or grill us or even fingerprint us. They didn't do anything interesting to us at all. Instead they made us sit in a stuffy room while Mother and Gordon, in an adjoining office, tried to talk the judge into letting us go so we could do our show that night. Then Mother put in a long-distance call to Grandpa in Seattle. Later the theatre manager came in and tried to get the judge to accept a fine as the court had done with Gus Edwards' kiddie revue. The walls were thin and we could hear every word.

"Gus Edwards was a different case altogether," the judge said. "There'll be no fine in *this* case. These children are illiterate!"

Mother screamed at him, "I'll sue you for that statement. My babies have a father and I'll prove it."

Then the phone rang, and it was Grandpa calling from Seattle.

"Oh, thank God we got you, Papa." Mother was laughing and crying at the same time. "They've taken the girls away from me, Papa. They say I'm not a fit mother. Papa, you've got to get on the phone and tell the judge who we are."

Fortunately, the judge was a Shriner. In the excitement, Mother had been too disturbed to see his Shrine pin, but when he learned that Grandpa was also a Shriner and that Mother was an Eastern Star, or practically one, he dismissed the case. But even so we missed the show that night.

From then on, it seemed that every time we opened in a new city, stern-faced policewomen would come backstage and question the boys and June and me. The questions were always hard. For example, when were we born? They always wanted the year. Months and days were easy but we had so many years to keep track of. On trains June was under five, I was under ten. In Syracuse we both had to be twelve. We couldn't play New York City at all, because the age limit there was sixteen, and even with lifts in our shoes we couldn't look sixteen.

Once a policewoman asked us to name the Vice-President under Wilson. June and I had never heard of Wilson. Another policewoman asked us who killed Cain. It went on like that until it became plain that, as much as Mother hated to spend the money, a schoolteacher had become a necessity. Finding the right kind of teacher was Mother's big problem. It was most important that they look the part. They had to have papers proving they were registered teachers, letters showing they had taught before. Mother didn't care where they had taught so long as it sounded impressive. Above all they had to be, as Mother said, troupers. The first one, Miss Hamilton, had the face for it and she had the papers, too, but she

was no trouper. She thought living in hotels was barbaric. Eating
in a cafeteria gave her indigestion. She couldn't sleep in an upper
berth; she was afraid she'd roll out. After a couple of weeks she
broke down completely and had to take a day coach back home. I
don't remember the second teacher too well. She was with us for
three days only. Mother and she had some slight difference about
salary.

Then when we were playing Minneapolis, Miss Tompkins
joined the act. She had just graduated from the Minnesota State
Normal School and we were her first pupils.

We liked Miss Tompkins immediately. She was delighted with
the prospect of traveling with a show troupe. She thought living
in hotels and eating in restaurants was a thrilling adventure. She
couldn't wait to sleep in an upper. The admiring glances of the
stagehands and musicians pleased her. She liked it when Mother
called her our tutor.

Mother had one misgiving about the new teacher; she was too
pretty. Mother would have preferred an older woman, a more
genuine type. Miss Tompkins was blonde, with blue eyes and very
pale eyelashes. Her figure was full. She wore high-heeled patent-
leather pumps. Mother made her buy a pair of sturdy ground grippers at once. Then she tactfully suggested that Miss Tompkins
wear her hair straight—marcels were a nuisance on the road, anyway
—and put on horn-rimmed glasses. "Not real lenses, of course,"
Mother said gaily. "Just glass in the horn rims for effect." Miss
Tompkins agreed.

Mother also toyed with the idea of a uniform. Gray serge with
a long cape for street wear, the cape to be lined with red flannel.
Very English-governess-like, Mother said. She and Miss Tompkins
settled for a black dress with white piqué collar and cuffs.

One morning, a few days after Miss Tompkins was hired,
Gordon invited photographers and reporters to attend our first class.
Miss Tompkins' black dress looked quite drab and Mother was
hopeful that, for all her prettiness, she would photograph badly.
That day we had real school desks in our dressing room. A large
blackboard hid the make-up shelf and Miss Tompkins had a desk
with a globe of the world on it. The globe was a prop from another

act on the bill. Miss Tompkins became very friendly with the reporters. While they set up their tripods, she said, "Oh, you don't want ugly me in the picture." They laughed and told her she was far from ugly, and one of the photographers told her to wet her lips so they would photograph more alluringly. Miss Tompkins' mouth was quite chapped by the time the pictures were finished.

While the pictures were being taken, a reporter asked Miss Tompkins what she thought about stage kiddies in general. "I find them above the average pupil in public schools," she answered quickly. "Little June has been on the stage since she was two and a half years old. She has never been to school. But actions speak louder than words. June, dear, how much is four times four?"

June stared at Miss Tompkins for what seemed a long time. There was something almost hostile in the stare, something Miss Tompkins couldn't account for. I felt sorry for her and decided to be helpful.

"We haven't got to our foursies yet," I said.   .

"Besides," June added, "we don't do it like that. We start from two times one is two, two times two is four, two times three is six and so on."

The reporter was satisfied and so was Miss Tompkins. Neither of them suspected that we learned our multiplication tables the way we learned a new song lyric. Skipping around was taboo.

When the pictures appeared in the evening paper, the caption of one said, "When is a school not a school? When it is backstage at the Hennepin-Orpheum." Mother wasn't at all sure she liked the sound of it. She preferred the one that said, "Dainty June and Her Newsboy Songsters at School. From nine until noon they study their readin', writin', and 'rithmetic—just like children leading normal lives."

At exactly noon the following day, June and I slipped into our coats and started to leave the schoolroom. We were at the door before June turned to Miss Tompkins and said, "We're going to the ten-cent store. Do you want to come wiff us?" June and I always took our noon exercise in the aisles of the local ten-cent stores—such nice smells of hot dogs and roasted peanuts, so many colorful things piled up on the counters, so many careless salesgirls. We usually wore coats with big pockets.

Miss Tompkins did want to come with us. She removed her horn-rimmed glasses before we started out—Mother had told her it was all right now that the publicity pictures had been taken—but she still wore the ground grippers and they made her walk strangely, almost as though she had snowshoes on. When people looked at June, with her blond curls and her animated little face, Miss Tompkins smiled proudly.

The dime store was down the street from the theatre. We forgot Miss Tompkins as soon as we got inside. We were too busy. June engaged a salesgirl in conversation and I clipped. Then it was my turn to talk to the salesgirl while June clipped. There was nothing systematic about it. We didn't take things we needed and we seldom took things we wanted. Quantity was what we were after. We had learned that to clip in quantity we couldn't specialize.

That day we didn't wait until we got to the theatre to compare our booty but began to empty our pockets as soon as we left the store. June won. She had a tin spectacle case, two compasses, a jar of pomade, a patent can opener and a tea strainer. I had two articles more, but mine were small compact things; June's were bulky. We were trading vigorously when all at once we heard Miss Tompkins gasp. It was almost like Mother's asthma gasp. June and I gave Miss Tompkins a sympathetic glance and went back to our bartering.

"Where did you children get those?" Miss Tompkins asked, her voice cracking on the last word.

June and I stared, first at Miss Tompkins, then at each other. "Woolworff's," June said. She still had trouble with her *th's* and Mother encouraged it because she thought it made June sound babylike. Usually Miss Tompkins, like most other people, smiled when June lisped, but she didn't smile this time. She seized our arms firmly and marched us back into the store. We didn't realize what she intended to do until we found ourselves standing before the cosmetics counter.

"Tell the lady you stole the jar of pomade," Miss Tompkins said to June. I was stunned and apparently June was too. As though in a trance she took the jar of pomade from her pocket and handed it to the open-mouthed salesgirl. Miss Tompkins forced her lips into a righteous grin. "Now ask her to forgive you," she said. "Tell her you will never steal again."

June's mouth began working. For a moment no sound came forth, then she managed to mumble, "I'm sowwy and I'll never steal again." The last words came very fast and June shut her mouth with a snap.

Miss Tompkins herded us to the next counter. Combs, brushes and spectacle cases were disgorged. I heard myself repeating June's speech and it didn't sound like my voice at all. It was more like a voice coming from the bottom of a deep well.

An hour later we were all in the dressing room. Mother was curling June's hair. She tested the hot iron on a sheet of newspaper that served as a cover for the make-up shelf. Then she placed a second iron on the flame of the Sterno can. When the stage electrician knocked and asked Mother about the light cues, Miss Tompkins offered to finish June's hair and took the iron from Mother.

June had been silent from the time we left the ten-cent store. Now, when she heard Miss Tompkins' voice, she banged her head on the make-up shelf with such violence that the thud made me look up from tying my shoe. June shoved her thin hands through her straggly blond hair and shrieked. Then she jumped up from her chair and backed into a corner of the dressing room. The shrieks became louder and louder. Miss Tompkins, holding the smoking iron in her hand, stared at her. I thought she had burned my sister and Mother thought so too. She rushed over to June and fell on her knees in front of her.

"There, there, she didn't burn my little angel on purpose," Mother said. "She didn't burn my little angel on purpose."

Then it all came out—garbled, disjointed, but true: how we had apologized to ten salesgirls, how we had returned fourteen articles. June didn't say stolen articles; she said "fings we got."

Mother picked her up and held her close. "Don't cry, Angel. Mommy is here. Don't cry." Mother began crying too, so I started—good loud bellows for the dignity I had left at the spectacles counter at Woolworth's. I threw myself at Mother and buried my face in her chest. June's knees hit me on the nose as Mother rocked her back and forth, but I didn't care. We were together. We were safe from outsiders who didn't understand us. Mother felt warm and smelled good. I cried louder.

Then, in a rush, Mother's mood changed. She put June on an army cot and pushed me aside. "How dare you?" Mother shouted at Miss Tompkins. June and I stopped crying and looked on. "How dare you subject that little bundle of nerves to such a strain?"

The little bundle of nerves sniffed loudly.

"How can the baby do her matinee in *that* condition?" Mother went on, her voice rising higher and higher. Miss Tompkins didn't even try to answer. In her very brief association with the troupe she had learned that much. She put the curling iron on the shelf and walked to the door.

"Get out!" Mother screamed. "You're fired!"

I was too scared to look, but I heard something heavy hit the door after it closed and I think it was a chair. When I opened my eyes, Mother was reheating the curling iron. June had stopped trembling. She dragged the upturned chair to the shelf and seated herself in front of the cracked, wavy mirror.

"She isn't really fired, is she, Mommy?" June asked.

Mother tested the curling iron with a wet finger before she answered. "Certainly not," she said. "Now sit still while Mommy does the bangs."

"Look, Mommy," June said a moment later, "I got three eyes."

Mother smiled. "No precious. That's just a defect in the mirror."

I jumped up to look. Sure enough, my sister did have three eyes.

6

Easter Sunday in Indianapolis was the best Easter we ever had because that was the year Gussie joined the act. Before the matinee June and the boys and I raced through the scenery and props finding eggs in the most unlikely places. Mother was very good at hiding Easter eggs. I found Gussie, a real live baby goose, sitting in a purple basket with two chocolate eggs under him. Mother had hidden him behind a canvas-covered tree stump used by Mantell, the India Rubber Man. I hadn't thought to look there, and if Gussie hadn't chirped I would never have found him.

He was so little I could hold him in one hand. Instead of feathers he was covered with pale yellow down. His flat bill was soft and leathery when I touched it. We had been given baby ducks and chicks for Easter before but no matter how careful we were they always died. But Gussie, from the very first, was a strong healthy goose, and every day he grew stronger and healthier. He grew bigger, too, and his pale yellow down turned into sleek white feathers, his flat bill grew hard and he learned how to hiss at people and snap at them. He also learned how to troupe.

Mother often said that Gussie was a natural-born trouper. Next to Life Savers, which he loved the best, he loved his little comedy hat with the feather in it, and next he liked rolled oats. On stage, in the cow number, June would hold a Life Saver in her hand and

Gussie, wearing his comedy hat, would waddle after her, trying
to snatch it from her hand. When the audience laughed he would
lean way over the footlights and hiss at them. That is all Gussie did
in the act, but it paid for his rolled oats.

It was a hot summer and Gussie felt the heat terribly. He
wouldn't eat, not even his Life Savers, and although he swam
twice a day in the bathtub between times he would sit for hours
with his feathers fluffed up and his bill open. Gussie, trouper
that he was, still yearned for a bit of outdoor activity.

After the matinee in Rockford, Illinois, Mother put his leash on
him and off we went in search of a river, or a park or a lake. We
walked until Gussie refused to take another step. Then Mother
picked him up in her arms. "You'd think," she said, "that in a town
the size of Rockford there'd be some place for a goose to cool off."
Mother petted him gently as we started back toward the theatre.

Across the street from the stage entrance a man was putting the
finishing touches on a window display. It was the window of a
sporting-goods shop and the man had built a miniature woodland
scene with real plants and shrubs to represent trees. There was a
waterfall in the background and a tiny figure of a little boy fishing
from a bridge into a pool of water with celluloid fish floating in
it. The window display looked so cool and peaceful that you could
almost believe you were in a forest. We followed Mother across
the street and stood beside her looking in at the woodland scene.

The man, wearing flannel covers on his shoes, stepped carefully
through the trees and lake. He placed a celluloid mermaid in the
water and stood back to examine the effect. We waited until he
climbed out of the window, then we followed Mother into the
store.

"I just wanted to tell you that you have the most beautiful
window display I've ever seen," she said to the man. "The realism is
unbelievable. That waterfall for instance. Beautiful! Simply beautiful. And that little bridge. It's like a hand painting!"

The man and Mother gazed over the wall into the window for a
long time. They were both carried away by the loveliness of it.
"But I have a feeling it needs *something*," Mother said. "I don't
know exactly what, but it needs something."

The man looked more closely at the window. He, too, thought it needed something.

"Movement!" Mother said. "That's what it needs, movement! It's beautiful, but it's static. You need some *wild life* in it."

The man snapped his fingers at the inspirational idea. "I've got just the thing," he said. "A stuffed raccoon!"

Mother looked at him in horror. "A stuffed raccoon?" she said, appalled at the very thought. "I said *movement*. There's no movement in a stuffed raccoon."

"I guess not," the man admitted. "I just happened to have a stuffed raccoon."

"Well, it won't do at all," Mother said positively. "I was thinking of a live animal, something like Gussie here."

The man hadn't noticed Gussie, who was lying listless and limp in Mother's arms. Now he poked a playful finger in his direction. Gussie was too exhausted with the heat even to hiss, let alone take a snap at the finger.

"He's a trained goose," Mother was saying. "You've probably seen him in our act. We're headlining in your lovely little theatre across the street."

The man said he hadn't seen our act yet, but he could tell just from looking at Gussie that he was an exceptional goose. He glanced over the wall at his window display. Then he looked back at Gussie. He was thinking very hard. Mother was thinking, too.

"Of course, Gussie is only on stage for a few minutes," she said. "And the theatre *is* right across the street. He could stay in your window after the show at night and spend most of the days here, too."

The man's gratitude was touching. "To think a stranger," he said, "a total stranger, would show such generosity and interest in my window."

Mother shyly brushed aside his compliments. "I love beauty," she said simply.

The man gave her a key to the front door and, tucking it carefully in her purse, she sailed happily out of the store. She held Gussie close to the window and let him look in. "Just think, Gussie, after the show tonight you'll be swimming in that pool. Won't that be lovely?"

At eleven thirty that night we let ourselves into the sporting-goods store. The man had thoughtfully left a light on for us, and Mother, leaning way over the wall behind the window, let Gussie, who was wearing his little comedy hat, drop gently into the woodland scene. Gussie blinked his eyes, then he waddled to the pool and stepped in. He stuck his long neck into the water, and throwing his head back he splashed the water over his feathers. His big webbed feet sprawled behind him as he swam the full length of the window and back again. Mother reached down and slipped the little hat off his head.

"It spoils the wild-life effect," she said.

Leaving his box of rolled oats on the counter, we tiptoed out of the store so Gussie wouldn't notice we were leaving him. He'd never spent a night away from us in all his life. We worried about his missing us, then we wondered if the man would remember to feed him in the morning. Although none of us mentioned it we worried most about what would happen in case of fire.

"We're doing this for Gussie's own good," Mother said on our way back to the hotel. "We mustn't worry about him. He's cool and comfortable and that's all that matters."

At eight thirty the next morning our phone rang, and rang. Mother, half asleep, walked over and took the receiver off the hook. I could hear the frantic voice screaming through the phone, but I couldn't make out the words. Mother blanched as she gripped the receiver tighter.

"Is Gussie all right?" she asked tensely. "I don't care about any of that, all I want to know about is Gussie, is he all right?"

At the mention of Gussie's name June and I jumped out of bed and began grabbing for our clothes. "I'll be there in five minutes," Mother said. "But I warn you, if anything has happened to that goose I'll sue you for everything you own!" Mother hung up the receiver and threw herself into her clothes. We tore out of the room and ran all the way to the sporting-goods store. Without a glance at the window Mother threw open the door and demanded that Gussie be handed over at once.

"Get him yourself," the man said through clenched teeth. His face the color of strawberry soda pop, he pointed a shaking finger toward the window. "Get that vicious goose out of here or I'll call the police."

There, in what was left of the woodland scene, was Gussie. A furious, hissing, snapping Gussie. Gussie, who believed that we had deserted him, had gone berserk. He had broken the little bridge and trampled it to pieces, the waterfall hose had been pulled loose and a stream of water sputtered from what was left of it, more water squirted through a hole in the hose, spattering the window glass with mud and bits of fern and leaves. The plants were chewed up and half eaten, the miniature trees were uprooted and lying with their roots and stumps in the air. The mermaid, bottom up, was stuck in a clump of mud. The woodland window display was an absolute, complete shambles.

"Gussie, darling, don't you know us?" Mother was saying. "It's your family, Gussie. We're here." Gussie flapped his wings in fury, toppling over a flower pot which had been hidden with moss.

"Get him out of here," the man screamed. "Get him out!" When Gussie heard the hateful, strange voice he kicked out a webbed foot and crashed down the cardboard background. Then he looked around wild-eyed for something else to destroy.

Mother spoke more firmly to the goose, "That's enough of this, Gussie," she said. She took his little comedy hat from her purse and waved it in front of his angry face. "See, Gussie, we've come to take you home." Gussie stopped hissing. His feathers flattened down and he tilted his head from side to side as he looked with one eye, then the other, at the little hat. He stood very still when Mother reached over the wall and lifted him out of the window. She put the little hat on his head and fastened the elastic under his chin.

"Come on, Gussie," Mother said softly as she buried her face in his long thin neck. "We're going back to the theatre where we belong."

There was some talk of the man suing us for damages, but Mother was ready to swear Gussie was a wild goose, therefore protected by the state conservation laws. Besides, as she said, Gussie had been an invited guest. We never knew what happened to the man's case, because after the show the following night we left for St. Louis.

7

THE BREVOORT
Hotel in St. Louis had been recommended by one of the stagehands.
We peered through the dingy window into the lobby. Theatrical
photographs covered the wall behind the reception desk. Even from
that distance we could see how yellowed and old fashioned some of
them were. Brown leather chairs, the springs sagging beyond hope,
were lined up in the window. Dented, dull cuspidors on rubber
mats that proved the bad aim of their users were placed between
them. The barbershop in the basement had a sign in the window
alongside a flowering begonia plant. The sign read: LEECHES FOR
BLACK EYES. The leeches clung to the inside of a fish bowl with
a piece of wire mesh on top. Their whitish stomachs looked flat
and slippery, all except one that was bloated and darker than the
others.

Mother tucked a few straggling curls up under her taupe-colored
cloche, then she and Gordon went into the hotel. "Let's hope they
have rooms for us," she said.

Miss Tompkins had left us at the theatre after arranging our
schoolroom. She told us she would make her own hotel arrangements and we all knew she was going to live at the Y.W.C.A. club
again. Mother couldn't understand why the schoolteacher preferred
living in those cold dreary-looking places. They were like institu-
tions, Mother said. Not at all homey like the hotels we lived in.

The boys and June and I sat on our suitcases near the entrance

to the hotel, but not so near the desk clerk could count us. Mother
was perfectly willing to pay a dollar a day for each of us but she
never mentioned how many we were. She would ask the desk clerk
for two double beds for the little boys and let it go at that. If the
desk clerk assumed there were only two little boys to a bed instead
of three that was his mistake, not Mother's.

To encourage this assumption our entrances into the hotels were
carefully staged. Three of the boys would go up to the room, and
one of them would come back down and go up with June and another boy and me. Then one of the others would come down and
go back up with the two remaining boys. It meant making a few
extra trips but it confused the desk clerks. There was too much
movement, too many children going in and out and up and down
for them to keep track.

Like most of the hotels we stayed in, the Brevoort was right
downtown. There was no place outside for us to play. Most times
we played in the hallways and got our exercise running up and
down the stairs. The hallways were fun to play in, but monotonous.
The maids' broom closets, when left unlocked, were a special treat.
The sharp evil smells of the disinfectants in the large drugstore-like
bottles were dangerous and exciting. Sometimes, stacked beside
the mops and buckets were old magazines, or funny papers we
hadn't read. Very often we found empty liquor bottles. We'd fill
them with water and drink it; then pretending to be drunk we
would stagger through the hall, throwing ourselves at the doors
and bumping into each other. When people would shout at us to
be quiet, we'd scoot up the stairs and wait, holding our breath for
the danger to pass. Riding up and down in the elevators was fun,
too, but after the first few trips the elevator boys weren't too
co-operative.

We weren't allowed to play in the lobby. Mother gave us strict
orders to walk, not run when we went in and out, and most important of all, we were not to speak to strangers. Unless, of course,
they were show people, then a few polite words were permissible.

Avoiding conversations with people outside our business was
sometimes difficult. It was especially difficult to know just when the
people *were* outside our business. A traveling salesman was easy,

Grandpa called me Plug.

My sister, June, could dance
on her toes when she was two and a half.

I was four
and couldn't do anything.

🦅 My specialty in the act was a "tough" number.
I sang it until I was 15,
mainly because I couldn't learn a new one.

Boussum

I performed in
Grandpa's lodge halls
when I was six.

Baby June and Her Pals.
The Military Finale featured a gun drill.

Sussman

Orpheum circuit
when I was ten.

Just like children leading normal lives...
A blackboard hid the makeup mirrors
and sometimes we had real school desks.

The Finale. The program read that June's gown was covered with
over a million rhinestones and that it cost $1,000.

Sussman

Dainty June and Her Newsboy Songsters.

Boardinghouses had back yards and places to play
...but hotels were homelike, too.

Campbell

Age-lis

It was June's song...I wore her costume just for the picture. Gigolo, the monkey, wasn't in the number, either, not since the time he bit my sister. Mother bit him back, but even so he wasn't to be trusted.

Age-lis

People stared at us when we walked down the street.

Mother was charming, courageous, resourceful, and ambitious. She was also, in a feminine way, ruthless.

anyone could tell he wasn't in our business, but what about the wrestlers who lived in the hotel? They rehearsed in the rehearsal room the same as we did. And what about the man who sold chances on the punch boards? During the summers he worked on a carnival and carnivals were a part of show business. And what about the lady with the red hair who wore a full stage make-up even on the street? June and I heard her talking to a man who was getting his hair cut in the hotel barbershop and from the conversation we were sure she was in our business. She was asking the man why he never got dates for her any more, and he answered her the same way the booking agents used to answer us before we got on the Orpheum Circuit.

"Don't blame me because you ain't working," he said. "All I can do is get you the dates. It's up to you to make good."

After hearing that we were sure it was all right to speak to her, but Mother made such a fuss when she heard about it that the manager of the hotel told her we could check out if we wanted to.

"I'm sure of my rent with her," he said, "which is more than I can say for everyone in this hotel."

Mother was so angry we would have moved out that same day if we hadn't already unpacked our trunks. It was a perfect example, she said, of how careful we had to be about talking with strangers.

The man who walked up to the desk a few days later wasn't really a stranger. That is, we had seen him around the hotel lobby before, but we didn't know for sure if he was in our business or not. Each time we had seen him he had been arguing with the desk clerk. But this day he was rather grand as he slapped a stack of money on the desk and demanded a receipt. "And I'd also like to have my baggage," he said. "The baggage you've been holding."

June and I were sitting on the top step overlooking the lobby. Mother hadn't said anything about sitting on the steps and we weren't actually *in* the lobby. It was like sitting in the balcony of a theatre. No one could see us, but we could see everything that was going on.

The porter brought out two large cases and placed them beside the man at the desk. June and I were used to unusual-looking baggage, but we had never seen anything as interesting as these. They were about four feet high and three feet wide, and were painted shiny black, with the letters WHAT IS IT? painted in white on the sides. Big white question marks were scattered all over, making them appear even more mysterious. In the lower corner in smaller letters was the name, DOCTOR GERBER AND CO.

The man didn't look like a doctor to me. His hands were shaking so hard he could hardly manage to lift the two gaudy cases. His eyes were bloodshot and his nose was like a chunk of red rubber sponge.

"Is it okay with you if I wait here for the wife?" the man asked. The desk clerk shrugged, and the man carried his two cases over to one of the brown leather chairs in front of the window. He sank into it as though it pained him to move.

I glanced around to see if Mother might be looking for us. The coast was clear so I walked down the steps and across the lobby to where the man was sitting. June followed close behind me. Standing in front of the man and his two shiny cases, my voice failed me. There was something about him that choked the words in my throat. Maybe it was his nose. It looked worse close to, as though it had been pasted on. It was bumpy and covered with thin blue streaks.

"My sister wants to know what you have in your cases," June said.

I gave her a sharp look. I did want to know, but I didn't think she should blurt it out like that. I was almost eleven years old and very conscious of formalities. The man peered up at June as though he hadn't heard her. Then he snapped out one word.

"Babies," he said.

June and I looked down at the cases and smiled uncomfortably.

"Not live babies," the man said, narrowing his eyes. "Dead ones."

June grabbed my arm with a hot damp hand. The desk clerk seemed so far away, too far away to help us. Aside from him we were alone in the lobby with this terrible man and his two cases of dead babies. He made a sudden move toward the case nearest him, and before June and I could run or scream for help he had unsnapped the catch and thrown it wide open. There were shelves on both sides, and each shelf was filled with wide-mouthed bottles. Each bottle held a baby. The babies were all sizes: some of them no longer than six inches, others almost a foot long. The larger ones were squeezed into the bottles so that the tops of their heads were all squashed down. The little ones floated around in a greenish liquid. Some of the bottles held nothing but a whitish mass of jelly-like substance. One bottle had a half a baby in it, sliced down from the top of its head to its tiny little foot. The man took one of the bottles off the shelf and held it close to me.

"See this one," he said proudly. "Negroid. Notice the white skin? All babies start out white. The color pigment doesn't change until the air hits 'em. This one over here is a six-month fetus. That one over there is a fiver. See the fingernails? Hair and nails at five months. Over here, now, we got an embryo. Three months. This one here is deformed. See the twisted foot?"

He was snatching the bottles in and out of the case so fast I couldn't keep track of which was which. It didn't matter. I didn't need his explanations either. Many things I had wondered about were suddenly and miraculously clear to me. Mother had once told me she found June in a rose and me in a cabbage leaf. I had hated being found in such an unpleasant vegetable, and now I knew that it wasn't true at all.

"—look at the umbilical cord hanging on this one—" the man was saying, and June and I gazed with wonder at the stringlike thing attached to the stomach. "It used to be a lot longer—I guess it rotted off." He shook the bottle upside down and sure enough there was the other piece of the cord.

There were a few questions I wanted to ask the man, but before I could get a word in, he jumped to his feet and greeted a florid-faced woman who strode into the lobby.

"Did you see Denham about the carnival dates?" he asked as he hurried over to her. "Did you tell him we got the babies back?"

"I sure did," the woman said, with a triumphant look at the desk clerk. "He greeted me with open arms. We got seven weeks of still dates lined up and a promise on the fairs."

The man walked jauntily back to where June and I stood, near, but not too near the cases. He snapped the case shut while his wife continued on toward the desk. She left a trail of whisky fumes as she passed. The desk clerk watched her warily.

"I'll thank you to leave quietly," he said. "We don't cater to boozers!"

Her husband, carrying the two cases of pickled babies, spoke to her from the door: "Come on honey. We got the act back and that's all that matters. Come on."

The woman hesitated a moment, then turned on her heel and walked unsteadily across the lobby and out the door. June and I waited. We didn't want to miss anything. Then, when we were sure the man and his wife weren't coming back, we scooted up the stairs to our favorite hiding place in the hallway. We snuggled down in the alcove under the canvas-covered hose that was rolled up like a worm with a sign above it, IN CASE OF FIRE ONLY, and sat there silently for a few moments, both of us in deep thought.

"That's why the woman in the revolving-ladder act got so fat she had to lay off," I said. "I bet she had a five-month flotus."

"Fetus," June said, correcting me primly.

"Why didn't Mother tell us about the embryos and the fetuses?" I said, almost to myself. "It's a lot more interesting than that old cabbage-leaf story."

June sat up very straight. There wasn't room in the alcove for her to turn completely to me, but she squeezed around as far as she could. "You didn't *believe* that silly story about the rose and the cabbage leaf?" she asked scornfully.

I had believed it, but I wasn't going to admit that to June. "Huh," I replied, "who'd believe a story like that!"

June wasn't convinced. "*You* did!" she said.

I jumped to my feet and slapped violently at the seat of my knickers to get the dust off them. "You think you're the only one that knows anything," I said hotly. "It so happens that I'm two years older than you are and I know a lot more than you do."

But while I was running down the hallway toward our room I knew in my heart that somehow my sister knew more about babies and where they came from than I did, and I wondered how I'd go about making her tell me without letting on I didn't already know.

The Brevoort, like most theatrical hotels, had a rehearsal room in the basement. There was a large mirror on one wall; a limbering-up bar running the full length of it. A piano and three chairs, one with the back broken off, were the only furniture. A bare electric-light bulb hung from a cord in the center of the ceiling.

Mother sat at the piano and told June and the boys and me to line up in front of the mirror. We didn't have many rehearsal days but when we did they were days of misery for me. Even the dances and songs I knew and could do on stage would go wrong at rehearsals. It wasn't just my awkwardness; my shoelace would come undone, the strap of my knickers would loosen. Sometimes I'd have a coughing fit and no matter how hard I tried I couldn't stop. Bubsy once accused me of coughing on purpose. "She's just trying to get out of learning the dance," he said. "She's always trying to spoil the act."

That wasn't true. I wanted desperately to sing and dance as well as June, but she learned everything so fast. The dances were easy for her. When I made a mistake the boys would call me "Plug" and giggle, and June would stand restlessly on one foot then the other. Worse than anything, though, was the big mirror on the wall. I couldn't help looking at myself and I hated the person I saw. I hated my brown straight hair, my ugly crooked teeth, and most of all I hated the knickers and the boy's clothes I wore.

That day I tried to look at my sister instead. She was wearing her duck dress, a black sateen pinafore with ruffled bloomers showing below it. The dress was trimmed with yellow to match the big smiling duck that covered the whole front. The duck had been painted on by hand with genuine oil paints, which had cracked in places, but you could still tell it was a duck. The rouge on June's knees, left over from the show the night before, was orange colored in the harsh light. There were faint traces of rouge on the knuckles of her fingers, too. That was a make-up trick Mother had learned from Francis Renault, the female impersonator. Even with her blond hair rolled up in curlers, June looked like an actress. Only actresses, I thought enviously, could be so pretty.

Mother struck a chord on the piano. "When I count four," she said, "I want you to start. Keep the line straight and pretend you have your guns. Ready?"

She played the introduction of "The Parade of the Wooden Soldiers," our finale music, and keeping time with her head, called

out the gun drill like a top sergeant. "Right shoulder arms, hip.
Left shoulder arms, hip. Hip, hip, hip—"

Tommy stopped dancing. "She's doing it again, Madam Rose,"
he said. "She's always doing it, and she throws us all off step."

"Doing what?" I demanded, because I knew he meant me. "What
am I doing that's so awful?"

"Counting out loud, that's what!"

"I am not!" I said indignantly. "He makes a mistake, Mother,
and he blames me. All the boys do. They're always blaming me for
everything."

Mother swung around on the piano stool. I thought she was
going to be angry, but her voice when she spoke was soft and low.
"What *is* the matter with you, Louise? Is it that you don't want to
do the dance? Is that it? What *do* you want? Would you like to
leave the act and live with Aunt Helma in Seattle?"

The boys were silent now. My leaving the act was a subject that
came up from time to time. None of the boys knew Aunt Helma but
they had heard Mother speak of her. Aunt Helma was my real
father's sister. Uncle Fred, her husband, was managing editor of
the Seattle *Times*. They were very rich and lived in a big white
house on Queen Anne Hill.

Twice before, I had almost left the act to live with them. One
time, I remembered, was before we met Gordon, when we were still
playing the lodge halls. Mother had taken me up to the big house
and on the way there she had told me how rich they were, and how
much they could do for me. Their daughter, Helen, had died when
she was twelve years old and Mother said Aunt Helma had never
quite gotten over it.

When we arrived at their house, Mother and Uncle Fred and
Aunt Helma went into the living room to talk, and Marion Bates,
who lived next door, took me up to Helen's room. Marion was my
age. Everyone said we could be twins if her cheeks were rosier, and
I was less chubby, but I thought she was prettier. She was wearing
a bottle-green velvet dress with a lace collar, and long white stockings that didn't have a wrinkle in them anywhere, not even at the
knees.

Helen's room was just as I remembered it from the last time I had visited there. Crisp white organdie curtains hung from the windows like starched petticoats. The bedspread, with a ruffle around the bottom, matched the curtains, and there was another ruffle on the vanity table. The rug was covered with flowers. The chairs were painted white with roses on the backs.

There was a niche in the corner of the room with glass doors, where Helen had kept her secret treasures, mostly sea shells and candy-box tops. On the top shelf was a silver loving cup with her name on it in fancy letters. Helen had won it for ice skating. How lovely it would be, I thought, to wake up every morning in a room like this.

Marion ran ahead of me to the window and opened it. "Look, Louise. You can see right into my bedroom."

I crossed over to where Marion was. When my feet touched the rug it was like walking in a garden. I wanted to take off my heavy oxfords so I could feel the softness, but I didn't think I should. Marion was a nice girl, and I liked her, but she couldn't understand certain things. Maybe that was because she had always lived in a house like Aunt Helma's.

"Helen was the prettiest girl on Queen Anne Hill," Marion said. "My mother says it's a wonder she wasn't spoiled with all the fuss everybody made over her. But she wasn't spoiled a bit. She was wonderful. I've missed her so very much since she went away to be an angel."

I looked out the window, the way Marion was doing. The stars were like rhinestones on a backdrop. The air smelled of cut grass.

"Let me show you Helen's hair ribbons," Marion said. She skipped over to the vanity table and opened one of the drawers. "Helen had the most beautiful curls you ever saw. Look at the ribbons. Aren't they pretty?" Her fingers played with the brightly colored bits of silk and satin. "Let me put one on you," she said suddenly. "Come on. Sit down."

Marion selected one of the ribbons and tied it to a strand of my hair, then into a big poufy bow. When she stood back to see the effect I could see her and myself in the mirror. Marion was too polite to laugh, but I knew she wanted to. I looked so silly, like a boy dressed up in girl's clothes.

She picked up a silver brush with Helen's initials on it and smoothed out my bangs. There was a mirror to match the brush, and a comb, a button hook, a shoe horn and all sorts of silver things. "They're from Tiffany's in New York," Marion said proudly. She handed me the brush, and sure enough there was the name on it in tiny lettering. "Helen had a real pearl necklace, too. Every birthday she got another pearl added to it. My mother says when you come here to live all these things will belong to you. Mother says you're the luckiest little girl in the whole world. Everybody doesn't get a chance to be adopted into such a nice family—"

The silver brush dropped from my hands. I looked at Marion in the mirror and saw that she really meant what she had said. "I'm not going to be *adopted*," I said. "I—I'm just coming for a visit, until Mother gets back on her feet—"

"Oh no," Marion said, shaking her head. "I heard my mother and father talking about it after dinner. They said the papers are all drawn up and all your mother has to do is sign them. Father says the—"

Aunt Helma stood in the doorway, with Mother behind her. Marion ran up to her and kissed her good night, then she kissed my mother, and waved her hand at me. "I just can't wait," she said. "We'll have such fun together—"

Mother didn't look at me as she came into the room and sat down on the foot of the bed, but I could tell she had been crying. Her eyes were red and swollen. Aunt Helma walked over to where I was sitting and put her arms around me. "What Marion said is true. You're going to live here with Uncle Fred and me, and be our little girl. Won't that be nice?"

I looked at Mother and waited for her to say something.

"This will be your very own room," Aunt Helma said. "Everything here will be yours. You'll go to school with Marion and her little friends, and in the summer we'll go up to the beach house and you can swim every day. You can have a pony if you like, and a boat—"

Mother had rolled her handkerchief into a tight ball. Once or twice she started to say something then stopped. Why did she stop, I wondered. Why didn't she tell Aunt Helma that she wouldn't

let me be adopted? Why didn't she say it was all a mistake, that
I was just visiting?

"You won't have to travel all over the country any more, living
in cheap hotels and being in the way—"

"I didn't say she was in the way," Mother said sharply. "Not
exactly. I only said that—" She unrolled her handkerchief and
blew her nose, then she turned to me, and when she spoke her
voice was quite different. "Louise, dear. You're old enough now
to know how hard life has been for me these past few months, what
a fight I've had just to keep our heads above water. It might be years
before June is where she belongs in the theatre. Years of hard work
and struggle. Your Aunt Helma loves you. She can do things for
you I can't do—"

"But if I'm adopted I won't be yours any more," I said. Mother
didn't seem to realize what being adopted meant. "I just couldn't
ever take Helen's place. I couldn't win a cup like hers, or look like
her or have long curls like hers—"

Aunt Helma began to cry. "You wouldn't have to be like Helen,"
she sobbed. "No one could be like Helen—"

I felt sorry for Aunt Helma, but I felt sorrier for Mother. She
looked so disappointed. "I'll work harder in the act, Mother," I
said. "I'll practice every day, honest I will. I'll do anything but,
please, don't let me be adopted."

I remember how Mother sighed and told me to go and get my
coat, and how Aunt Helma and Uncle Fred waved good-by to us
from the front porch of their big white house. I took Mother's hand
as we walked down the street. "I'll make up for it some way," I
said. "Just wait and see."

Mother looked down at me, and smiled, then with a sigh she took
the hair ribbon off my head and folded it up carefully and put it in
her purse.

Mother was speaking my name impatiently, and I forgot about
Seattle and Aunt Helma and how I was almost adopted. "Answer
me," she said. "Do you want to do the dance or don't you?" Tommy
and the boys were watching me. I knew they were hoping I'd cry.
"I *do* want to do the dance," I said, keeping my eyes down and
biting back the tears. "I don't want to go and live with Aunt

Helma. I want to stay with the act—more than anything in the world. It's just that I—"

"That you *what?*" Mother was losing her patience. I could tell from the way she tapped her fingers on the piano. "Don't just stand there," she said. "What is it this time?"

I wanted to tell her I wouldn't be so clumsy if I could wear a dress like June's, and have my hair curled and wear pink socks, but I couldn't. Not in front of the boys. It didn't do any good to tell Mother anyway. I had told her before and all she said was I had to learn how to make the best of what I had. She said everybody couldn't be blonde and dainty like my sister. That I had to learn how to hold in my stomach and not look at my feet when I danced.

"Play the music again," I said. "I'll try harder, this time. Honest I will."

8

WHENEVER WE
worked on the bill with big stars, Mother would see to it that June
and I watched every single one of their performances. Sometimes
the stars weren't too pleased to have us crouched down in the wings,
show after show, learning every word and gesture of their acts.
Eva Tanguay for one put her foot down firmly. "Get those little
monsters out of the wings," she screamed, "or I don't go on!"

Mother couldn't have cared less. She didn't consider Eva Tanguay a real star at all, and she said so loud enough for everyone
on stage to hear. "Come along, girls," she added. "There's nothing
I want you to learn from *this* freak attraction!"

Fanny Brice's act was a different thing altogether. From the
moment we knew we were to be on the bill with her Mother
began making plans for us to watch each performance.

But her plans took a sudden change when she received a telegram from Mr. Nash, the manager of the Orpheum Theatre in
San Francisco. He wired Mother to notify him at once if there
was anyone in our act who could play a scene with Fanny Brice.
The part called for a teen-aged girl capable of speaking five lines.

Mother sat down in the dressing room and began composing an
answer. "Have perfect girl for part," she wrote; then she scratched
it out and began again, "Capable actress available . . ." June looked
down at the paper Mother was working on.

"Teen-aged means somebody over twelve, doesn't it?" she asked.
Mother was too busy to answer right away. "How can I be over
twelve," June said, "when I'm only nine?"

Mother added her name, Madam Rose, to the bottom of the
message she had written; then she took down her beaver coat from
the hanger and put it on. "You girls wait here for me," she said.
"I have to send this telegram."

"I won't do it," June said flatly.

"Won't do what?" Mother asked from the doorway.

"I won't play in that scene with Fanny Brice."

Mother smiled down at my sister, "Of course you won't, dear,"
she said. "Mother wouldn't want you to. Louise is going to play
the scene."

Mother had closed the door behind her before I realized what
she had said. *Louise is going to play the scene.* I had never spoken
a line on the stage in my life. I was still doing "I'm a Hard-boiled
Rose" because I couldn't learn the words to a new song. I, who
couldn't sing or dance or do anything, was to do the scene with
Fanny Brice. It was frightening and wonderful at the same time.

"Mother was only joking," June said. "You're only eleven, you
can't be a teen-aged girl any better than I can."

But Mother wasn't joking. Instead of wiring Mr. Nash, she
telephoned him long distance, and for the rest of the week she
pounded the lines she had copied down over the phone into my
head. By the time we arrived in San Francisco on opening day, I
knew the five sentences by heart. But I didn't know the cues;
Mother had neglected to ask Mr. Nash for those.

While I waited outside Fanny Brice's dressing room, I went over
the lines, "Take your hands off me! Who do you think you are?
Mary Rose, what's that to you? I don't like it. I'd rather have a
name like Ruby." The lines didn't make sense to me but I went
over them again, anyway.

I could tell from the way she looked at me that Fanny Brice was
disappointed. I was a little disappointed in her, too. I had expected
her to be swathed in furs, and jewels, with a train on her dress
and feathers in her hair, like Eva Tanguay. Instead she wore a
plain black dress, with a cloth coat over it. Her jewelry was a gold

wedding ring. She didn't look like my idea of a big star at all. But there was something nice about her, anyway.

"So you're going to play Mary Rose, huh?" she said, looking at me from my brown scuffed-up brogues to the tweed boy's cap on my head. "How old are you?"

I hesitated. I was going to say I was a teen-aged girl, but I wasn't sure of what that implied so I told her the truth. "I'll be twelve on my next birthday. I'm big for my age."

"You sure are," she murmured.

"I know my lines," I said. "I've been studying them very hard." Then to prove it, I raced through all five, making them one sentence; "Take your hands off me who do you think you are Mary Rose but what's that to you. . . ."

"Hey, wait a minute," Fanny Brice said. "I've got a couple of lines in there myself."

She told me to sit down in her dressing room; then she explained the scene to me. "It opens," she said, "with me leaning against a lamppost in front of this waterfront scene. I sing a verse and chorus of my song; then Clancy, the cop, brings you on. You're a drunken flapper, and this cop is arresting you. I talk him out of it, then I ask you what your name is, and you tell me Mary Rose. But you don't like this name, see? In fact, you're a know-it-all kid that's heading for the gutter, only I step in and straighten you out. Do you think you can play it?"

"I know I can," I said fervently. I wasn't sure I could, but I wanted so hard to do it that I would have said anything.

"Have you got an evening gown?" she asked. Then without waiting for my answer she said, "No. I didn't think so. Adele! Unpack that dress I just got from Madam Frances. My friend here is going to try it on."

Adele, the maid, brought me an orange chiffon dress that was so beautiful it made my eyes blur. It had narrow jeweled shoulder straps and rows and rows of orange ostrich feathers on the full flowing skirt.

"Put it on," Fanny Brice said, "I want to see if it fits."

I looked around the room for a place to undress where she and the maid couldn't watch me. I couldn't bear the thought of them seeing me in my long underwear with the baggy knees and the sewn-in garters. There was no screen, nothing to hide behind. "I know it will fit," I said. "I'm sure of it."

Fanny Brice was losing her patience. I could tell from the way she tapped her foot. I made a fast decision and quickly, before I could change it, I pulled off my sweater and unfastened the belt to my knickers and let them fall to the floor. Fanny Brice and her maid both gulped when they saw my underwear. I knew they would and I wanted to die right on the spot. The maid was awful about it. "Where did you *find* underwear like that?" she asked.

"Mother buys it for us when we play Canada," I replied coldly. "It's one hundred per cent pure wool."

The maid was going to say something, but Fanny Brice stopped her with a look. "You can't wear it under this gown," she said, slipping the orange chiffon over my head. "Now, go on, unbutton that union suit. It's almost matinee time."

The dress fitted perfectly. I held in my stomach as I turned from side to side, gazing at myself in the mirror. I couldn't believe it was me. I looked taller, and thinner, and even older. Fanny Brice looked at me appraisingly. "You might get away with it at that," she said. Then we both looked down at my feet in the scuffed-up oxfords with the underwear dragging over them.

"See if you can squeeze into these." She handed me a pair of gold brocade shoes with high Louis heels. "They might be a little tight, but you can stand it for the few minutes you'll be on stage."

After our act was over I had almost an hour to change from a newsboy into a teen-aged flapper, but I couldn't wait. The moment the military finale was over I put on the orange chiffon dress and squeezed into the gold shoes. June watched me owl-eyed as I wobbled across the dressing room on the high heels. "Does Mother know you're wearing a dress like that?" she asked. I didn't answer her. It was hardly the question, I thought, to ask someone who was trying to get into character. Besides my feet hurt. I was nervous, too, and my throat was dry. I pulled off the gold brocade shoes and rested my feet on the cool cement floor. Then, so I wouldn't muss it, I took off the orange chiffon dress and hung it carefully on a hanger. June was looking at me with a wise little smile, but I didn't care. Suddenly I heard someone calling my name. The call boy was shouting for me. "Rose Louise. Places please. Miss Brice is on!"

At first I couldn't believe it. I had never been paged before in all my life. Then in a panic I grabbed the gold shoes and tried to shove them on my swollen feet. Half running, half limping, I was in the hall before I realized I hadn't put on the dress. I darted back and slid it over my head. June pushed me out of the room. "Go on," she said. "You can hook it up while you're running."

Clancy grabbed my arm and dragged me on stage. I had one shoe on, the other in my hand. The hooks of the dress were undone and one shoulder strap hung loosely. I tried to pull away from him. "Who—who do you think you are?" I heard myself saying. "Take your hands off me!" In a haze I saw Fanny Brice watching me and I waited for my cue to speak again. The words tumbled out one after the other, as though they were being said by someone else. My legs felt numb as I followed her to the center of the stage and sank down onto the box as she had told me to do. The gold shoe hung limply from my hand. I had been on the same stage less than an hour before but somehow everything seemed different. The spotlight that encircled us and threw shadows on the backdrop was different; the theatre seemed larger and more beautiful. The blackness that was the audience seemed more alive. The orchestra leader seemed different, too. His hands, like pink wax birds, floated as though in space. Over the words of the song I could hear the muted strains of a violin.

Then, too soon, the blue footlights turned to white and the song was over. The curtains closed in slowly and Fanny Brice walked through them to take her bows. I sat on the box behind the folds of heavy velvet and listened to the applause and hoped with all my heart that some of it was for me. The stagehands began clearing the set. I put on the gold shoe and hobbled back to my dressing room on an orange-colored cloud. "Someday," I thought, "someday I'll be a real actress."

My sister threw her arms around me. "You were wonderful," she said and her voice sounded surprised and proud. "I watched you from the wings and I couldn't believe it. You even remembered your words!"

The boys began piling into the room whooping and yelling. "Boy, wuz you good!" Bubsy shouted. "I never seen such good acting. Me and my brudder cried honest to God tears, din't we?" Sonny and the boys danced around the room. Then Mother and Gordon came in and both of them were hugging me. "I knew you could do it," Mother whispered in my ear. It was the biggest, happiest day of my whole life and I hated for it to end. I was too excited to eat dinner. I couldn't wait for the night to come. But for the next performance I was careful to be on time. The orange chiffon dress was hooked up and my hair was smoothed down with Bandoline. I had both shoes on, too, and I didn't wobble on the high heels because I had been practicing in them. The second show, I knew, was better than the matinee. I read my lines carefully, without that awful breathlessness, and because I was more sure of myself I added a few things. I staggered the way Colleen Moore did in a picture I saw and once or twice I hiccuped. When Fanny Brice finished taking her bows I followed her down the hallway to her dressing room. "It was better that show, wasn't it?" I asked, tagging along beside her. "I mean, there was more character in it, wasn't there?"

"Yeah, a lot more." She walked so fast I could hardly keep up with her. Then when she got to her dressing room she stopped with her hand on the doorknob. "You were fine in the scene," she said. "It has nothing to do with you, but, well—I'm taking it out of the show. The act needs a comedy number in that spot. The ballad is too draggy. I already rehearsed the new song. It'll go in for the matinee tomorrow."

"No!" The word came out of me in a gasp. I put my hand to my mouth quickly before I said anything more, before I started to cry.

"I'm sorry," Fanny Brice said. "I never did like the number. I don't know why I decided to do it in the first place—" She pretended to be busy unbuttoning her sweater, but I knew she was doing it because she didn't want to look at me. I didn't want to look at her, either. I was so ashamed I wanted to run away somewhere and hide. "Mother will be worrying about me," I mumbled, "I'll have to go. Is it all right if I bring back the dress tomorrow?"

"Adele will pick it up," Fanny Brice said, "and look—about the scene, don't feel bad about it. It was too much to ask of a kid your age, with no experience."

I closed my mouth with a snap. No experience, I thought bitterly. But she was right. The years I had been on the stage didn't count. How could I ever get experience doing "I'm a Hard-boiled Rose"? How could I ever learn anything when I was just atmosphere?

"I enjoyed working with you," I said politely. "Thank you very much."

The door closed and I stood there for a moment then started down the hallway to my own room. Mother was angry about something. Her voice rang through the hall. Some of the other dressing-room doors were opened a crack so their occupants wouldn't miss anything. I held up my head and walked on, trying to keep steady on the high heels, fighting back the tears. I hated to open the door. I knew they would all be in there waiting, and I knew what each one of them would say and do. Gordon would look at Mother with that knowing smile and pretend to be sorry when he wasn't sorry at all. Mother would shake her head hopelessly the way she did at rehearsals and the boys would probably giggle. Mother's voice was louder. I could hear snatches of what she was saying. "The humiliation—a headline act—how dare she—" Then Gordon interrupted her. "Your asthma, Rose." I took a deep breath and opened the door. They stopped talking when they saw me, and Mother, with a forced little smile, put out her arms. "Louise, dear," she said softly, "I—I have some bad news for you."

"I know," I said. "Fanny Brice just told me."

Mother's smile vanished in a flash. She doubled up a fist and pounded it on the make-up shelf. "It's an outrage, that's what it is. Someone ought to write a letter to *Variety*. I have a damned good notion to do it myself."

She took my knicker suit from the hook and laid it on a chair for me, then she began unrolling my long brown stockings. "It's a pure case of jealousy," she said. "Pure dyed-in-the-wool jealousy.

Why, from the moment you walked on stage, not a person in that audience looked at her. I was out front and heard the comments. They were raves."

I wanted so hard to believe Mother but I couldn't. I knew better. I knew I'd never be an actress. I knew I'd never be anything. I unfastened the hooks of the orange gown and Gordon mumbled something about waiting for us outside. When he left, the boys followed him silently, one by one. June jumped up from her chair and ran after them.

At the door she turned and looked at me. "You *were* good, Weese," she said. "I don't care what Fanny Brice or anyone says."

Mother put my oxfords on the floor near my chair. "Hurry dear," she said. "It's getting late."

I hung up the orange chiffon dress and covered it carefully with a wardrobe sheet, then I wrapped up the gold brocade shoes in newspaper. I knew it was getting late. It must be almost midnight, I thought, as I pulled on my long underwear with the baggy knees. It had to be midnight because I was turning back into a pumpkin.

9

FROM SAN FRANCISCO
we jumped to Vancouver. We liked playing Canada but getting
across the border was always difficult. They had strict child-labor
laws and even stricter anti-rabies laws. The immigration authorities
always demanded birth certificates from us and health certificates
for the dogs.

Because of Mother's conception of Christian Science she didn't
believe in having the dogs inoculated, and the immigration authorities balked at accrediting the health papers she showed them, which
was understandable considering Mother wrote the papers herself.
When that hurdle was passed, and it was never easy, we had the
birth certificates to worry about. Mother couldn't show June's because the age limit in Canada was twelve and June was only nine.
We had a signed affidavit from Grandpa stating June was of age,
but it was never accepted at the border without a lengthy argument.

"I'm not going through this again," Mother said as we finally
got past the Canadian border. "One way or the other, we have to
have a *real* birth certificate for June."

Finding a man in Vancouver who was clever at copying documents was easy. As Mother said, the woods were full of them, and
because of the large Chinese population and the United States laws
on quotas and aliens, most of the copyists specialized in birth certificates. Mother ordered one that would prove my sister was twelve

years old. She would like to have made it sixteen but she was afraid she couldn't get away with that; June was small for nine. Besides twelve was a nice age as far as the child-labor authorities were concerned.

Fortunately June had been born in Vancouver when Mother and Father were visiting Grandpa Hovick, who was an architect and working there on a building. Mother wasn't good at keeping track of birth dates even in those days and June arrived two weeks before she was expected. At the time it had been very awkward. But, as Mother said nine years afterward, "Everything happens for the best. Where else could I have found a man artistic enough to make such a beautiful document?"

It was so beautiful and such a good copy that Mother had the same man make health papers for the dogs.

The day she visited the recording clerk's office, with the birth certificate tucked carefully into her purse, Mother took me with her. Introducing herself as Mrs. Holbrook, she told the clerk she was looking for the birth certificate of a relative on her husband's side of the family.

"I lost my husband last year," Mother said with her eyes downcast. "Since then the will has become so complicated and so involved—I—you see I'm not much of a businesswoman and there are so many greedy relatives—I don't want anything for myself, but I have my child to think of. . . ." I cast my eyes down, too, when the man looked at me.

The recording clerk couldn't have been more helpful. He took Mother and me into a room where all the birth certificates of the city were filed in metal cabinets that covered the walls from the floor to the ceiling. A ladder ran along a track beside the file cabinets.

"My goodness," Mother said, her blue eyes wide with awe, "how do you *ever* manage to find anything?"

"Everyone to his own trade," the clerk said humbly. Hopping up on the ladder and holding on with only one hand, he slid it down the track. "What was the name of the party?" he asked.

That, Mother said, was the main difficulty. She wasn't absolutely certain of the name, nor was she sure of the date, but she thought the name began with an H. With a nimbleness that brought a gasp of admiration from Mother the clerk flicked open a file case and ran a finger down the papers, dusty and yellow, that were crammed into it. "Hancock—Hardwood—Harmon—" As he called off the names it sounded like a vaudeville act. "You're sure it starts with an H?"

"Please let me help," Mother said, looking so very young and artless. "I'll remember it if I see it."

The clerk made room for Mother on the ladder and she clung tightly to his arm as he slid them back and forth on the track, much faster, I thought, than was necessary. But the H's Mother was looking for were in a lower file, and just as she found what she wanted, a wave of dizziness made her stagger against the file case, a finger resting on a birth certificate that began, "Hovick, Ellen June—"

"I—I'm afraid I feel faint . . ." Mother said apologetically. "Could I bother you for a glass of water?"

The distressed clerk tore out of the room, leaving Mother slumped over the file case. The moment the door closed behind him, Mother revived and motioned for me to stand guard at the door; she quickly switched birth certificates. The artistic forgery was placed in the file case, and the dusty original was tucked carefully into Mother's purse.

Mother drank the water the clerk brought her, and thanked him kindly for his thoughtfulness. She was feeling too ill, she said, to continue the search, but could she come back another day?

"Any time at all," the recording clerk said. "That's what I'm here for, to be of service." He took the empty glass from Mother and walked with us down the long corridor to the exit. "Next time we'll stay off the ladder," he said, and he and Mother both laughed.

The following week when we were playing Portland, Mother, using her right name, that is one of her right names, wrote the recording clerk's office requesting a copy of June's birth certificate, and a copy of the forgery was sent to us. It was such a valuable paper that Mother even kept the envelope it came in. It put an end to those unpleasant questions from the child-labor authorities and it also put an end to Miss Tompkins. A girl twelve years old had presumably graduated from grammar school.

Mother was sorry to see Miss Tompkins leave, but relieved too. As she said the day we put the schoolteacher on a train heading for Minneapolis, "Some people never learn to be troupers."

"She tried," Mother said fondly, "but it just wasn't in her."

My sister and I couldn't spell, and we hadn't learned our multiplication tables beyond the foursies, but our school days were over.

※※※

The circus acts we worked on the bill with would rehearse every morning at the theatre. Before Miss Tompkins left, while we were still having school lessons, we would see them there working on their trampolines, webs and trapezes. The boys in our act weren't interested in learning the circus tricks but my sister and I were, and the performers were happy to teach us.

The Flying Nelsons taught us how to balance on revolving ladders. The Medinis tied ropes around our middles until we learned how to do flip-flops and nip-ups. Odiva taught us to swim in her glass tank of cloudy water that smelled a bit fishy from the seals. Maude Elliott and Her Girls of the Altitude taught us to do the splits on a web, the long white rope that hung from the flies. We went into the cage with Princess Pat, the lioness, and let General Pisano shoot balloons off our heads.

Then in Portland we worked on the bill with Orrin Davenport and his horses and I discovered there was something I could do as well as June. With only one lesson I could ride a horse bareback without holding on to anything except the thin rope around his neck.

Orrin Davenport's horses had broad backs almost as flat as a table top but even so it was supposed to be hard to stay on. It wasn't hard for me. Before I knew it I was able to stand up on the horse's back. It was a wonderful feeling to go jogging around the ring with the great strong animal beneath me snorting and shaking his powdery mane.

I loved the smell of the shavings kicked up by the horse's hoofs and the noise of the ringmaster's whip that snapped like a firecracker. I felt light and graceful as I knelt on the broad back of the animal and held one leg up in the air. "Yah, doss is goot," the trainer would say and it sounded in my ears like an accolade.

Then the week was over and the Orrin Davenport troupe was going south and we were going east. After the last show I watched them take down the ring and pack away their props and lead the horses out the stage door to the vans that waited to take them to the depot. I went out into the stage alley and watched until the vans were out of sight. Then I went back into the theatre and closed the door behind me. In my heart I felt that I was closing the door on the greatest opportunity in my whole life.

※※※

Opening day in Cincinnati we scrambled out of the taxicab in front of the theatre. A man on a ladder was putting up the names of the acts on the marquee. A few letters of June's name were already up, but above it, in much larger letters, was the name Cantor J. Rosenblatt. Mother repeated the name out loud, a look of bewilderment on her face. "Why," she said, "I never heard of the act."

Other stars had been billed over us on the Orpheum Circuit. Alice Brady had top billing when we worked with her. Fanny Brice had headlined, and so had Sophie Tucker and Olga Petrova. Mother didn't like it, but if the act was, in her estimation, a real star act, she would begrudgingly take second billing.

"What's the meaning of this?" she said. "Gordon, take a look at that billing!"

Gordon was busily taking the luggage out of the taxi and piling it up on the sidewalk. It was a nondescript assortment of luggage: black fiber dog bags, the monkey box, Gussie's crate, his own Gladstone bag with the frayed torn luggage stickers, cheap cardboard suitcases, Mother's pin-seal fitted overnight case with its protective canvas cover, paper bags overflowing with things we had forgotten to pack in the trunks at the last moment, and a net shopping bag filled with oranges and what was left of our train lunch. Gordon counted the eighteen pieces several times while Mother kept asking him, "Who is this act?—who is he?"

I knew Gordon was trying to put off answering Mother. He

pretended to count the luggage again. "Who is he?" Mother demanded. "Answer me, Gordon!"

"Look, Rose, I can explain," he said, with an uncomfortable eye on the billing. "When they told me he . . ."

"Oh, you knew about it, did you?" Mother's hands clenched into fists. "And who are *you* to let them bill some unknown act over us?"

"I had nothing to do with it," Gordon said patiently, "but if anyone deserves top billing this man does. He's the most famous cantor in the world, Rose. He makes Victrola records; people come from miles around to hear him sing in a synagogue."

"I don't care where he's played," Mother said evenly. "I've never heard of him and his name comes down, and June's goes up, or we don't go on!"

Gordon sighed as he always did when Mother put that edge to her voice. I really didn't like Gordon, but I felt sorry for him when Mother delivered her ultimatums. He picked up his share of the luggage and walked slowly into the theatre. The boys and June and I grabbed up our bags and followed. Mother let the dogs out of their carrying cases so they could run around a while before being closed up in the dressing room. Opening days were hard on the dogs, too.

Gordon never used the stage door on opening days. He didn't think it was fitting for an act of our standing. Instead he would enter through the front of the theatre. Then, standing in the aisle in the darkness, he would yell, "House lights! The Dainty June Company is here!"

When the house lights went on, we would troupe down the aisle, single file, and up the steps to the stage. The stagehands and other acts on the bill would watch us silently as we piled up the steps, loaded down with luggage, the monkey screeching and Gussie honking and hissing.

Gordon would usually pass out cigars immediately. He often said that stagehands and musicians could make or break you and he never waited, as some acts did, until the week was over. "There'll be more closing night," he would say expansively, and sometimes, if we got everything we wanted, he would keep his word.

That day his greetings were brief. He was much too concerned about our dressing rooms to spend time on the cigar passing. When an act was billed over us they usually had the star dressing room, too, and Gordon knew Mother was in no humor for that. He read the dressing-room list on the call board. I stood beside him, looking as he did for our name. There it was, on the very top of the list, "Dainty June Company, dressing rooms A and B." I read it again to make sure. There was no dressing room listed for Cantor J. Rosenblatt.

"Maybe the sign out front was a mistake," I said to Gordon. "Maybe it's from last week's show and they didn't take it down yet."

Gordon was looking across the stage at a man who sat, stiff and straight, on a chair against the back wall, with his hands folded on his lap. "That's him, over there," Gordon said, taking off his hat. "That's Cantor Joseph Rosenblatt."

I looked at the man again, then I looked at Gordon to see if he was looking where I was looking. I was sure Gordon meant someone else. The man I saw couldn't possibly be billed over us. His black suit was shabby and not even very clean. He was almost comical with his long, curly brown beard and the skull cap on the back of his head.

"It's a great honor for us to be on the bill with that man," Gordon was saying. "Every penny of his salary is going to the synagogue."

"Why?" I asked. "Do they need the money?"

Gordon shrugged. His hands spread out like a fan from his elbows. "Everybody needs money," he said.

I knew all about synagogues and shul and Rosh Hashana from Gordon. June and I would count the stars for him on Saturday nights. When we had counted five he would smoke a cigarette, his first one after the Jewish Sabbath. We had often waited for him while he prayed. June and I said our prayers in bed at night, but Gordon's prayers had to be said at prescribed hours and the hours weren't always convenient. Once we had to wait for him to pray even though we were hurrying to catch a train.

There was a mysticism about Gordon's religion that fascinated me. Among the books I trouped was a Gideon Bible, and Gordon and I would read the ancient laws put down in Leviticus. During those times I almost liked Gordon. His dark eyes seemed to glow when he read the words and his voice vibrated dramatically. It was scary, but I liked it. He once told me his religion was the most important thing in his life.

"Even more important than Mother?" I asked.

Gordon hesitated a moment before he answered me, then he nodded his head. "Yes," he said, "even more important than your mother."

One year I observed Yom Kippur with him. I didn't go to the synagogue because Gentile girls weren't supposed to, but for twenty-four hours I fasted with him. I didn't even brush my teeth because I had promised myself I wouldn't touch a drop of food or water. I wasn't hungry or thirsty at all. I felt like an elf, as though I were lighter than air; but after the show that night I fainted and Mother wouldn't let me keep Yom Kippur again.

Mother didn't disapprove of Gordon's religion, but she did remind me that I had been baptized a Catholic. That had been my Grandma Dottie's idea. It had also been her idea that Mother go to a convent as a girl. Mother was just part Catholic now. She was also part Christian Scientist and Unitarian but because we were either playing a matinee or traveling on Sundays we seldom went to church.

"You just live by the Golden Rule, dear," Mother would say to me, "and you won't need church. Do unto others before they do you."

Gordon felt different about religion. I knew the Cantor was someone important in his church and I felt sorry for Gordon because he was going to have to fight with him over the billing.

"Maybe the rabbi could burn some fat on the altar," I suggested.

"Burn some *what?*" Gordon said, staring down at me.

"Like in Leviticus," I said. "If he burns some fat from the victim on the altar it washes away the sin."

Gordon didn't have time to answer, because Mother was walking prettily across the stage. The dogs strained at their leashes as she paused, nodding from side to side at the stagehands, who looked at her admiringly. She came up to Gordon and smiled the smile she reserved for him. "I've been talking this over with the theatre manager," she said, "and I've decided it wouldn't look right for us to be billed over a religious act."

Relief covered Gordon's face as he looked down at Mother. His eyes crinkled at the corners and I could see how very much he loved her. Mother was still smiling up at him. "Religion or no religion," she said, "he's going to have one hell of a time following us."

The opening matinee we stopped the show cold. June had to take bow after bow, and Mother finally had to tell her to make her little beg off speech before the audience would let her go. Mother threw a towel over June's perspiring shoulders and led her back to the dressing room. "Let him try and top that," she said with a satisfied smile.

Later June and I wandered out onto the stage and crouched down in the wings to watch the end of the act preceding the Cantor's.

We had worked on the bill with the act before and knew every joke and every song in it. It was called "Ball and Skein" because their scenery and costumes were all hand crocheted. Mrs. Ball had crocheted the drop and the wardrobe herself. She wore an all-crocheted dress, with a crocheted hat to match and crocheted gloves and purse. Mr. Ball wore a crocheted suit. His tie, spats, vest and even the umbrella he carried were hand crocheted. June and I sang along with them as they did their closing number, "Fifty years from today, when the men wear crochet . . ."

With a drum roll and a cymbal crash the orchestra stopped playing. All the lights in the theatre went on, not just the stage lights, but the house lights in the audience, too. The manager of the theatre stepped through the curtains and said, "We are proud to introduce Cantor Joseph Rosenblatt." He pointed to the wings as he exited, and after a long stage-wait the man with the beard and the little skullcap walked slowly to the center of the stage. There was no music to bring him on, no spotlight on him. Before the show that day he had asked for this. Plain white lights, he had said, and no entrance music.

The garish white lights made him look even more shabby. His suit was wrinkled and one trouser leg was caught up in the top of his high-laced shoe. The silence in the audience and the stillness in the orchestra pit were strange and untheatre-like. He blinked his eyes at the brightness, then suddenly, almost frighteningly, one note broke through the silence. It was a high, piercing sound like a wail. There was a sadness in it that choked me. The note faded away and I could hear the audience catch its breath almost as though it was one person.

The orchestra played softly as the Cantor began to sing. It wasn't a song I had ever heard before and I couldn't understand the Hebrew words but I knew he was singing about all the sadness in the world. He had the clearest, purest voice I had ever heard. There was a gentleness and strength and warmth in it. I felt that if God were to sing to us, this is how His voice would sound.

Abruptly, and much too soon, it was over. The Cantor just stopped singing and without a nod or a bow he turned toward the wings and walked slowly off the stage. The cheap, coarse material of his coat brushed against my arm as he passed me. He walked straight toward the stage door and out onto the street. The stage door closed behind him.

The hushed silence in the audience broke as though someone had cracked a whip. Applause filled the theatre. Then someone shouted, "More, More!" and someone else began to stomp his feet. Soon the theatre rang with the noise of their shouting and stomping. The aisles began to fill with people rushing toward the stage. "Encore. Encore, more!" they yelled.

Backstage there was panic. The stage manager was shouting out orders, "I don't care where he went, find him! He's got to go out there and take a bow! Find him for God's sake before we have a riot on our hands."

The applause and shouting from the audience were a deafening roar. The musicians crouched close to the wall in the pit away from the railing where the audience pushed and shoved as they shouted for the Cantor to come back. The moving-picture screen was quickly being lowered behind the front curtain, the stage manager screaming into a phone to the front booth, "Get that newsreel on, hurry! We've got to quiet this mob!"

Then the orchestra leader tapped the stand with his baton and the musicians came to attention. "The Anthem," he said hoarsely, and as they played "The Star-Spangled Banner" the audience quieted down, and in a little while they filed reluctantly out of the theatre.

Before the show that night the stage manager told the Cantor that singing in a theatre was different from singing in a synagogue. "You have to take bows," he explained. "You have to sing an encore or two—"

The Cantor listened patiently, nodding his head from time to time in agreement. But when he finished his act that night he walked straight across the stage and out the stage door. But this time the stage manager was prepared. The moving-picture screen was in position and the newsreel flashed on the screen the moment the Cantor exited. Every show that week, it was the same way. The newsreel would go on and the audience would applaud all through it, shouting and screaming for an encore, but the Cantor had gone back to his Synagogue.

Mother said it was the greatest piece of showmanship she had ever seen. Later, she agreed with Gordon that the Cantor had more than just showmanship. "He could be the biggest thing in vaudeville," she said, "if he'd just dress up the act a little."

10

K̲ANSAS CITY WAS A
big mistake. Even Gordon, whose idea it had been to go there, admitted that. Mother said it was a disastrous move. The railroad fares
from Chicago, where we had been laying off most of the time since
we closed on the Orpheum Circuit, had left the money bag very
flat. There was a lot of work in and around Kansas City, but not for
us. Not after what happened in Wichita.

I had warned Mother and Gordon about Wichita, but they
wouldn't listen to me. I had seen a black cloud hanging over a big
W in Mother's tea leaves and I knew it was a bad omen. Sure
enough, after our opening matinee, the theatre manager tried to
cancel the act. He claimed it had been misrepresented to him.
Shaking our photographs in Gordon's face, the manager said they
weren't our pictures at all. Of course that wasn't true. The pictures
had been taken three years before and we had all grown a lot, but
they were most certainly of us. We finished the four-day engagement, but the manager sent a bad report of the act to Kansas City
and that was the end of any further bookings in that territory.

There was one bright spot, though. The blankets on the hotel
beds in Kansas City were pure white wool, soft and downy. Mother
said they were the most beautiful blankets she had ever seen. She
rubbed one of them against her cheek. "How I'd love to have a coat
made of this," she said. The name of the hotel, in big Spencerian
letters, was stitched across the blanket. Mother ran a worried finger

over the stitching. "Thank heavens," she said, relieved and pleased. "For a minute there I was afraid it was printed on."

Stitching, she knew, could be picked out, but when the hotel name was printed on, the blankets were useless as far as we were concerned. Mother began calculating on her fingers: "Let's see now, my coat will take two blankets, June's will take one blanket and another blanket for your coat, Louise, makes four blankets. We'll have to work fast."

There were only three days left of the week, before we were to open in Omaha, and clipping four blankets isn't easy, but the chambermaid in Kansas City was careless. She was always leaving her passkeys hanging from the keyholes, and when a guest would check out she would leave their doors wide open. Even so, as Mother said, we had to work fast.

Getting the blankets out of the hotel once they were clipped was a problem. They were too bulky to fit in our wardrobe trunk, and our suitcases were so full as it was that we had to sit on them to get them closed. Mother solved the problem by wrapping the blankets around herself and covering them with her beaver coat. Gordon went ahead to the depot with our trunks and Mother, because she handled the money, checked us out of the hotel.

As she waddled up to the cashier's desk she looked like a beaver-covered barrel. There was a slight discrepancy in our bill. At least that is what the cashier called it. Mother said it was highway robbery. She said she distinctly remembered hearing him say, when we checked in, that her single room with bath was the same rate as those double, without. It made a difference of seven dollars, and Mother argued heatedly over it. "It's not the principle of the thing," Mother said. "It's the money." When Mother was angry she used her hands and arms a lot. That day as she pounded on the desk and waved her arms about to emphasize her point, the blankets began to slip.

By the time the cashier had agreed to split the difference and had taken the three and a half dollars off the bill the blankets were hanging inches below the beaver coat. Mother didn't know this and there was no way we could warn her. All we could do was form a solid front and surround her as she waddled toward the revolving door. Three of the boys walked at her side, facing the cashier; the rest of us provided protection from the rear.

When we met Gordon at the depot Mother was still angry. "If I'd known they were going to overcharge us like that," she said, "I would have taken those lovely bath towels."

In Omaha, the day after we opened, I cut the patterns for the white wool coats, and before the week was over I had made all three of them. They were made alike with big shawl collars and dolman sleeves. Mother, modeling hers, turned from side to side as she admired herself in the mirror.

"There isn't a reason in the world," she said, "the way Louise sews, that we don't have a half a dozen of these."

I taught myself to sew by making clothes for Gigolo, my pet monkey. In his wardrobe trunk, which was originally a cigar box, he had a red chiffon evening gown, a bathrobe, overalls, a bathing suit and a fur jacket from the leftover scraps of Mother's beaver coat. Those were his best clothes. For everyday wear he wore sweaters made from Gordon's old woolen socks. I would cut off the heels and toes and use them for sleeves. The top of the socks made a roll-down collar.

Mother attached an almost magical importance to my being able to sew. Perhaps that was because she couldn't sew at all. She thought I must have inherited the talent from my Big Lady, who had won prizes with her needlework, and who, besides making fancy hats and shimmies and corsets, had embroidered an altar cloth for the nuns that was the pride of the Sacred Heart Convent.

My sewing wasn't always too neat, and sometimes the stitches didn't hold, but Mother didn't notice things like that. "It's the flash that counts," she would say.

I made Gigolo a coat from the leftover scraps of the blankets. It had a shawl collar too, and dolman sleeves, and a tam o'shanter to match. June wanted me to make a coat for Sambo, but Mother told her there were enough blanket coats in the family.

Closing night in Omaha Gigolo strangled to death in his blanket coat. I had left it on him all night because it was cold and he twisted it around and around his neck until he couldn't get free. I found his tortured little body in the hateful mess of white wool when I opened his box in the morning. The moment I opened the closet door I knew something was wrong. He usually talked to me when I woke him up for breakfast but that morning the silence frightened me. I lifted him out of the box and his arms hung down limply, like a child's. One little hand held a fragment of wool he had pulled away from his throat. I wiped the froth off his mouth with the hem of my nightgown, and I must have cried out because I felt Mother's arms around me, then everything went black.

When I woke up I was lying on the bed with a wet towel on my head. The shades were down and Mother and June and Gordon were looking down at me. "Where is he?" I asked.

"We've taken him away, dear," Mother said softly. She came over and lifted me up. "Your sister brought you some warm milk. Drink it slowly." She held the container to my lips and I could feel the warm liquid trickle down my chin.

"It was God punishing me," I said. "He took him away from me because we stole the blankets."

Mother handed Gordon the container of milk and held my shoulders tightly. "That isn't true," she said. "Never say a thing like that again. Those blankets were coming to us, and God never punishes you for taking what you deserve. Gordon and I will find you another monkey. . . ."

I closed my eyes to shut in the tears. Mother held me for a moment then she let me fall back on the pillows. I heard them tiptoe to the door and when it closed I knew they had left me. I was glad to be alone. I didn't want sympathy, and I didn't want anyone to see me cry.

Mother and Gordon took away Gigolo's wardrobe trunk and all his little clothes and the things that would remind me of him, but they couldn't make me forget. His death was the first real tragedy of my life. Sambo's death had been sad, and I had cried for days when Gussie died from eating rat poison backstage in Toledo, but Gigolo's death was my fault and I knew it.

After the show that night we took a day coach to Detroit and I sat by myself and looked out the window at the darkness. Then when the lights in the coach dimmed and everyone slept and the only sound was the creaking of the car and the wheels on the rails I promised God I would never take anything again that didn't belong to me, even if I deserved it.

11

GOING TO DETROIT had been Gordon's idea. Besides the Regent and Miles theatres, right in town, he said he could book the act in Ypsilanti, Pontiac, Flint and Wyandotte. Now, after laying off for almost four weeks, he wasn't so sure. "The agents won't even see me," he told Mother. "Wichita hurt us a lot, and Omaha didn't help, either. Bad news travels fast."

Mother paced back and forth in the hotel room. There wasn't much space for pacing since we had the cot moved in to cut down on expenses. I sat on the edge of it and picked up my feet each time she passed by. Gordon, his hat pushed back on his forehead, leaned on the washbasin watching her. "It's radio, Rose," he said. "Radio has damned near ruined vaudeville."

"Radio!" Mother snapped. "Those earphones will never take the place of vaudeville."

"—Besides, the kids aren't babies any longer. June can't get by with what she used to get by with—"

Mother's face got red and the cords in her neck tightened. "You dare say a thing like that!" she said, her voice high and shrill. "*You*, who've lived off that baby for four years, dare to stand there and tell me she has no talent!"

"I didn't say that," Gordon said, backing away from Mother's fury. "What I said is she's not a baby. She's almost eleven years old—it's time she—"

Mother flew at him and began pounding his chest with her fists. "Shut up!" she said. "She'll always be a baby. She'll never grow up. Never, do you hear me? Never, never—"

I snatched up my cap and sneaked out of the room. Mother's anger embarrassed me. I was embarrassed for Gordon, too, cringing under her fists and trying to protect his face from her fingernails. I closed the door behind me and rang for the elevator. While I was waiting I heard Benny, the trained seal in the room next to ours, splashing around in the bathtub, applauding himself with his flippers, then Mother's voice got louder and just as the elevator arrived I heard something heavy hit the door. The elevator boy gave me a knowing look. "They're at it again, huh?" he said cheerfully. "Do'ya know what I'd do if I was him?"

"I'm not interested," I replied, stepping into the elevator.

"I'd haul off and hit her back. That's what I'd do."

"Down, please," I said, looking straight ahead.

Next door to the Dixieland Hotel was my secret hiding place. Even June didn't know about it, or the hours I spent there. I looked up and down the street, then I ducked in through the doorway. It was a strange, wonderful place with batik scarves on the walls and small tables and chairs placed in the dimly lighted corners of the room. Candles, stuck in bottles, threw flickering lights on the bookshelves. It was named the Seven Arts Book Store. During the late afternoons the place would be crowded with young men and girls who looked almost alike with their shaggy haircuts and low flat shoes. The books in the store fascinated me, as all books did, but the people sitting at the tables fascinated me more. While I browsed and pondered over what I'd buy with my saved-up allowances, I could hear them talking about F. Scott Fitzgerald and James Joyce and Carl Van Vechten.

The manager of the bookshop was young and delicately handsome. He walked softly on the toes of his feet and when he took the books from the shelves he handled them gently. His voice was gentle, too, and his eyes were sympathetic and warm. His name was George Davis. It didn't seem to matter to him that I had very little money to spend, or that I had been in the bookshop every day for a week and still hadn't made my selection. No one else appeared to be buying books either, at least not often. They were all talking about books and their authors, but that was all.

My books had already broken the bottom out of the trunk June and I shared for our toys. Mother never censored my reading but she did weigh the books I bought. When the trunk, that had been reinforced, collapsed again, Mother put a limit on the number of books I was allowed to troupe.

Deciding what to keep was difficult. Miss Tompkins had told me before she left us that books, even though some of them weren't entertaining, were always stimulating to the mind. Most of the books she had selected for me were weeded out by now. I had gradually replaced *Sarah Crewe*, *A Child's Garden of Verses* and *Tanglewood Tales* with Boccaccio's *Decameron*, *Indian Love Lyrics*, *The Blind Bow Boy* and *Das Kapital*. I also trouped Huneker's *Painted Veils*, *The Rubáiyát of Omar Khayyám* and an old copy of Balzac's *Droll Stories*. June had nine Oz books in the trunk, and between us we shared a collection of back-dated *Weird Tales* magazines.

I had read every book I owned several times, but I didn't feel exactly stimulated in the mind over all of them. In fact, a few of them had puzzled me considerably, and bored me besides. Some of my books had been bought for their impressive covers, others because they looked like grownups' books but mostly because they were the cheapest ones on the stands.

In the candle-lighted bookshop I hesitated between a copy of Firbank's *The Flower Beneath the Foot*, which had a lovely picture on the faded gray cover, and *Marius the Epicurean*. I knew if I bought either one I would have to make room for it in the toy trunk. I was wondering more about which of my old books would have to go than about which of the two new ones I would buy, when the manager of the store spoke to me. "Have you read Shakespeare's sonnets?" he asked, offering me a slender cloth-covered book.

I hadn't and I didn't particularly want to, but I did want to be a part of the group in the bookshop. For a whole week I had listened to them and watched them and been apart from them. I thought perhaps the slender cloth-covered book of sonnets was the bridge I needed. "I don't care much about reading plays," I said, trying to look grown up and worldly. "Being in the theatre my-self I—"

"These are poems," George Davis said.

I didn't like poems either, and I already had two books filled with them, but he was looking encouragingly at me so I bought the book. I glanced at it casually, then when a group of laughing young men came into the shop I wandered as close to them as I dared, holding the book in my hand so they could see the title.

"—his very lack of pretension is pretentious," one of them was saying and the others agreed. "Having asthma doesn't make a hack writer another Proust."

Standing under a batik scarf I pretended to read by the light of the candle, holding the book in such a way that the title would show. The voices went on and I edged closer. "Anyone can write," one of them said. "Who was it said every man has one book in him?"

The strap of my knicker was loose. I could feel it creeping down my leg, but I didn't bother to pull it up. I was in too much of a hurry. Holding my book of sonnets close, I ran out of the shop and into the lobby of the hotel. I remembered seeing writing desks in an alcove back of the elevators and I hoped, as I ran, there would be no one there. The alcove was deserted. I snapped on the light over the desk nearest to me and snatched the hotel stationery from the slot. Quickly, before the inspiration left me, I dipped the pen in the inkwell and held it there while I decided on my opening words. The pen scratched on the paper as I wrote: "Page one. Scene one." I paused for a moment, then added, "I enter."

The ink was thick and it made a blob on the paper. The letterhead with its picture of the hotel disturbed me. I turned it over and began again. "I enter—" I looked at the words for a long time. Who was I? What would I say? What would happen to me? Faintly, and in reverse, I could see the lettering DIXIELAND HOTEL. I rolled the paper into a tight ball and threw it in the waste-basket, then I pushed back the chair and went up to our room. I'd write a play some other day, I decided. When I had more time and the pen wasn't so scratchy.

June was standing outside in the hall, the parchesi game in her arms, her ear pressed close to our door. "They're still fighting," she whispered. "First it was about me, now it's about money."

"—everything going out, nothing coming in," Gordon was saying. "We're damned near broke."

"And whose fault is that?" Mother demanded. "The act is as good as it ever was. It's your fault we're not back on the Orpheum Circuit, where we belong. A fine man you are, blaming your failure on a baby—a child."

June and I took the parchesi game and moved down the hall.

Twice during the game we moved farthur away from our room. The yelling was disturbing us. Then suddenly the door flew open and Gordon, with his black overcoat flung over his arm, stood with his back to the hallway. "You've told me to get out for the last time, Rose," he said, in a loud angry voice. "I'm leaving, and so help me God, I'm not coming back."

He almost stepped all over our parchesi board as he stomped through the hall and ran down the stairs, his overcoat dragging behind him. In a moment Mother slammed the door shut. June and I went on with our game. The fight hadn't lasted nearly as long as we had expected it to. Later, when our game was finished, we tiptoed to the door and listened, taking turns pressing our ears to the keyhole. Mother was crying. I knew she had her face buried in the pillow because her sobs were muffled.

At dinnertime, the boys gathered around outside Mother's door. June put her fingers to her lips and warned them to be quiet. "They had another fight," she whispered. "Mother's crying."

None of us had dinner. We weren't hungry anyway, and besides Jack's mother had sent him a fruitcake and this was a good excuse to eat it. Three of the boys slept on the floor that night so June and I could have their bed; we didn't want to disturb Mother.

The next morning when we listened at Mother's door, we could hear her breathing heavily. We knew she had stopped crying and was having an asthma attack so we tapped softly on the door. We heard the bed springs creak and in a moment Mother opened the door. The window shades were pulled down and the air was heavy with the fumes of her asthma powder. June and I tiptoed in, the boys behind us. We watched Mother gravely as she sank back on the bed and began to weep. Her face was red and swollen and her pillow was wet with tears. The dogs whined softly at the door. "Gordon's left us," Mother said. "He's gone—for good."

June put out her hand and touched Mother gently on the shoulder. "He'll come back, Mother," she said. "He always does."

Gordon didn't come back. He didn't telephone, and he didn't write. For ten days Mother stayed in her room with the window shades pulled down. Each day the boys and June and I would tiptoe in and wait until she stopped crying long enough to give us money for dinner. We would take the dogs with us and bring back something for Mother to eat. The next day we'd find the food almost untouched; the sandwich dried up with a bite or two taken from it, a thin skim of film on top of the coffee that had soaked through the container.

The desk clerk began looking at us suspiciously as we went in and out of the hotel by ourselves. We knew the chambermaid had told him about Mother crying all day in her room with the shades pulled down, and about Gordon's things being moved out of his room. We knew this because one day when the maid was in there we heard her talking to the clerk on the telephone. Gordon's Gladstone bag was gone and his toothbrush was missing from the glass on the washbasin. The only thing left was a photograph of Mother in a leather frame on the bureau. "I think he's skipped," we heard the maid say. "Can't say I blame him with all that fighting that went on."

Other guests in the hotel were talking about us. We heard one of them telling the desk clerk that it was a disgrace the way we were running in and out of the hotel at all hours of the night. "Like a band of wild Indians," the woman said indignantly, "and if you don't do something about it, I will!"

We scooted up the stairs as fast as we could and locked ourselves in the boys' room. We sat huddled together on the bed and listened for strangers' footsteps in the hallway.

"She'll call the Child Labor Board," Bubsy said. "I betcha she will." June looked at him with wide, frightened eyes. "Well, she might," Bubsy insisted. "And if she does and my fadder finds out about it, he'll make me and Sonny go home."

"Pop hates cops," Sonny said solemnly.

"I could write a letter to Grandpa," I said. "I could tell him

Mother's sick. He'd know what to do."

"That's no good," Bubsy said impatiently. "By the time he got the letter we'd all be shut up in some jail with bars on the winda."

That evening when we tiptoed into Mother's room we found her dressed and sitting in a chair near the window. The shades were up, and the late sun was shining down on her lusterless hair. All the curl was out of it, and it hung down around her swollen face in dull scraggly ends. The wardrobe trunk was opened against the wall, and Mother's dresses were thrown over the top of it.

"Get your things together, children," she said. "We're leaving for New York tonight."

Bubsy's and Sonny's faces fell. "New York?" they said in a dismayed chorus. "Gee, that means we gotta live at home with Mom and Pop—"

Mother went on as though she hadn't heard them. "I'll show him. I'll put this act back on the Orpheum Circuit if it's the last thing I do. He'll come crawling back on his hands and knees. Mark my words. On his hands and knees—" Her voice faltered and ended with a choked sob. The boys and June and I started packing without looking at her. There was something in her sobs that shut her away from us, and made me feel as though we shouldn't be there at all.

It was an overnight jump from Detroit to New York, but we took a day coach to save money. I sat at the window and remembered that night long ago, when we left Detroit with Gordon. I remembered how he and Mother had sat together and how they had laughed and talked and planned, and how Mother's eyes had sparkled when she looked at him.

I glanced over at her now and wondered if she was remembering, too, but I couldn't tell because her eyes were closed tight, her mouth a thin white line. Then her dry lips began to move and I heard her say, "I'm going to try and pick up the tangled threads of my life."

June moved restlessly on the seat in front of us, and Mother leaned forward and helped her cover her eyes with the collar of her coat. "I'm going to start in all over again," she said almost to herself, "—alone with my two babies against the world."

12

People had been looking at us strangely ever since we arrived in New York. A man had even followed us to the coffeeshop once, and stood peering in at us through the window while we ate. Mother couldn't understand it. "You'd think," she said, "in a city the size of New York they'd be used to show people."

Mother and June were wearing their blanket coats. The dogs trotting along beside us wore black-and-white-striped sweaters. June's blond hair hung down from under her huge tam o'shanter. She wore white Russian boots and knee-length socks. It was very cold so June and I both had our hands shoved in the little fur muffs Mother had just bought us. They were made to look like puppy dogs, with zippers down their backs and a pocket inside for a handkerchief. June's muff was white fur to match her coat, and mine was brown with black ears. The muffs had been quite expensive and I was too big to carry such a thing. But Mother bought them anyway. She thought their publicity value was worth the investment. Now, as the woman spoke to us, it seemed that Mother's hunch was right.

"I see the girls are carrying 'Snuggle Pups,'" the woman said. She beamed down on June as she patted the nose of the little muff. "I handle the firm's publicity, and I'm always so happy when one of our puppies finds a good home."

She and Mother laughed gaily at the little joke. "They were given to the girls by the theatre manager in Boston," Mother said, making up the story on the spur of the moment. "A little reward for breaking the house record."

"I knew it!" the woman said. "I just knew you were in show business. Louis B. Mayer is a good friend of mine and I've met so many show people through him I feel as though I'm almost in the business myself."

At the mention of Louis B. Mayer, Mother took off the glove that covered her diamond rings and scratched her nose delicately. "I haven't seen him in *years*," Mother said. "Not since the girls were out in Hollywood making movies. How *is* he?"

"Fine, just fine," the woman replied. "Still out in Hollywood, of course."

June stood on one foot then the other. It was cold and the wind whipped around the corner of Forty-fifth Street where we were standing. She sniffled loudly and tugged at her half socks. Her bare knees were chapped and blue and she began jumping up and down to keep warm. Mother and the woman were so busy trying to impress each other they didn't hear June sniffle. The woman was telling Mother her name was F. E. Gorham, and she had just taken over the "Snuggle Pup" account. More as a lark, she said, than anything else. Then she asked Mother if we could use a song in our act about the Snuggle Pups. Mother was a bit doubtful. She had discovered long ago that when she took a doubtful attitude with song pluggers, they usually made it worth while to use one of their songs.

"What kind of a song is it?" she asked.

F. E. Gorham hummed a few bars of music, then stopped suddenly as a thought struck her. "I have a copy of the song in my locker at Penn Station," she said. "Let's run down and get it."

Before Mother had a chance to make up her mind, we were hustled into a taxicab and a few minutes later were following F. E. Gorham to the locker section of Penn Station. She took a key from her alligator purse and opened the locker door. Mother had been eying her a bit suspiciously in the taxicab, but now as the locker door flew open, I could see her doubts disappear in a flash. The locker was filled with Snuggle Pups. There were curly-haired Snuggle Pups, sleek-haired Snuggle Pups, black ones, white ones, little ones, big ones. There must have been fifty Snuggle Pups crammed in the locker. F. E. Gorham rummaged through the pile of fur until she found the lyrics to the song. They were written on a piano lead sheet, the title penciled in on top: "I Want a Snuggle Pup All My Own"; the words and music, I noticed, were written by F. E. Gorham.

She smiled shyly at Mother. "I was afraid if you knew I wrote the song you wouldn't be interested."

She was about to close the door when suddenly she snatched out a curly-haired Snuggle Pup and gave it to June. Then she plunged her hand into the locker again and pulled out one with blue eyes for me. While we were thanking her, she slammed the door of the locker, then grabbed Mother's arm. "Now," she said, "let's all have lunch and talk."

That was how we met F. E. Gorham. It is rather difficult describing her. Every time we saw her she looked different. One day she would wear glasses, the next day not. She wore her hair curly, then straight. That first day her hair was a rusty blond color worn in a dip over her forehead. Her eyes were a watery blue and the skin around them was crinkled. The only make-up she wore was an orangish rouge on her cheeks, and pale brown eyebrows penciled on quite differently from her natural eyebrows, which grew out in a stiff stubble. She wasn't at all pretty, but her gestures and mannerisms were those of a pretty woman.

The hotel dining room she took us to was elegant and expensive looking. We waited in the entrance, which was flanked with imitation potted palms, while Mother checked the dogs at the cloak-room. A string quartet on a trellised platform played softly. F. E. pulled off her clumsily-mended gloves as she waited for the head-waiter. Then, glancing around the room as though looking for some-one she knew, she let her sealskin coat fall down over her shoulders. I hadn't noticed how shabby her clothes were until I saw her in the bright light of the dining room. Cloth violets hung by a safety pin to the collar of her coat. A sleazy pink blouse was tucked carelessly into a tweed skirt. She was as out of place in the room as we were.

The headwaiter, after a fast appraisal, led us toward a table against the far wall of the room, but as we passed a large center table, F. E. held up an imperious hand. "This one will do very nicely," she said. She made the seating arrangements and, taking a pair of glasses from her purse, scanned the menu. I glanced down at my menu and gulped. I had never seen such high prices. Asparagus was a dollar and a half. Fillet of sole three dollars. Coffee fifty cents. Mother was looking at her menu, too, and I could see she was alarmed.

"Let me do the ordering," F. E. said gaily. "This is my party." Her coat was flung over the back of the gilt chair and the torn soiled lining hung down, showing the inside skin of the fur. The part of her glasses that fit over the ear was broken and had been repaired with a piece of string. As she tapped the menu with them the string flew back and forth.

"We'll start with the fruit cup supreme," she said to the waiter, "then a *crème de volaille,* and a bit of fish to follow . . . the *truite meunière,* I believe, and a nice *châteaubriant,* for four, medium rare. We'll order dessert later."

She closed the menu with a snap and handed it to the waiter, then she turned to Mother. "Now," she said, "tell me all about yourselves."

Mother began as she usually did, from the time of her first divorce. I had heard many versions of the same story but this time it was closer to the way I remembered things. Mother didn't go into any of the sad stories about being alone in the world with two babies to support. She didn't tell the whoppers about how successful the act was either. She told the woman quite simply how we came to New York looking for work after Gordon left the act, and how difficult it had been to find bookings, how bad conditions were and how we had been forced to take one salary cut after another. F. E. chewed her food thoughtfully as she listened to the story. She stacked up the empty plates and pushed them aside. When the waiter went past she interrupted Mother.

"We'd like to order our dessert," she said. Taking the menu, she glanced down the list. "Let's see now—what would be nice and partylike—oh, yes, of course! We'll have a Baked Alaska. The girls would enjoy that, and demitasse for two. Milk for the children."

When the waiter left, F. E. put her elbows on the table and looked closely at Mother. "How much money do you have left?" she asked.

Mother turned her rings around and around on her fingers. "Three hundred dollars," she whispered truthfully. "Of course," she added, "if worse came to worse I could always hock my diamonds —and there's Papa, he wouldn't let us down."

"How would you like to play the Roxy Theatre?" F. E. asked with a lift to her penciled eyebrows.

"The Roxy?" Mother gasped.

"Roxy Rothafel is a close friend of mine," F. E. said. "He'll book any act I recommend. I'll telephone him in the morning and call you after I speak to him. Is ten o'clock all right for you?"

Mother nodded her head. She picked up a bread crumb and rolled it between her fingers, glancing around the room as though she might be checking for a fire exit. June and I exchanged a quick look. If Mother got up to leave, and I expected the move any moment, we were ready to follow in a hurry.

"Roxy can thank me for bringing him some of the biggest stars in the business," F. E. was saying. "One word from me and you'll have a contract in your pocket."

Mother was fumbling for her gloves when F. E. suddenly and loudly began clapping her hands together like a little girl. "Look at what's coming! It's our dessert. Isn't it lovely?"

The waiter, making his way through the tables, carried a silver platter high in the air. On it was a flaming melon-shaped mound topped with a design in cherries. People in the dining room stopped eating to watch the waiter as he placed the rather terrifying dessert on a serving table near F. E. and plunged a knife through the flames.

"Isn't it fun?" F. E. asked. "Of course, it's only ice cream, but it's so gay and impressive." She leaned over to Mother and whispered confidentially, "A Baked Alaska was the first gastronomic disappointment in my life."

"Oh, that's too bad," Mother murmured sympathetically. "Thank heavens I don't have trouble with my stomach."

The waiter placed a serving of the dessert before each of us, and went back to the kitchen with the platter. As he disappeared through the service door F. E. dipped into her alligator purse and brought out a small matchbox. She opened it under the table, but not so far under that Mother and I couldn't see what she was doing. With two fingers she removed a medium-sized dead cockroach from the box, which was filled with other kinds of dead bugs: flies, bedbugs and water beetles. Peeking around furtively to make certain no waiters were about, she dropped the dead cockroach into her Baked Alaska. Then she picked up her fork and began to eat.

"Isn't it delicious?" she asked June and me. "I think of all the—" She stopped suddenly and the smile froze on her face. With a cry of revulsion which was loud enough to bring two waiters scurrying to our table, she pushed back her plate and grabbed frantically at her throat.

"Oh, quick, help me," she gasped. "Help me, I'm going to be ill."

The waiters ran to her side and as she leaned weakly on the starched shirt of one she pushed at the dead cockroach with her fork. "Look—" Her lip curled with repugnance, "look what I found in my Baked Alaska!"

The waiters stared in fascinated anguish at the dead cockroach, the one almost dropping F. E., who had, by then, fainted dead away. Two other waiters and several men from adjoining tables ran over to help. It was quite a struggle, because F. E. came out of her faint in a state bordering on hysteria. Four waiters managed with difficulty to whisk her away to the manager's office. The string quartet played loudly to drown out her moans as she sprawled in the waiter's arms.

There were several embarrassing moments while we waited at the table for F. E. to return. The offending cockroach had been removed, but the waiters hovered over Mother in case she too should faint. At last the door to the manager's office opened and a pale, trembling F. E. emerged. She was smiling wanly as she leaned on the manager's arm.

"I'll be all right, really I will," she said faintly. "I want just to get out into the fresh air."

The dogs were rescued from the cloakroom and we were escorted to a taxicab, the fare paid in advance by the apologetic manager. As we drove away, F. E. began to recover her vitality. She popped an after-dinner mint into her mouth and settled back comfortably in the seat.

"He was afraid I was going to sue him," she said with a pleased chuckle, "but I never do. Live and let live, that's my motto."

F. E. dropped us off at the Langwell Hotel on Forty-fifth Street, where we were sharing a suite with Danny and Johnny. The other boys were staying with their parents while we were in New York. Danny and Johnny slept on a day bed in the sitting room and Mother and June and I shared the bedroom. The rooms were small and we were crowded, but we were retrenching. We had been retrenching a lot since Gordon left. We laid off a lot, too.

Most days when we were laying off, we started making the rounds of the booking agents' offices at eleven in the morning. That morning we didn't get started until late because Mother was waiting for the telephone call from F. E. Gorham.

"Well," Mother said, "it's past noon; we might as well get dressed." We helped her clear away the evidence of our breakfast. The canned milk went on the window sill, the sugar and cups and coffeepot went in the bottom bureau drawer, along with the electric stove. Mother was friendly with the chambermaid, but she didn't believe in taking chances.

It took Mother and June longer to dress than it did me. They had so many more things to put on. Mother paced about the room nervously as she buttoned up the knitted suit Big Lady made her while visiting friends in Walla Walla. "Expecting us to believe that she knew Roxy Rothafel," Mother said irritably. "I'll bet she didn't write that 'Snuggle Pup' song, either." She tucked her curls up under the crocheted hat that matched her dress and put on her sealing-wax beads. "It just proves how careful you have to be talking to strangers."

June was dressed before Mother. She sat on the edge of the red velour chair, her blanket coat bunched up around her, and picked at a tiny seed wart that had formed on her chin. It was a strange little wart, opening out at the end like a flower. It was pale, the same color as her skin and not noticeable at all unless you were close to it. But it bothered June, and when Mother wasn't watching she would pick at it.

"Stop fooling around with that wart," Mother said without even looking at my sister. Mother had a way of knowing when we were doing something we weren't supposed to that was very disturbing. She picked up her gloves and the brief case and, as she gave the boys their last-minute instructions, June and I ran ahead to ring for the elevator.

The boys never had to make the rounds of the booking agents' offices with us. I asked Mother once why they didn't have to go, and she told me she didn't want outsiders knowing our personal business deals. "Little pitchers," she said mysteriously, "have big ears."

Making the rounds of the booking agents' offices was boring and sometimes humiliating. The agents never stood up to greet Mother; mostly they glared at us over their stubby cigars and went right on barking into a telephone. There were always two or three telephones on their desks and we would have to pretend we weren't listening while they shouted and yelled into one after the other. Sometimes they cooed and pleaded into the phone and that was worse, because their faces belied their voices.

Mother would try to sell them our act between telephone calls. She would take our photographs, a few newspaper clippings and a contract or two from the brief case. The contracts and clippings were old, the photographs weren't recent ones either, but it didn't matter; the agents never looked at them. The faded words of the clippings, "Child Star Stops Show"—"Baby June Solid Hit"—and the heading "Orpheum Circuit" on the contracts gave Mother courage to face these interviews.

While we waited to see Jack Linder I thought of Gordon and remembered how much easier it had been when he was with us. He would sit on the edge of the agents' desks and offer them cigars and slap them on their backs. He never got angry or insulted the way Mother did when they offered us dates below our established salary. He would laugh at them, and walk jauntily out of their offices. His shoulders never sagged and his smile never faded until the door closed behind him.

Of all the agents, Jack Linder was the most polite. Mother was sure he would have something for us. The theatres he booked couldn't pay us our standard salary, but we hadn't gotten that in so long we hardly expected it any more. The date he offered made Mother so angry she began shoving the clippings and contracts back in her brief case. "Why, that's an insult," she said. "Two hundred and twenty-five dollars for eight people! You know our salary and you know how our little act goes over. You've been booking us long enough to—"

"Take it or leave it," the agent said. "Plenty of acts around will grab it if you don't."

Mother rose and motioned for June and me to follow her; then, at the door, she turned and forced her lips into a smile. "I'll call you later, Jack. Maybe they'll up the money. We'll take it at two hundred and fifty."

"Don't count on it," the agent said, picking up one of his telephones.

In the outer office, we ran into Flora and Frank Maynard. They didn't do a real kiddie act, but in a way they were competition. They used to bring their three children on stage for bows, and little by little the children began doing more and more in the act until it was now called "The Maynard Family." Mother and the Maynards had been friends since our second season on the Pantages Circuit. When they were broke and laying off in Chicago, Mother and Gordon had loaned them money, which they had never paid back. Not that Mother hadn't reminded them of it often enough, but it seemed that every time we ran into them they were still broke.

That day they were all dressed up and breezed into the office as though they owned it. Flora had on a new leopard fur coat with a beaver collar and Frank wore a pale beige polo coat with a long belt tied around his middle. They were very happy to see us, but careful, too.

"How's Gordon?" Frank asked. "Where is he?" Flora gave him an exasperated look and he quickly changed the subject. He began telling us about his new superheterodyne radio that weighed two hundred pounds, and about their new Hudson sedan and the new costumes for the act. He would have gone on if Flora hadn't interrupted him. "In fact," she said hurriedly, "we bought so much new stuff we're flat broke."

Frank caught the cue and laughed to cover the awkward pause. "Yeah. You know us, Rose. Easy come, easy go. That's us."

"Yes, I know," Mother said coldly. Then glancing down at Flora's hand, she added, "I'm glad you finally got your wedding ring out of hock." Wrapping herself majestically in the blanket coat, she advanced to the door. June and I jumped up from the bench and followed her. "Sorry we can't chat for a while," she said, her hand on the knob, "but we have a rehearsal. We're going back on the Orpheum Circuit next week."

Mother was so angry when she stormed out of the office and down Broadway that June and I could hardly keep up with her. "—two hundred and twenty-five dollars for five days in Kingston," she muttered. "I'll see the Jack Linder office in hell before I accept it."

As soon as we were in our hotel room, Mother sat June down on the red velour chair and began tying a piece of thread around the wart. "I have a strange presentiment," she said, "that this is going to do the trick." Mother said the same thing each time she tried a new wart remedy. Once she had rubbed the wart with bacon and buried what was left of it in the potted palm in the hotel lobby. The theory was that when the bacon rotted the wart would disappear. Another time she painted the wart with iodine. It looked so awful that Mother tried to cover it with make-up but that made it look worse. It took days for the iodine stain to go away, but the wart remained.

Mother was cutting off the loose ends of the thread when the boys burst into the room. They had their roller skates slung over their shoulders and I knew they had been skating on the cement floor in the furnace room even though that had been forbidden. Danny ducked behind the door so Mother wouldn't see his skates. Johnny was too stupid to hide his, but Mother wasn't looking anyway.

"Did you get the messages at the desk?" Danny asked. He had ditched his skates and he faced Mother with a big innocent smile. "Mrs. Gorham called three times. She said for you to meet her at the side entrance of the Roxy Theatre at eleven o'clock tonight."

"The Roxy Theatre!" Mother jumped up so fast she almost cut June with the scissors. She ran to the wall phone and began jiggling the hook up and down. "She didn't leave her number," Danny said nervously. "I asked her and asked her. Honest I did. Johnny can tell you. She just said it was important and you should bring the girls. Why can't we go, too?"

"Quiet," Mother said, "I want to think." She sank into the red chair, a dubious, perplexed expression on her face.

"Are we going to go?" June asked.

"I don't know yet," Mother replied. "Go play, all of you. I want to think."

13

THAT NIGHT F. E. WAS
waiting for us at the side entrance of the Roxy Theatre. She led us
through the door to an elevator and pushed a button. She appeared
to be quite familiar with the routine. She knew just which button
to push in the elevator and how to hold her finger on it so the
door wouldn't close too soon. As we ascended, she gazed possessively
and fondly at all of us. She fluffed the hair around June's face and
checked my knickers to see that they were pulled up.

"Roxy's a dear, sweet man," she said to Mother. "But he's
peculiar in some ways. Let me do the talking. I know how to handle
him."

Mother, clutching the brief case, nodded in agreement. She was
doing exactly what she had said she was going to do before we left
the hotel. "I'm going to give her the rope," she had said, "and see if
she hangs herself."

F. E., unaware of Mother's feelings, hummed a little tune, a bit
off-key, as the elevator went past one floor after another. She had
changed her pink blouse for a navy-blue beaded tunic which she
wore over the same tweed skirt. It was probably my imagination,
but I thought her hair looked more pink than it had the day before.

The elevator stopped and the door automatically opened. F. E.
led us down the hall to a door with an engraved card over the bell.
The card read: MR. S. L. ROTHAFEL, PRIVATE. She put her finger

on the bell and pressed it firmly. "Remember," she said, "let me
do the talking."

It was gloomy and silent in the hallway. I could hear the bell
ringing far away on the other side of the door, then a sound of
footsteps coming toward us. They were slow, measured footsteps
and a panic seized me. What if it isn't Roxy Rothafel on the other
side of that door at all, I thought. What if it's a white slaver, or a
killer, or a madman! The footsteps were coming closer; they sounded
to me like the footsteps of doom. I wanted to run as fast as I could
and take my mother and my sister with me.

Then, all of a sudden, the doorknob turned and a man's voice
said, "Come in." When I opened my eyes all I could see was F. E.
She had her arms flung around the man who stood back in the
doorway. Her sealskin coat almost completely covered him. His
glasses slipped down on his nose as she kissed him on one cheek,
then the other.

"How happy I am to see you again," she cried. The man adjusted
his glasses and, patting F. E. perfunctorily on her shoulders, managed to pull away from her embrace. "So this is the little act you
phoned me about," he said, looking from June to me, then to
Mother. F. E. introduced us to Roxy Rothafel.

June dipped into her curtsy. I bent a knee as gracefully as I
could; then Roxy shook hands with Mother and led us into the
huge room he called his office. "I'm so glad you could see me this
late at night," he was saying. "During the day there are so many
interruptions, telephones ringing, people—"

"You should just see this place in the daytime," F. E. said loudly.
"It's a regular madhouse."

Roxy rested his eyes on F. E. for a brief second, as though trying
to place her; then he helped Mother off with her coat and seated
her in a chair in front of a gate-leg table. The table was placed beside a red velvet sofa. Three chairs, like the one Mother sat in, with
high carved wooden backs, were grouped around the table, which
was set for five people. June and I sat on the sofa and stared around
the office while F. E. and Mother settled themselves.

It wasn't like any office I had ever been in before. It was more
like a hotel lobby, not the kind of hotels we stayed in, but big

expensive hotels like the Taft. There were other groups of carved-back chairs, with tables between them, and standing lamps beside them with long fringe on the lamp shades. Maroon velvet draperies hung on spears over the windows and a thick rug covered the floor. The only officelike note was a nest of telephones on the huge almost-bare desk. I counted six of them around a mahogany box with buttons on it. In the far corner stood a parlor grand piano painted gold and vermilion, an embroidered Spanish shawl draped over it. Photographs in silver frames rested on the bunched-up fringe of the shawl. It was all so beautiful and luxurious it took my breath away.

"I hear you girls like hot dogs," Roxy was saying. I pulled my eyes away from a Buddha that sat, holding burning incense in his hands, on a console table. "Do you like mustard or catsup?" he asked, pointing to a bottle of one and a jar of the other. I nodded my head in the general direction of the mustard.

"She likes a lot of it," June said. "I like catsup."

Cream-colored candles lighted up the copper chafing dish and the matching bun warmer; the Sterno in stoves under them burned blue and yellow. Roxy lifted the lid from the chafing dish and forked out a hot dog and placed it on a bun.

"You girls help yourselves," he said. "Don't be shy; dig in." He handed Mother the hot dog, which she accepted gingerly, as though she had never eaten such a plebeian dish. "I let my man go for the evening," Roxy said. "I thought we'd manage all right by ourselves."

"The less servants know about your private life the better off you are," F. E. said, spearing a hot dog for herself and spreading it lavishly with mustard. "I had a butler once that tried to blackmail me. Did I ever tell you about him, Roxy?"

Roxy chewed into his hot dog and waited until he swallowed before he answered. "I don't believe so," he said. He made it quite clear that he didn't care to hear about it, either. I was disappointed. Blackmail sounded interesting.

There was a long silence. The conversation hadn't been exactly strained—F. E. saw to that—but even so there was something strange and unpleasant about the party. There were too many long silences, punctuated with the sounds of silver clinking against the

chafing dish and the self-conscious sounds of people chewing
politely.

"How's business holding up?" F. E. asked, breaking one of the
silences. She wiped her lips daintily with a paper napkin. "Is that
Lilyan Tashman picture pulling them in?"

"Excellent," Roxy said. "Fine picture. Good business."

"I'm so glad to hear that," F. E. said, her voice ringing with
sincerity. "Lilyan's a sweet, lovely girl, and she deserves a break.
I was really worried about her there for a while. With all that—
you know what."

There was another silence. F. E. poured herself a cup of coffee
and sipped it thoughtfully. "Do you hear anything from Monte
Blue?" she asked. Roxy didn't answer.

"Funny fellow, Monte," F. E. said reminiscently. "You know, it
was through me he got his first break in the movies. I saw him
walking down Hollywood Boulevard one day and I said to myself,
that boy's a movie star if I ever saw one—that same day I—"

Roxy dropped his paper napkin on the table and, getting up
suddenly, went over to the gold and vermilion piano and sat down
to play. He reminded me of Grandpa as he sat there studying the
keyboard and cracking his knuckles, one after the other. Then he
began to play, and any resemblance to Grandpa disappeared in a
flash. Roxy's virtuosity was truly something to watch. He slid back
and forth on the bench, elaborately crossing one hand over the
other. To emphasize a musical point he would raise both hands high
in the air then let them fall with a crash. Grandpa never threw his
head around so dramatically, either, nor did he attack the keys with
such an abandoned fury. In fact, I had never seen anyone play the
piano the way Roxy did. Then, all of a sudden, in the middle of
the loudest part, he let his arms fall limply to his sides and the
piano kept on playing by itself!

With an impish grin, Roxy swung around to us, waiting for our
reactions. Mother and June, after a confused silence, applauded
politely. I was too stupefied to do anything but stare at the piano
keys as they moved up and down by themselves. F. E. pounded the
table with her fork. "Encore—encore," she cried. Her coffee slopped

over into the saucer and she pounded harder. "You're a scream, Roxy, you ought to go on the stage yourself." She was still laughing and pounding on the table when Roxy got up and crossed over to his desk.

"Now," he said, "let's talk a little business."

Mother, whipping out the photographs of the act from her brief case, almost ran to the desk. I think she had given up hope that any business was to be discussed. She placed one photograph after another before him, explaining the act as she went along. "This is the baby doing her Russian toe tap dance," she was saying, "and this is the newsboy opening with all the children on stage—" As she piled the photographs up on the desk, one of our Orpheum contracts fell from the brief case. Mother picked it up quickly. "How in the world did *that* get in here?" she said, shoving it carelessly into her purse, but not before Roxy had seen the salary, $1,250.

The piano was playing too loudly for me to hear everything they were saying. F. E. had joined them, now, and was trying unsuccessfully to get a few words in. Roxy was nodding his head and Mother was acting out the cow number. I knew it was the cow number from the way she held her hands to her head describing the horns. From time to time, Roxy would glance down at the photographs; then over to June who sat with her lips in a tight grin, her eyes staring straight ahead. June hated to have Mother call her a baby. Each time Mother would say it, June's mouth would get tighter.

Roxy opened a drawer in his desk and brought out a set of contracts. With his fountain pen he filled in all the blank spaces and gave Mother the contract for her signature. Mother's hand shook as she signed her name. She kept one copy and gave the others to Roxy; then quickly, as though she were afraid he might change his mind, she told June and me to get our coats on.

"It's very late," she said, "and we have a lot of hard work ahead of us. Thank Mr. Roxy for the lovely hot dogs."

June and I thanked the man, and dipped once again into our curtsies. Roxy stood up to see us to the door, but Mother waved him back to his chair. "Don't you bother; you've done enough for one night. We'll let ourselves out."

Holding the brief case close to her chest, Mother led us through the ornate office into the gloomy silent hall. This time she pushed the elevator button, holding her finger on it so the doors wouldn't close too soon. She knew just which button to push in the elevator, too.

F. E. was sullen and silent until the elevator began to descend; then she turned angrily on Mother, "I told you to let me do the talking!" she snapped.

Mother wasn't disturbed by the tone of F. E.'s voice; I don't think she even heard her. "Just think," she said in a sort of trance, "two weeks at the Roxy Theatre. And seven hundred and fifty dollars a week!"

"If you'd kept your big mouth shut," F. E. said, "I could have got us a thousand."

I didn't say anything, but I had a feeling that F. E. had never met Roxy Rothafel before in all her life.

※※

During our lay-off before the Roxy opening we saw F. E. every day. She would appear when we were having breakfast in our room, or we would find her draped over a stool at the counter of the Dew Drop Inn when we stopped by for dinner. Sometimes she would be waiting for us in the lobby of our hotel when we returned from making the rounds of the booking agents' offices.

"Why do you bother with those small-time agents?" she asked Mother. "The Roxy contract, as bad as it is thanks to you, is better than anything they can get."

There was no way Mother could explain that the contract was her reason for making the rounds. Good or bad, it impressed the agents and friends like the Maynards. Mother did admit she might have been hasty in signing the contract. There were many things wrong with it. There was no billing clause, for instance. No clause that we were to have the star dressing room. Most disturbing, it wasn't a contract for the Roxy Theatre on Broadway at all. It was for Roxy's other theatre, the Academy of Music on Fourteenth Street. But Roxy's name was on it, and the salary was the highest

we had received since the Orpheum Circuit. The Roxy Theatre
would follow, Mother was sure of that. "Once we've opened and
he's seen the act," she said, "the rest will be clear sailing."

One afternoon when we returned to the hotel we found F. E.
pacing up and down the lobby. She grabbed Mother's arm and insisted that we all go for a walk with her at once. We had been
walking from booking office to booking office all day and were
tired, but rather than have a scene in the lobby, we went.

Leading the way, F. E. walked us briskly down Sixth Avenue.
She didn't wait for the green lights at the crossings but dodged in
and out of the cars, a pink ostrich feather bobbing up and down
on her green hat, as she scurried around trucks and taxicabs. Then,
all at once, she stopped. A happy, relieved smile covered her face.
"The doors are still down," she said. "Thank God we made it in
time."

She was looking at a tall building ahead of us that was being
remodeled. Carpenters had torn down the original façade and bricks
and boards were piled up on the sidewalk. Part of the demolition
work was covered with a wall of old doors which had obviously
been removed from the building. The doors were painted all colors.
Some of them cheerful yellow, but mud stained now and streaked.
Others were pink, or blue, or gray. One had LADIES on it in faded,
chipped letters. It looked like a fun house at an amusement park.
Workmen were piling great slabs of slatelike material onto a truck.
To make it easier, they had taken down a section of the painted
doors, and the remains of the old walls were exposed. Jagged pieces
of wood stuck out like prongs, and huge bent nails held fragments
of old two-by-fours and splintered moldings. It was rather sad-look-
ing, I thought. Like a discarded Christmas tree lying in the gutter.

F. E., taking long firm steps, held Mother's arm tightly as she
walked ahead of June and me toward the demolished building. One
jagged board protruding from the wall extended a few inches over
the sidewalk. Before I could call out and warn her, F. E. walked
straight into it. I could hear the thump as her forehead bashed
into the jagged wood. With a startled shriek of pain, she staggered
against the wall and slid down into a faint on the sidewalk. Mother
dropped to her knees beside her. Taking a handkerchief from her

pocket, she tried to wipe away the blood that gushed from a wound on F. E.'s forehead.

"For God's sake, Rose, leave me alone," F. E. hissed. She let her head fall forward and that made the blood rush faster. "Don't just sit there," F. E. said. "Call an ambulance. And get the supervisor of the building."

Mother didn't have to call either one of them. In a matter of minutes, we heard the ambulance screeching down the street, the siren going at full blast, and a man who said he was the building supervisor was leaning over F. E. "How could such a thing have happened?" he said. "This is a dreadful accident."

F. E. looked up at him. Blood covered her face and dripped down horribly onto her sleazy pink blouse. Her hat, with the pink ostrich feather in it, was lying on the sidewalk, spattered with blood. "Look at that board," she said, pointing to the jagged two-by-four that now hung loosely because of the impact with her head. "Do you see a red flag on it?" she said accusingly. "Do you see any warning around here at all of the dangers to pedestrians?"

The man began to bluster. "Just a minute, now, my men have complied with every safety law. It's our policy to—"

F. E. interrupted him. "I have three witnesses to this gross negligence on your part. Mrs. Hovick here and her two little girls saw the whole thing. You certainly aren't going to call those two innocent little children liars, are you?"

A crowd had gathered, and to a man they were on F. E.'s side. They moved in closer to the building supervisor eyeing him with menace.

"But there must have been a red flag somewhere," the man said nervously. He turned to me, "You saw a flag, didn't you?"

I felt so sorry for him I wanted to lie, but I didn't. I didn't tell him F. E. banged her head into the board on purpose, either, and I could have, only I wasn't sure.

"Tell him the truth, Louise," F. E. said. "Did you see a flag?"

Her pale blue eyes were icy as she peered up at me, her lashes clotted with blood. She's mad, I thought. Not just crazy in a nice, amusing way but really mad. "Tell him!" she said. I pushed my way through the crowd and threw the words back over my shoulder as

I ran. "There was no flag!" I yelled it as loud as I could. "No flag —no flag!" I ran all the way back to the hotel without stopping. My chest ached and I was so out of breath I wanted to throw myself down on the sidewalk, then I would think of F. E.'s icy blue eyes and my fear made me run faster.

I waited in the lobby, where there were people around me, for Mother and June to come back, and prayed that F. E. wouldn't be with them. Then when I saw Mother and my sister and knew they were alone the relief made me weak. I held on to Mother's arm in the elevator and walked close beside her down the hallway to our room. She was silent and thoughtful until she closed the door behind us. "I don't know what it is," she said taking off her hat and shaking out her curly hair, "I can't put my finger on it, but there's something about that F. E. Gorham I don't trust."

That night when we were having dinner at the Dew Drop Inn F. E. threw open the door and strode in. She stood dramatically at the end of the counter, one hand on her hip, the other resting on the cash register. "A fine friend you are!" she said staring at Mother. "After all I've done for you, the least you could do was go in the ambulance with me to the hospital!"

She was still wearing the blood-stained blouse. There was a clumsy bandage on her head and the green hat with the pink ostrich feather sat precariously on top.

She glared at Mother and their blue eyes met. Mother glared her down. "We did enough as it was," she said. "Taking everything into consideration, we did plenty!"

F. E. shrugged her shoulders. "Well," she said, "everything worked out all right anyway." She took off her fur coat and hung it on a hook, then she sank onto a stool and ordered a hot roast-beef sandwich. While the counter boy was fixing her order she fingered the bandage on her head. There was a faraway look in her eyes. "Did you ever see anything funnier than that building inspector's face?" she said. "You should have seen him at the hospital, you would have died laughing. I'm a bleeder, you know. Some people are, and some people aren't. I'm one of the lucky ones."

I looked down at the catsup on my hamburger and tried to remember it was really catsup. I tried not to look at F. E. and the

soiled blouse, but she was laughing now and it was hard to keep
from laughing with her.

"There I was bleeding all over the place," she was saying between
bursts of laughter. "He was begging me to settle then and there.
He kept pushing the money at me and I kept pushing it back—"

The counter boy placed the hot roast-beef sandwich in front of
her and F. E., still laughing, dug her fork into the mashed potatoes
that were there on the plate like a gray snowball. "I finally settled
for a thousand dollars," she said, wiping a bit of gravy from her chin.

Mother stirred her coffee thoughtfully. "A thousand dollars,"
she said. Her eyebrows were squeezed together and I knew she was
thinking very hard. Then she shook her head, ever so slightly, and
began to sip her coffee.

For a moment I had been afraid of what Mother was thinking,
and I was relieved and pleased when I knew that, whatever it was,
she had dismissed it.

14

Peering out into the black void of the theatre I could see the white collar of Mother's dress. She was checking the acoustics of the Academy of Music Theatre before rehearsal opening day. As June and the boys and I spoke our lines from the act Mother would move to a different section of the house.

"Now let me hear you, Sonny," she said and her voice came from way over to the left.

"M is for the many things she gave me. . . ."

"Very good. Now you, Louise."

"I'm a Hard-boiled Rose."

Acoustics, Mother often said, are funny things. Sometimes in the smallest theatres we had to shout the loudest. But the acoustics here were fine. Mother said you could hear a pin drop. "Now you, Johnny," she called out and her voice was thin and hollow. I couldn't see her white collar at all, then way at the very back I caught a glimpse of her. Johnny stepped forward to sing his line, but he stopped when the house lights went on as a group of men began walking down the aisle. Sudden changes frightened him and he moved close to the other boys. Two of the men who were walking down the aisle carried a table with buttons on it and electric cords hanging down from the sides.

Until the lights went on I hadn't realized how huge the theatre was. The red velvet seats went so far back I couldn't see the last rows. A crystal chandelier, almost as big as our hotel room, hung down from the domed ceiling.

"It's like being back on the Orpheum Circuit," June whispered and I nodded my head, too impressed to speak.

The men in the aisle cleared a path for Roxy, who walked through it, his teeth clamped on a cigar, a green visor, like Gordon used to wear when he worked on our scrapbooks, on his head. He sat behind the table and snapped on a shielded lamp, then he pushed one of the buttons and the house lights dimmed. He pushed another and the stage lights began to come on almost magically. A gold velour curtain was slowly and silently closing in behind us.

"Clear the stage," one of the men shouted. "Everyone off the stage for rehearsal."

The lights were turning from red to blue as the boys and June and I groped our way to the wings. For a fleeting instant I wondered if I should curtsy to Roxy, then I decided against it; he was too busy with the buttons. Mother hurried down the aisle headed in his direction but one of the men surrounding him shunted her off and up the stairs to the stage.

"Everyone stand by for rehearsal!" someone shouted and it made my blood tingle with excitement. I got that same choked-up feeling I always had on opening days.

Back of the gold velour curtain the stagehands were pulling our scenery out of the trunk. The blue sateen traveler I had made in the hotel in Detroit looked old and shabby beside the satins and velvets that belonged to the theatre.

"Is this all of it?" the stagehand said. He had the curtain spread out on the stage and he looked down on it with disgust. "There isn't enough stuff here to hang in the men's room!"

"You can mask it in," Mother was saying, a note of nervous hysteria in her voice. The stagehand began shoving the scenery back in the trunk and Mother stood by helplessly. "We can't go on without our scenery," she said. "It sets the entire mood for our act—" The stagehand crammed the last bit of scenery into the trunk and slammed down the lid. "We'll fix up something for you," he said. "We got a warehouse full of stuff."

The musicians were tuning up in the basement. Mother bit her lip; there was no time now to argue with the stagehand. Our costumes had to be unpacked, an on-stage dressing room set up for our quick changes. The make-up had to be spread out on the shelf, our dancing shoes, rubbed with vaseline, lined up below. The gilded guns had to be placed in the wings so we could grab them up quickly. The cow head had to be unpacked. The boys and June and I had special jobs assigned to us and the discordant noises coming from the musicians' room made us quicken our steps.

Then it was time for us to go on for the dress rehearsal, and made up and dressed for our newsboy opening we stood in the wings waiting for our cue. Mother, wearing the gray wig for the tableau, gave the electrician our light cues. "Remember now," she said nervously, "when the baby says, 'I'm glad I'm an adopted child,' start your dimout, and when she says, 'My family picked me out but your family had to take what they got,' blackout, and the spotlight will pick up the baby for her ballad."

June fumbled with the oversized safety pin that fastened the ragged sweater around her waist. "I wish she would stop calling me a baby in front of people," she said. She snapped her hat, with the feather in it, back and forth on her head, stretching the elastic way out each time to make sure it would work all right on stage. "I'm not a baby any more. I'm almost eleven years old. She makes me lisp and wear these awful baby clothes and I hate it. I hate the whole act."

"Not so loud," I said. "Mother will hear you."

"I don't care if she does. I wish something terrible would happen to me. I wish I could get sick, so I didn't have to go on. I wish I could die, right now!"

"Don't say that. It's bad luck to say such a thing."

June pulled her arm away from me. "It's all right for you to talk. You don't have to go out and sing and dance and do the same old silly things you did when you were a baby. You don't have to do anything in the act. You never have to do anything. I'm the only one, and I hate it!"

The orchestra played the introduction to "The Bowery," our opening number. I grabbed my sister's hand and we ran as fast as we could to the center of the stage so we'd be there when the curtain opened. "I'm sorry, Weese," June whispered as we ran. "I didn't mean it. Not about you, I mean."

"I know you didn't," I said, and we smiled at each other as the curtains began opening.

"—but when your family got you they had to take what they got!" The lights dimmed down and the boys and I stood quietly in the darkness as June stepped into the spotlight and began to recite her ballad. As she spoke the lines the orchestra played "Pal o' Mine" softly in the background. "My little dog—I taught him how to do some tricks, and he could jump as high as the shelf. I didn't teach him gratitude, he learned that by himself; for one day when we were playing in the street, there was a great big truck I didn't see—"

June stopped and the drum roll ended with a crash. She held her little round fists to her eyes. When she took her hands away and looked up into the balcony tears glistened and rolled down her cheeks.

"—if it hadn't been for him, it would have run right over me." Her voice cracked on the last word, and she dropped her head. The music swelled and June, holding her head high now, sang the last eight bars of the song, her voice clear and sharp, her face wet with tears, "They needed an angel in heaven, so they sent for that pal o' mine."

With an embarrassed little smile, she wiped her nose on the back of her hand, and the curtain closed in slowly. The opening number was over. June had cried real tears again and I was glad because I knew Mother would be pleased.

The boys and June and I raced to the change room while Georgie did his eccentric tap dance. When it was over we were ready for our next cue. We danced, then we ran, we sang and we ran again. Back and forth we ran from the wings to the change room, and each number was worse than the one before it. Our music was all wrong, we didn't recognize the violin trills and the strange noises from the French horns and the oboes. The light cues were mixed up and we bumped into each other in the dark. Twice Mother tried to make us stop the act and start in again from the beginning, but Roxy called out from the audience, "It's just a rehearsal. Keep going—go on!"

Sonny's voice cracked a bit as he began the chorus of his ballad. Mother, behind the curtain, wearing the gray wig and a fichu over her dress, sat in a rocking chair with a Bible on her lap. Tommy knelt at her feet, and I stood behind them, leaning on the back of the chair with my eyes cast down. On cue the curtains slowly parted and we froze for the picture. I could feel Mother go tense when Sonny's voice wavered.

> M is for the many things she gave me.
> O means only that she's growing old.
> T is for the—

At that moment a small sandbag fell from the flies, missing us by inches, and broke with a plop on the stage. The Bible clattered to the floor and Tommy fell over backward as Mother jumped to her feet. "What the hell's going on up there?" she shouted to the flyman. Her wig slipped down over her forehead as she slid around on the spilled sand. "Of all the stupid, careless, unforgivable things—"

The music went on, and Sonny, after losing a few notes, caught up with the orchestra.

> H is for her heart of purest gold.
> E is for—

"Close the curtain, goddamnit," Mother screamed.

> Put them all together they spell Mother,
> A word that means the world to me—

The curtain closed in and Sonny and Tommy and I ran to change for the finale.

When the act was over we stood in the wings, breathless and wet with sweat. June tugged at her rhinestone dress fretfully. "It's too tight on me, Mother," she said. "I can't dance in it at all any more."

"Quiet," Mother said. "The stage manager has some notes he wants to give us."

His notes were short and to the point. Because the show was running overtime there would be a few cuts. "You'll open with the newsboy number," he said, "and close with the little girl's ballad."

"*Close* the act with June's ballad?" Mother said. "There must be some mistake. That number runs only six minutes! What about the cow number? That's the biggest number in our act. . . ."

The stage manager left us without another word. Mother put a towel around June's shoulders and we all walked close together across the huge stage and up the three flights of stairs to our dressing room. "I'm sure there's some mistake," Mother said. "I'll speak to Roxy about it myself."

Roxy was too busy to see Mother that day. In fact, he was too busy to see her for the whole two weeks of our engagement. Then on closing day Mother received a note from him. She looked at the envelope with his name on it for a long time.

"Go on, open it," F. E. said. We hadn't seen much of F. E. since we opened, but that day, our closing day, she was there in our dressing room with us. "Read what it says."

Mother tore open the envelope; her eyes sparkled as she read the note. "He wants to see us!" she said. "I knew it. It's about the Roxy Theatre booking. I just know it is."

F. E. grabbed up her coat and started to follow Mother out of the room.

"He wants to see the baby and me alone," Mother said firmly. "Make yourself comfy here with Louise. We'll be right back."

F. E. puttered about the dressing room while Mother was away. She wandered over to the make-up shelf and looked at herself critically in the mirror. She put on some lipstick, and a lot of blue eyeshadow over her eyes, then she painted on darker eyebrows and gazed at herself, pleased and happy with the effect. "Wonder if your mother got paid yet?" she said.

I didn't have to answer her, because just then Mother and June came back. June was crying, and Mother was so angry I thought she was going to have an asthma attack. She threw her coat over the back of the chair and glared around the room at us. F. E. pattered about, agitated and nervous. "What happened?" she asked. "What did he say?"

June held her tear-stained face up to Mother and cried out, "Tell her, Mother. Tell her what he said!"

"It was a lot of foolishness," Mother replied. "He was just talking to hear himself talk."

"That isn't true and you know it!" June stood with her hands clenched close to her sides. She wasn't crying now; her eyes were fierce with anger. "He said I could be a big star if I was properly trained. He said I should have singing lessons, and dancing lessons, and acting lessons. He said he'd pay all the bills and everything if Mother would promise to not interfere for a year."

The outburst exhausted her. Her shoulders sagged and with a little moan she sank into the chair and buried her face in the make-up towel. F. E. looked down at her, then over at Mother. "What's there about that to get sore over?" F. E. asked. "That's a great compliment. What's the matter with you, Rose?"

"Compliment?" Mother shrieked. "How dare he suggest such a thing! My baby is a big star right now. Show me one child who has press clippings like hers. What school can teach her anything she doesn't already know?"

"What did you tell him?" F. E. asked after a long pause.

"What did I tell him?" Mother said. "I told him to mind his own business, that's what I told him! There's no man in the world going to take my baby away from me." Mother was packing everything we didn't need for the last show. She left a small chunk of Crisco on a towel so we could use it to take off our make-up, and packed the can away in the trunk. Then she packed our military costumes and the extra dancing shoes. "The nerve of him," she said, as she began wrapping each one of the gilded guns in newspaper. "And just what does he expect Louise and me to live on while the baby is away in this school?"

F. E. picked up one of the guns and began to help. "You could get a job," she said. Mother shoved the gun in the trunk and reached for another one. "A job?" she repeated. "What could I do to earn a living?"

"Oh, I don't know." F. E. shrugged her shoulders casually. "All sorts of things. Look at me, for instance. I manage."

Mother snatched the gun from F. E. and shoved it away in the trunk with the others. "God forbid," she muttered, under her breath. "I'd rather starve."

That night when we were alone in our hotel room Mother decided we would move. We had enough money now to pay our back room rent without dipping into our nest egg, but that wasn't Mother's only reason. "It's F. E." Mother said. "I'm afraid of her. . . . She's up to something. I don't know what it is, but I don't like it." It didn't take us long to pack the next morning. We closed up the wardrobe trunk and put our few overnight things in a suitcase. When we finished breakfast the cups and coffeepot would go in one of the dog bags and we would be ready to leave.

There was a knock on the door, and Mother, from force of habit, shoved the coffeepot under the table. But it wasn't the chambermaid after all. It was F. E. She had a bag of doughnuts with her.

"Going some place?" she asked, eying the trunks and bags lined up near the door.

Mother glanced at them uneasily. "No, not at all," she said. "Just cleaning up a bit. I thought I'd put those things in the storage room. Would you like a cup of coffee?" Without waiting for an answer she brought out the coffeepot from under the table and poured a cupful. June and I began dividing the doughnuts and we sat down to finish breakfast. Bootsy and Runty, the poodle we bought after Mumshay was killed in the folding bed in Syracuse, looked at Mother with pleading eyes and she filled a saucer with coffee for them. Danny and Johnny snatched up their doughnuts and went over to the sofa. The strange, unfriendly silence was broken with a gentle tap on the door. Mother hid the coffeepot, then she went to the door and opened it.

"We heard you were looking for boy dancers," a young man said. "My partner and I'd like to try out for the job." He didn't look like a dancer, neither of them did, and they weren't wearing dancing shoes. Besides they were much too old for our act; they looked at least eighteen.

One had a scar on his lip and the other was short with a thick neck. They both carried caps in their hands, and they twisted them nervously.

"There must be some mistake," Mother said. "We do a kiddie act and I'm not looking for boys anyway." She started to close the door and the one with the scar on his lip pushed his way into the room.

"This is a stickup," he said pulling a gun from under his cap. "Keep your mouths shut and nobody'll get hurt."

They slammed the door shut and grabbed Mother's arm. "Where's the rings and the money?" one of them hissed. Mother twisted away from him and lunged for the gun, but before she could snatch it, he flipped it over in his hand and brought the butt of it down on her head. With a startled moan Mother fell to a heap on the floor.

It had happened so suddenly that none of us realized the danger until we saw Mother fall and the blood flow from a cut on her head. With a savage scream June threw herself at the gunman, then the boys and I rushed at them and began beating them with our fists and yelling for help. The dogs, barking shrilly, snapped at their feet, and Mother dragged herself to the window. "Help, murder!" she cried, the blood pouring down her face. "Help! Help!"

We were still screaming and bumping into each other when the room began filling with people and policemen. The two men were gone. We tried, incoherently, to explain what had happened, but everyone had a different version. The chambermaid had seen the two men rush out of the room and was sure she could identify them. The elevator boy remembered them as being tall and dark. The desk clerk said they were short and mean looking. Then another policeman came in with the gun. He had found it, he said, on the roof. There were no identifying marks on it, no bullets in the chamber.

"They must of known their way around; sure you never saw 'em before?"

We all answered him at once. Even Mother, who was having the cut on her head sewn up by the doctor, told him the men were strangers to us. The doctor had given her two pills to ease the pain and her eyes were heavy lidded.

The policeman closed his notebook. "Funny how they knew their way up to the roof," he said. "I'll make a report on this, but I might have to ask you a few questions later."

In a little while everyone had gone. The shades were pulled down and Mother was lying on the bed, her head swathed in bandages. "You were all very brave," she said in a tight, pained voice. Smiling wanly at the boys and June and me, she patted the money bag that was under her padded robe. The pills had made her drowsy and her gestures were slow and heavy. "Thank God they didn't get our rings or the money," she said. Then suddenly her eyes were wide and frightened. "Where's F. E.?" she whispered. I had forgotten all about F. E.

"She—she's gone." I said, looking around the room. None of us could remember when she had disappeared. She had been there when the gunmen came into the room, we all remembered that, but where was she when the police arrived? Where was she now?

Mother jumped up from the bed. "She instigated that robbery, I know she did. She's been planning it for a long time. I knew she was up to something. I felt it in my bones. Quick, get the dogs in their bags, pack the coffeepot. We have to get out of here."

The bandage was slipping from Mother's head as she raced around the room, packing the last-minute things, and opening and closing bureau drawers. June and the boys and I looked under the beds and in the closet and when we were sure we hadn't forgotten anything we called down for a bell boy to help us with the trunks.

"The policeman!" I said suddenly as I remembered. "He said he might want to ask us some questions. We should tell him about F. E."

Mother put her hat on over the bandage and grabbed up her brief case. "What could we tell him? We don't know where she lives, what her telephone number is. . . . We don't even know if F. E. Gorham is her right name."

We crowded into a taxi with the trunks and suitcases on it and drove down Eighth Avenue looking for a place to live. "We'll just wipe her off our list," Mother said. "We'll find a nice quiet apartment somewhere and forget she ever darkened our lives."

15

OUR APARTMENT AT
the Henry Court in New York was one of the cheaper ones,
with no outside windows. There was ventilation of a sort from
the windows facing the court, but no daylight. We had to burn
electricity all day, and it was very expensive. There was a meter
on the wall in the sitting room and it seemed we were always
putting quarters in it. We could tell when the quarter was almost
used up because the lights would dim for an instant before they
went out completely.

One of the advantages of the apartment was that June could play
outside on the street. There were many children living on the
block and June made friends with them. The oldest of her friends
was twelve, and a rather snively twelve at that. I was fourteen and
thought of myself as a bit above the children in the neighborhood.
None of them collected stamps the way I did, and they had never
heard of the books I read. My vocabulary was better than theirs, too.
They didn't like me any better than I liked them. Sometimes when
I would be sitting on the brownstone steps in front of our apartment
house, they would race by me screaming, "Stuck up, stuck up,
she's covered with mud and she's stuck up."

"I am not!" I'd yell, and taking off after them I'd chase them up
the block. I didn't wear boy's clothes or knickers any more, I wore
pleated skirts, but I could still run fast in a skirt.

June said it was my own fault that the kids didn't like me.
"You snoot them," she said. "Nobody likes to be snooted and you
do it all the time. You even snoot me."

"I don't care if they like me or not," I said, which wasn't exactly
true; even snively twelve-year-olds are better than no one at all.
"They're gauche, that's what they are. And you're gauche, too,
or you wouldn't play with them."

June ran screaming into the apartment, "Mother, Mother," she
yelled. "Louise just called me a dirty name!"

I had to show Mother the word *gauche* in the dictionary before
she'd believe me. "It isn't a dirty name," I said. "It means ill
bred and that's what June is and you have to admit it."

"I'll admit nothing of the kind," Mother said. "She's as well bred
as you are. You're both well-brought-up young ladies, and if I hear
you call your sister a name like that again, so help me, I'll take
every one of your books and burn them."

Mother cooked for us in the apartment. There was a dark kitchen
back of the sitting room and every time we turned on the kitchen
light the cockroaches would scurry across the floor to their hiding
places. "How F. E. would love this kitchen," Mother used to say.
"She'd think it was a gold mine."

We hadn't seen F. E. since the attempted robbery months before,
but we thought of her a lot. Not just when we saw the cockroaches,
but when we saw a building being demolished, or when we passed
the Roxy Theatre. "What a misdirected life," Mother would say
on these occasions. "Why, with her personality she could have been
another Aimee Semple McPherson."

There was always enough to eat; Mother saw to that. We ate
beans, stew, cabbage, all wholesome food, Mother said, and plenty
of it. "The Maynards don't eat any better than we do," she would
add. "And we can be thankful that we don't owe a penny to a
living soul."

Perhaps if we had known anyone with money we might have
borrowed it, but most of the acts we knew were as broke as we were.
Then when the money bag was flat, the diamonds were in hock
and the rent was past due, the telephone would ring and we'd be
offered a date in Greenpoint, or three days in Utica. During the

frenzy of packing the costumes and telephoning the boys Mother would stop, a grateful smile on her face. "God's watching out for us," she would say. "I knew He wouldn't let a little act like ours lay off."

One by one the boys in the act were being replaced. Johnny had gone home to Shenendoah, then Jack's parents had sent for him. Georgie had left the act after an alarming incident in Kingston, New York, involving a waitress. June and I never knew all the details, but considering that Georgie was only fourteen and the waitress almost thirty it must have been a most strange affair.

Then Danny skipped out one night and joined a flash act without even leaving a note. Mother said later she hadn't expected gratitude from him but he could have at least said good-by. After that the only boys left of the old group were Bubsy and Sonny. Sonny's voice had changed. It was a gradual change. First, when he would try for a high note his voice would crack, then little by little it deepened until it wasn't a tenor voice any more at all. Bubsy could still dance, but he was taller than Mother. It was plain to see the boys' theatrical careers were over. Bubsy said so himself. He told Mother one day they had to find jobs that would pay them a salary.

"We gotta help Mom," Bubsy said. "We just gotta earn some money for her."

"Yeah," Sonny added. "Pop's in jail again."

"It's a bum rap," Bubsy said loyally, "he wuz framed. But we—we got to leave the act."

It was warm and humid. The window to the court was open, but the frayed lace curtain hung still. A radio from someone's apartment blared noisily through the court. A frantic voice was shouting through the static, "He made it! Lindbergh has crossed the Atlantic! Three thousand, six hundred and ten miles in thirty-three hours, twenty-nine minutes and thirty seconds—two ham sandwiches—a tiny kitten in his pocket—"

Mother stepped over to the window and listened more closely. Her lips set in a thin angry line. "If he wants to kill himself it's all right," she said, "but I certainly think the A.S.P.C.A. should have stopped him from taking a kitten on such a dangerous trip."

Someone in the building was cooking cabbage and the odor of it choked me. I snatched up my book of sonnets and went to the door. "Where are you going?" Mother asked.

"Just out on the front steps."

Mother didn't hear me. She was too busy sorting out Bubsy's and Sonny's clothes. There was a pitiful nothingness to the shabby socks and sweaters she shoved in the paper bag. The boys watched her gravely. "Gee, we're going to miss the act and everybody," Bubsy said. I closed the door softly behind me.

Outside June was playing across the street with her friends. They were chasing each other and screaming and yelling in the angry way they played. It made me feel grown-up and old to hear them. I couldn't remember ever having been as young as they were. I sat down on the warm brownstone stoop and opened my book. I wasn't reading it. I was thinking of Bubsy and Sonny and all the time they'd wasted in the act. Then I wondered what they'd do now that they weren't in show business any more. I remembered the time we visited some of our relatives in Portland and hoped the boys wouldn't have to live with civilians like those. I tried to think of a worse kind of life, but it was inconceivable. I realized again how lucky I was to have a mother like mine who belonged in show business and a sister like June who made it possible.

A man shuffled past. The sound of his footsteps slowed, then stopped. I looked up and recognized the overcoat. It was shabbier than I remembered it, and not very clean, but I would have recognized it anywhere. "Gordon!" I said. Our eyes met for an instant, then with long strides and without looking to see if a car was coming or not, he hurled himself across the street. "Gordon," I called out, chasing after him. "It's me. Louise." He didn't stop. June must have heard me because she came running toward us, her blond hair flying and her bloomers showing. "You've come back to us, Gordon!" she cried. "I knew you would. I just knew it."

Gordon picked her up the way he used to when she was little and held her high in the air. "How big you've grown," he said. "Why, you're almost a grown-up young lady."

Reminded of her age, June scrambled to her feet, and pulled down her dress. "Mother will be so glad to see you," she said. "She thinks you're dead. Doesn't she, Louise? She said if you weren't dead you would have found us and come back to us a long time ago—"

Gordon pulled back from her. "I don't want to see her," he said sharply. "I never want to see her again. Never, do you hear me?"

The smile faded from June's face. "But—aren't you coming back to us?" she asked. Gordon didn't answer her. "Why are you here if you aren't? What are you doing to—live? How can you earn any money without us?"

There was a grayness in Gordon's face. His eyes were too bright and something must have happened to his teeth, because his mouth dented in strangely. He felt me looking at him and turned his head away. When he spoke it was to June, not to me. "I have an invention," he said. "A great new invention. I'm going to have my own company, my own factory, salesmen all over the country. I'll have a big office with my name on the door—"

"What kind of an invention?" June asked, her eyes wide with awe.

Gordon took my hands and held them up to my chest. "The ordinary brassière," he said, measuring his words carefully, "depends on shoulder straps and elastic that cut into the flesh and flatten down the natural contour of the body. Now, Louise," he said, "I want you to cup your hands."

A few of June's friends had gathered around us and the boys among them were giggling and nudging one another. I didn't want to cup my hands, not with them watching me, but Gordon insisted so I did.

"Now lift!" he commanded. "See what happens? No flattening of the contour, no elastic, no shoulder straps!"

There was a pause while Gordon waited for the full significance of his words to sink in. One of the boys snickered and I let my hands fall to my sides.

June cleared her throat and moved uneasily from one foot to the other. "How does the brassière stay up?" she asked.

"With wires!" Gordon exclaimed. "I have invented a *wire brassière!*" He waved his hand at us as he began to back away. "Don't tell your Mother you saw me," he shouted, then suddenly he turned and broke into a run. The last we saw of him was his black overcoat as he darted around the corner of Eighth Avenue.

"He must be crazy," one of June's friends murmured.

June turned on him in anger. "He is not!" she said. "He—he's just sick—" Burying her face in her hands, she ran across the street toward our apartment house. I followed, more slowly, after her. I wondered if I should tell Mother, then I decided against it. She thought Gordon had loved her, and I didn't want to be the one to tell her that wasn't true, but I made up my mind then and there that I wouldn't believe any man who told me he loved me.

16

THE NEW BOYS IN the act weren't nice at all. In fact, most of them were awful. Mother had to pay each of them a salary and that was bad enough, but they wanted their money the very night it was due. They were arrogant and nosy and asked all sorts of questions such as where were we booked, and how much money was the act getting. They wanted to tag along when we made the rounds of the booking agents' offices, and tried to pry into all of Mother's private business matters.

When the act laid off, and we laid off a lot, they would grumble and threaten to quit. They had no respect for the act, either. They said it was old-fashioned and dated. The two who worked in the cow skin grumbled the most. Especially Henry, who was the rear end. He was getting thirty dollars a week when we worked and still he grumbled. Most of the other boys got twenty-five. The only reason Mother paid Henry more was because he was such a good rear end. He also drove the car.

Mother had discovered the advantage of traveling by automobile when we were offered three weeks' consecutive work in and around Buffalo, New York. The railroad fares would have consumed any profits to be made. Besides, with the railroad companies, we had to pay cash, and we could buy an automobile with a little money down, and the rest each month if we had it.

Mother bought a second-hand Studebaker because it was roomy.

The man who sold it to us said it had originally been owned by an undertaking establishment. He said that meant the car had not been driven fast, and although it was several years old, the mileage on it was quite low. The Studebaker wasn't exactly a hearse; it was the car used to transport the mourners to the funerals, and it seated nine people comfortably.

Mother had a neat tarpaulin made to fit over the top to cover our scenery, which traveled there. A heavy-duty rack held our trunks and the cow head. The suitcases went on the running boards. The spare tire behind the trunk rack had the name of the act, DAINTY JUNE AND CO., printed on it in white letters. Below, in smaller letters, was the word ENROUTE.

Mother had learned about taking care of a car from the old National sedan, but she had never learned to drive. Among the boys in the act, there always had to be one who was a careful and, as Mother said, conscientious driver. There had been others before Henry, but even with his grumbling he was the most conscientious. He was seventeen and had blondish kinky hair. He was from the Lower East Side of New York and called girls "goils" and anything with feathers, including chickens, "boids." Neither June nor I liked him very much, but we had to admit he was a good driver and he was the best rear end of a cow we'd ever had. His partner was a tall, silent boy named Manny, who had worked in his father's drugstore before he decided to go into show business. He did impressions of Pat Rooney, George M. Cohan and Bill Robinson and managed, somehow, to make all three of them alike.

Two of the other boys, Tommy and Bingo, looked like the gunmen who had tried to hold us up at the Langwell Hotel. They were perfect for the newsboy opening, but aside from that there wasn't much else they could do. The act called for six boys and Mother had trouble finding talented ones who would work for so little money.

Bobby was talented, but he was peculiar. Mother said you could tell he came from a nice family from his manners; he would stand up when she entered a room and wait until she sat down first. He had nice table manners, too, but he was erratic. He was always experimenting with his specialty. Each show would be different.

The orchestra leaders would complain and when Mother spoke to him about it he would threaten to quit. "I'm an inspirational dancer," he would say. "I'm too creative to get one routine and stick to it. This is how I am and if you don't like it I'll find some other act that does."

Mother most certainly didn't like it, but when Bobby was good he was very good and he wasn't fussy about his salary, so Mother kept him on.

Stanley was seventeen, too, but he was different from the other boys. He was clever, and ambitious and very handsome. June said he was conceited but she didn't know him as well as I did. He might have been self-confident, but he wasn't conceited. He was an eccentric dancer and used to stop the show with his specialty. I knew that because I watched him from the wings every single show.

He would crouch down low when he danced, his hair hanging black and shiny over his face, his teeth flashing in a wide smile. He danced to "Me and My Shadow" played in stop time, all but the last sixteen bars when the orchestra played forte for his figure eight and over the top. He used a lobster-scope for that part, making him look as though he were dancing in slow motion. When the lights came up full, and his dance was over, he would sell it on one knee, his arms stretched out as though to embrace the audience.

The lobster-scope, a metal disk that fitted over a spotlight, was his own, and on opening days, he would give it to the spotlight man himself. "Be careful of it," he would warn. "Anything happens to that lobster-scope and the whole act's a flop."

Stanley had a few habits I didn't like. He bragged a lot, and he used to change his money into one-dollar bills and make it into a roll with a ten-dollar bill on top. I thought that was cheap looking, and I told him so. "It makes you look show-offy," I said, "and you aren't like that at all."

"Funny you should say that," Stanley said. "Everybody thinks because I stop the show all the time I've got a big head."

"They're probably jealous," I murmured.

"Say, I never thought of that." Stanley sat forward on the bench where we were sitting in the stage alley in Trenton. The autumn moon was so full it was almost as bright as daylight. Stanley weighed the possibility of anyone being jealous of him. "What's there about me to be jealous about? Sure, I stop the show, but what's there to that?"

His feet were moving in a time step as he sat looking up at the moon shining through the fire escape. His feet were always moving in dance steps. He would dance while we waited in line in a cafeteria, while he put on his make-up, and even when we were watching the movies together backstage in the darkness. He wore double cleats on the tips of his shoes so he could hear the taps better.

"I like being with you," he said suddenly. I leaned back against the brick wall so my face would be in a shadow. "You aren't like most of the girls I know, giggling all the time and always talking about themselves. I like serious girls."

"I have a very serious nature," I said. "Maybe that's because I read a lot. Do you like to read?"

Stanley didn't answer me. He was doing a triple wing and concentrating on the intricacy of the dance step.

"Thus by day my limbs, by night my mind," I quoted, "for thee, and for myself no quiet find—that's from Shakespeare's sonnets. Have you ever read them?"

Stanley jumped to his feet, and stood with his back to me silhouetted against the moonlight. "This sure is a dumpy theatre, isn't it?" he said. "I never would have joined this crumby act if your mother hadn't told me we were going on the Orpheum Circuit."

"Oh, we'll be going back," I said hurriedly. "It's just that vaudeville is in a slump right now. Mother says that's because of the talking pictures."

"Other acts keep working, I notice. Talking pictures haven't hurt them any." Stanley strode up and down the alley, a scowl drawing his dark eyebrows together. "I'm not going to keep on playing dumps like this, laying off all the time, living in cheap hotels and traveling in that old wreck of a car. I'm going to get a girl partner and teach her everything I know. It'll be my act, Stanley Glass and Company. When I got it broken in and just how I want it, all I have to do is have the right people see it."

"Who do you want to have see us—you, I mean?"

"Agents," Stanley said. "Those are the important guys. But I'll be

ready for 'em. That's why I always wear my dancing shoes; you
never know when you're liable to run into 'em. I might be standing in front of the Palace Theatre someday and along would come
this agent. I'll give him my time step, then I'll give him my triple
wing—"

His arms spread out and the iron cleats on his shoes glittered
in the moonlight as he did a triple wing. His teeth flashed in a
smile and his black, oily hair fell over his face. "Hum me some
music," he said as he was dancing.

I hummed "Me and My Shadow" and Stanley did the figure
eight and over the top. I knew I was closed out of his thoughts but
I didn't care. It was enough to be humming for him and to be
with him.

"This agent stops and his face lights up when he sees me dancing," Stanley was saying. "He knows talent when he sees it—and
he knows I got it. I go into my knee drops. . . ."

I stopped humming. "Right there in front of the Palace Theatre
you do the knee drops?"

"Anywhere," Stanley said. "Don't talk, keep humming—this
is my big chance. The agent's watching me, I give him my nip-ups;
then I go into my after-beats—a crowd gathers and they're all
cheering me and I keep on dancing and dancing. . . ."

Stanley danced until he fell exhausted and out of breath on the
bench beside me. He spread out his legs and dropped his head
between them. His broad shoulders heaved as he breathed heavily
and his shirt, wet with sweat, stretched tight across them. He
reached over and took my hand, then quickly, like the fluttering of
the moth around the electric light bulb over the stage door sign,
he kissed me. My mouth burned from the light touch of his lips. I
pressed back further against the wall, deeper into the shadow so
he couldn't see my face.

"As soon as I get some more money saved up I'm getting out of
this act," he said. My hand was free now and I held it close to me
because it was damp from his touch.

"What—what kind of a girl were you thinking of getting for your
act?" I asked.

Stanley was doing a waltz clog step and he leaned forward to look at his feet. "I hadn't thought too much about it. She's gotta be able to hoof, of course. She's gotta be pretty. But mainly she's gotta know I'm the boss. Why?"

"Oh, I was just wondering," I said.

"Louise, are you out there?" Mother stood framed in the stage door. Then she looked up and down the alley and saw me. "What are you doing out here? I told you to rehearse the finale with the boys between shows."

I jumped to my feet and ran to her in the light of the stage entrance. "I did, Mother," I said. "I went over it three times. You can ask Stanley—"

Mother hadn't seen Stanley in the shadows; now as she did she looked back at me, a slight frown on her face. "I don't like you being out here in the night air, without a sweater. Come along now."

"My book," I said. "I have to get my book off the bench."

"The boys absolutely refuse to do the dance with you unless you pull yourself together," Mother was saying as I ran back for my book. It was so close to Stanley I touched his hand when I picked it up.

"You're supposed to count four, then start," Mother said.

As I ran after her through the stage door, my foot caught on a loose board and I tripped. I felt Stanley's dark eyes on me and I grabbed the railing to steady myself. The sounds of the cleats on his shoes tapping on the cement walk followed me as I ran, angry at myself and ashamed, to my dressing room.

We had a long lay-off after Trenton. It wasn't easy to keep the act together during that time, but somehow Mother managed, and when the booking agent in Kansas City offered us four weeks in that territory the same boys went with us.

We played Sedalia, North Platte, Toledo, all the theatres we had played over and over since I was a child, but now there were only four vaudeville acts on the bill and the talking picture had top billing. Sometimes Bingo, or Bank Night or Dish Night was billed over the picture. The dates were for three or four days each with long lay-offs between.

Topeka was a four-day stand. The Jayhawk Theatre was very

nice but the salary was low. Mother had turned it down at first, but later when nothing better came along she accepted it. Closing night, after she had paid the boys, there was practically nothing left.

A drizzly rain was turning to snow. I waited at the parking lot for Stanley to go by. He had to pass there on his way to the hotel and I waited a long time for him. The parking-lot attendant watched me idly and I pretended to be busy tightening the straps that held our trunks into the rack of our car.

I wasn't quite sure what I would say to Stanley when he passed by, but I wanted to walk with him back to the hotel. I hadn't seen him alone since that night in Trenton. We had watched the movies together backstage, and I had sat next to him in the car each time I could, but that wasn't really being alone with him and walking with him through the snow.

After a while the parking-lot attendant turned out the light in his shack and locked the door with a bolt. "You'll catch cold out here," he said, and he waved good night as he walked down the street.

I went back to the hotel alone. The lights were off in the lobby, too. The night clerk was sleeping with his mouth open in one of the big leather chairs. I tiptoed past him and took the key to the room off the board where it was hanging. June must have gone into our room through Mother's door, I thought; then I saw that Stanley's key was there, too.

I started up the stairs to our room, when I heard Mother scream. It was a thin scream and it seemed to tear through the cold dark hallway. She screamed again and again, and I ran as fast as I could to the door and threw it open. Mother was sitting on the edge of the bed, her eyes staring vacantly at a piece of hotel stationery she held in her limp hand. The window was open and, as the cold wind stirred the paper, I saw my sister's handwriting on it.

"She's gone," Mother said dully. "She's eloped with a boy in the act. My baby is gone—"

Mother's face blurred. I reached for the bedpost to steady myself. Stanley! The name choked in my throat. I bit my lip until I could feel my teeth bite into the flesh. Stanley! She had to be pretty, he had told me, and she had to be able to dance—he meant my sister all the time. That was why they had been whispering back-

stage during the show and while we were packing the car. That was
why they stopped short each time I came near.

"They're married," Mother was saying. "She told them she was
eighteen and they believed her. A *baby* and they believed her. He's
taken her away from me—my baby is gone."

The note fell from Mother's hand and I reached over and
picked it up. I read the round, childishly scrawled words, "—we
were married two weeks ago in North Platte so you can't have it
annulled. Please don't try to find me. I can't go on doing the same
act all my life. I'd rather die. Bobby loves me and he—" I read the
name again. *Bobby*—not Stanley. *Not Stanley.* I sat on the bed
next to Mother and the tears came easily now. I could feel them
hot and wet on my cheeks. He did mean the kiss, it wasn't June he
had been thinking of at all. I wept for Mother, but in my heart
there was a gladness. My sister had eloped with Bobby, not Stanley.

"—she's only a baby," Mother was saying. "She's thirteen, Louise.
Thirteen years old! She can't leave me like this."

Then Mother's shoulders sagged and she leaned heavily against
me. "But she has left me—you're all I have now, Louise. Promise
me you'll never leave me. Promise me that, dear. Say you'll never
leave me!" She held my arms tightly and looked hard into my
eyes. "Promise me!"

"No, Mother. I can't promise that." The dreary hotel room, like
so many I'd known, seemed to dissolve around me. Somewhere a
radio was playing and I thought of Stanley and the act he was
going to do. I would be wearing an orange chiffon gown with rows
and rows of ostrich feathers on it, and I would be dancing beside
him. The orchestra would be playing "Me and My Shadow" and
I would be dancing in the spotlight. I knew why my sister had run
away and I didn't blame her. If I'd had the chance I would have
run, too, as far as I could.

There was a tap on the door and I took Mother's hands from my
shoulders and went over and opened it. Henry walked slowly into
the room. "I'm sorry, Madam Rose," he muttered. "I—I knew all
about it, but I couldn't tell ya. You understand that, don't ya?"

Mother nodded her head numbly.

"They're all gone," Henry said. "All the boys skipped. They

knew there wasn't any act any more without—June."

"No—there's no act any more," Mother said.

"I thought you'd need somebody to drive the car." Henry looked down at his feet idly kicking at a tear in the carpet. "I couldn't leave ya here in Topeka wit no one to drive ya wherever you're goin'."

No act any more—wherever we're going—the words crowded into my head. June is gone. Stanley is gone. There is no act any more. No place to go.

Mother put the leashes on the dogs and picked up her brief case and her coat. "We'll go home," she said, and the word *home* sounded strange coming from her lips. "We'll go home to Seattle."

A C T   T W O

17

HOME WAS A STRANGE word coming from Mother. I thought of it again and again as I sat at the window in the back seat of the car and watched the frozen miles go by. Home, to us, had always meant the hotel, or the theatre. Now it meant Grandpa's house in Seattle. Or did it? I wasn't sure just what it meant. The snow was banked high on the sides of the road, glittering white ahead and behind us. An occasional rooftop or tree thrust itself, brown and gaunt, through the whiteness. We were going home.

Mother sat in the front seat of the car with the dogs at her side, the road map on her lap. Henry, his hands blue with cold on the steering wheel, squinted his eyes against the dazzle of the frozen patterns etched on the windshield. We would be in Wamsutter, Wyoming, on my birthday, my fifteenth birthday. Mother had measured it out on the map and made the announcement that morning. It was the end of my childhood, she said, and the word *childhood* sounded strange, too, like the word *home*.

"What do we call that middle part of our lives?" Mother said, groping for the word. "First it's childhood; then it's—oh, what *is* that word?"

"Adolescence?" Henry suggested hesitatingly.

"Why, yes," Mother replied, surprised and not too pleased that Henry, of all people, should know. She turned a bit in the seat, not enough to disturb the dogs, but enough to look back at me. "Well, anyway, that's what you're coming into. Your adolescence."

She paused to check a road sign, and verified it on the map. Her cheerfulness was forced and as bright as the sun on the snow. "Just think," she said, "of the girls who would give anything to have shared your childhood. The music, the lights, the applause, the people you've met, the excitement—you've had a real fairytale childhood."

The car skidded and Henry, white-faced and taut, brought the wheels back into control. I looked through the rear window to see if the trunks were secure, if the cow head was safe. There were fewer suitcases on the running boards now. The empty seats in the car were a constant reminder of those who had left us. None of us mentioned this. Mother's reference to my adolescence was the closest we'd come to speaking of the future. We were going home to Seattle and that was all we knew.

Home, not to the theatre or the hotel, but home to Seattle.

It began to snow. Large, soft flakes fell on the hood of the car and melted from the heat of the motor. The snow covered the ice on the road and Henry drove slower. "They're big flakes," Mother said. "That means it won't last long." Mother knew many signs like that: leaves showing their white undersides meant rain, a sunshine shower wouldn't last a half an hour; she could even tell if a thunderstorm was coming from the way a cat would sleep with its head under its paws, but I had never heard the one about the big snowflakes before. "It's a sure sign," Mother added. Henry and I didn't question her. We wanted to believe the snowstorm wouldn't last.

It was getting dark and we hadn't passed a house or another car in miles. By Mother's figuring we were about fifty miles from Wamsutter. The car, top heavy and unevenly balanced, swayed and skidded on the road. Each time we skidded I could hear the load on top shift. The tarpaulin was frozen and, as the scenery slid from side to side, it cracked the icy coating, sounding like shattering glass.

"When we get a little money ahead, we're going to buy a heater for the car," Mother said. She had said it many times, but heaters were expensive and we never seemed to get that far ahead. Henry slowed down for a curve and the car swayed dangerously over on its side. "Use your brakes!" Mother said sharply and Henry, although he knew better, slammed down his foot on the brake pedal. For a frightening instant we seemed to fly through space; then with a jolt that threw me to my knees on the floor of the car, scattering my bag of jelly beans through the air like hailstones, the car stopped.

We were in a ditch ten feet from the road. "I couldn't help it, Madam Rose," Henry said, dazed and bewildered at what had happened to us.

"Of course you couldn't," Mother replied matter-of-factly. "Thank God we have that shovel I found."

She hadn't exactly found the shovel. It had been lying with other tools near an excavation on the side of the road. There had been two round, black oil lamps marking the hole. Mother took one of the oil lamps, too, but we had to throw that out a few miles farther on because it smelled so bad. Besides, we didn't have the proper oil for it. I hadn't wanted Mother to take the shovel or the lamp, not after the promise I made when Gigolo died. But now I was glad that we had the shovel, regardless of how we came by it.

Mother took the blanket from her lap and opened the door of the car. "We'll take turns shoveling," she said. An icy wind blew through the car, and Mother closed the door.

"I'll go first," Henry replied. "I got this heavy overcoat on."

It wasn't a heavy overcoat at all. It was a dark-blue topcoat with a frayed velvet collar. A button was off and Mother had given Henry a safety pin to hold the front together. His blond kinky hair was covered with a cap he wore pulled down over his ears. "Don't let the motor stop running," he said, adjusting the throttle. "If it freezes on us, we'll never get outta here." Mother tied her scarf around his neck before he got out of the car.

Clouds of snow flew about as he emptied shovelful after shovelful over his shoulder. Mother took Woolly Face, my pet monkey, and tucked him under her coat and told me to get out and help. I took the shovel from Henry, but it was heavy, and when it was filled with snow I couldn't lift it. Henry blew on his hands and laughed at me. "You shovel," I said to him. "I'll dig with my hands, I can do it faster." It was almost dark now and I dug frantically, fear and cold biting at me. From far off I heard the howl of an animal.

"Coyotes," Mother said. She was beside me and digging, too, her bare hands clawing into the snow around the wheels. "They're more afraid of us than we are of them."

Then the wheels were free and Mother and I stood back from the car while Henry got in and tried to drive it out of the ditch. The wheels spun and the snow flew in a flurry, but the car didn't move. It was in too deep. Mother threw a blanket under the wheel for traction and even that didn't help.

"I'll have to go look for help," Henry said, tying the scarf tighter around his neck. His pants legs were covered with snow and his patent-leather dancing shoes were caked with ice. "If I keep walkin' straight ahead I gotta find somebody."

He left us sitting in the front seat of the car and showed us how to keep the throttle open. "Don't waste the battery," he warned. "Keep the lights off and the motor goin'."

We left the headlights on to guide him back to the road. The snow was so deep he staggered as he pulled one leg out of it, then the other. When he disappeared into the darkness, we turned off the lights, all but the one on the dashboard. The dogs whimpered and Mother patted them mechanically; she was looking at the gasoline meter and the arrow that was pointing to below the quarter-full mark.

"It's a good thing we have that box of Fig Newtons," she said, pulling the blanket close to her shoulders. Our breath froze on the windows and made slim icicles. The howl of the animal came closer, then there was the sound of another, and another. They were so close now I could hear them sniffing, like dogs, around the car. A round spot melted on the window and something black pressed against it. Mother drew closer to me. The dogs growled and she held their faces so they couldn't bark. Another black spot appeared at the window and I knew then it was an animal's nose. They were scratching on the doors and the sides of the car, and one black nose, then another, would press against the window and disappear. I thought of Henry out there in the darkness, staggering through the deep snow, and closed my eyes at the thought.

After a little while Mother asked me to reach back for the box of Fig Newtons and we ate them slowly and silently in the dim light from the dashboard. Mother held the crumbs in her hand for the dogs to lick up. Their ears were high and their eyes showed white as they growled softly at the black spots that came and went on the windows; then a pointed claw scratched through a crack in the window where the stripping had come loose and Mumshay barked and snapped at it. Mother held the blanket to the window. "They can't get in—can they?" I asked. "Could they break the windows and get in?"

"I don't think so," Mother whispered. Then we heard the sound of a gun being fired, the noise of men shouting. Through the frosted windows we saw the lights of their lanterns and, in a moment, Henry opened the door of the car. "I found help for us," he said. The hair of his nostrils was matted with icicles and his face was white from the snow. "They were clearing the railroad tracks and there's a whole lot of 'em." He shoved two salami sandwiches at me and staggered back through the snow to the men who were there to dig us out.

We slept in the garage in Wamsutter that night. The hotel was very expensive and Mother didn't want to waste the money, we had so little left. It was warm in the garage and the mechanic worked the whole night fixing the broken steering knuckle of our car. We took turns helping him, handing him tools and fixing him hot coffee from his thermos. It was dawn when the job was finished. Through the window I could see that it had stopped snowing. A sharp, cold wind blew through a broken window pane.

"That'll be thirty-seven dollars," the mechanic said, wiping his hands on a greasy rag. "I gotta charge you overtime for workin' at night."

Mother took out her purse and emptied it in the man's hand. "This is every cent I have in the world," she said. It was $11.82. "We hoped by being careful it would take us to Seattle. We're with a show troupe, and we have a booking there—"

The mechanic looked down at the money in his hand, then at the car, and then at Henry's patent-leather dancing shoes. "Gee, lady, I only work here. I don't make the prices on the jobs. The boss'll be here at nine o'clock—"

"But we can't wait," Mother said frantically. "We have only two days to make Seattle. We'll have to drive night and day as it is. If we don't play this date I don't know what will happen to us. . . ."

She fumbled with a little enameled watch pinned to her dress that she had bought for six dollars in Kansas City. There was a lily on the cover and two four-leaf clovers worked into the enamel; it didn't run, but it was very pretty. Mother held it out to the mechanic. "It was my grandmother's," she said softly. "Please take it. When we get to Seattle we'll send you the money and you can return the watch—I feel I can trust you."

The mechanic held the tiny watch in his greasy hand. "I don't know what the boss'll say," he murmured. Mother closed his hand over the lily and the four-leaf clovers. "You'll make him understand. I'm sure you will."

Henry helped Mother get in the front seat, and the mechanic leaned in through the window and spoke to her. "You got a valve and piston job coming up on this old baby," he said, patting the side of the car. "If you take it easy though it oughtta get you to Seattle okay." He dropped the $11.82 on Mother's lap. "You'll need that," he said. "The watch'll keep the boss quiet until I hear from you."

Mother wiped a tear from her eye. She didn't try to thank the mechanic, and I knew he was glad of that because he was embarrassed. Henry put the car in reverse and backed slowly out of the garage. The mechanic waved good-by to us from his place near the grease pit. "Turn left at the next block," he yelled. "It'll take you back on the main highway. You can't miss it."

Mother rolled up the car window, and felt under her dress for the money belt. She put back all but five dollars and eighty-two cents along with the forty dollars left of our nest egg. Mother wasn't taking any more chances; the next time she emptied her purse into someone's hand there would be less money in it.

"I hope I can pick up another cheap watch," she said, "just in case we have trouble with that valve."

Grandpa was waiting for us in front of his little house. His hair was whiter and his cheeks were rosier than I had remembered. His trousers hung loosely from the striped suspenders over his shoulders. His elbows came through the holes in his gray sweater. "Welcome home," he said, holding out his arms to us. Mother ran to him.

"Now, now, Rose," Grandpa said as he led her, weeping, into the house. "Your Papa knows, but we don't want the neighbors to see you crying."

Henry waited on the front porch. He wasn't quite sure what he was to do, or where he was to go, and I wasn't sure, either. Later, Grandpa went out on the porch and brought him in. "You did a fine thing, boy," Grandpa said with his arm on Henry's shoulder. "That was a good Christian act, bringing my girls home."

Mother looked up at him warningly; Henry wasn't a Christian, but Grandpa didn't mean what Mother meant. Or maybe he did, and thought Henry would be pleased. "We'll fix up this sofa for you right here next to the stove."

Grandpa brought out a pillow and blankets and made a bed for Henry in the living room. "Many's the time I've slept out here myself when the Big Lady and the girls were home. I guess it's just as well she isn't here right now." Grandpa's smile was cheerful, but I thought there was a note of bitterness in his voice. "Some fellows found a lapis lazuli mine around Carson Sink and your grandma went down to look it over."

Snow covered the little house that night, but it was snug and warm inside. In the moonlight coming through the bedroom window I could see Mother looking up at a crack on the ceiling.

"Louise?" she whispered.

"Yes, Mother?"

"I didn't forget your birthday," she whispered, "We'll do something to celebrate it real soon. As soon as I get my bearings."

It didn't take Mother long to get her bearings. In less than three weeks she began making plans. There weren't going to be any boys in the new act. Mother was definite about that. Henry would

drive the car, and be the rear end of the cow. The rest of the act
would be all girls. They were easier to handle, Mother said, and
certainly more trustworthy. None of the girls was to receive a
salary; the experience would be worth more than money to them.
Henry, when he had paid back the money he owed Mother after
the long lay-off, was to receive thirty dollars a week.

"We'll comb the city of Seattle for talent," Mother told Grandpa.
"We'll cover every dancing school, every amateur contest. We'll
get the cream of the city's crop."

Grandpa was more agreeable about this act than he had been
about the old one. Mother didn't have to remind him that we had returned every penny he had advanced us, or that we had paid for
the new roof on the house. The Model T Ford sedan under the
lean-to tent in the back yard had been a present from us, and the
radio also that sat like a behemoth on the console table. Grandpa
knew we had made money with the old act. But he couldn't understand how we had spent it all. We didn't have any expensive
clothes, or jewelry besides Mother's rings; we hadn't made any
investments; and we had only twenty-six dollars in the nest egg.

"I may not have any money," Mother admitted, "but I have a
million dollars' worth of know-how in my head."

Grandpa's agreeableness to back us might have stemmed from
Mother's restlessness at being cooped up, as she put it, in Seattle.
There were so many minor irritations that upset her: the sameness
of the days, the neighbors who dropped in at all hours and asked
such unfortunate questions, the beds to make and the dishes to
wash. Grandpa's lodge meetings were tiresome, too. On Ladies'
Nights, Grandpa would expect Mother to go. She came home from
one of the meetings swearing she would never go through such an
ordeal again. "My God, Papa," she said, "how do these women
stand it? How can they live such stagnant lives?"

There were endless funerals we were expected to attend. Not
just the funerals of lodge brothers, who were dropping off with
alarming frequency, but the funerals of their relatives who also
passed on, as Grandpa said, to greener fields.

Grandpa had an arrangement with his lodges where he would

Aleksander

I made all the costumes for the act...even my black
velvet trouser suit that Mother insisted
I wear because I was the tailored type.

Bloom

Roberts

After I bleached the girls' heads.

Nancy
and Porky

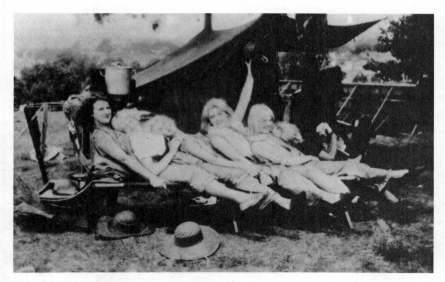

Living in a tent was fun...for a while.

The scenery rode on top of the car,
the cow head on the trunk rack, and our makeup
and shoes went on the running boards.

This was my favorite costume because it was grown-up looking. I would have liked it more had Mother allowed me to wear a brassiere.

The top was orange velvet, the skirt was black net…

🎬 Mother had the tears painted on…

Billy Minsky told me to wear my hair straight.
He said it was more ladylike.

My first high heels.

drive the mourners to the burial grounds and back in his Ford. He was paid a dollar and a half for each mourner he transported. On good weeks, Grandpa said, he could clear from three to five dollars. And, he added, it was found money because he would have had to attend the funeral anyway.

The Studebaker was ideal for this purpose. The trunks and the cow head were removed from the rack, along with the spare tire with the name of the act and ENROUTE painted on it. The scenery and tarpaulin were stored in the tool shed and the car was put back into its long-past original service. Henry drove the car for the funerals and Grandpa gave him cigarette money out of the profits.

"It seems to me," Grandpa said one day, "that an able-bodied boy like that Henry could get himself a decent, upstanding job in the neighborhood."

"Oh, Papa," Mother said impatiently, "Henry's a dancer. He can't take an ordinary kind of a job."

Grandpa looked over at Henry with a peculiar expression on his face. Grandpa didn't know much about dancers, he said, but he did know a bum when he saw one.

Grandpa found a room for us in the basement of one of his lodge halls where we rehearsed the new act. A sewing machine was set up in one corner, and between rehearsals I sewed the new costumes. They were made of cretonne and organdie, with ruffled bloomers, and big matching hair bows. As Mother said, they were youthful and girlish. They were also cheap and easy to make.

Mother wasn't too happy about the girls she found for the act. She was sure someone had combed the city before she did. Even Grandpa, who thought all little girls were pretty, had to agree that, if this was the cream of the city, someone had scooped the top off the bottle.

There were six girls in the act, besides me. The oldest, little Mary, was sixteen, but she was so tiny everyone thought she couldn't be over ten. She sang June's "Vamp a Little Lady" number and wore the black sequin dress my sister had outgrown. She lisped, too, and had many of June's mannerisms.

Two of the girls, Nancy and Millie, were sisters. Their father worked at the shipyards and, because he knew all about metals, he melted down old pots and pans and made the dancing cleats for our shoes. Their mother was also very helpful. She used to send the sisters off to rehearsal with a basket lunch that was big enough for all eight of us. The sisters were going to be comediennes in the act so they didn't have to be pretty. Nancy's blond head sat on her long, thin neck like a jonquil. She was to sing June's cow number and wear the same costume, pigtails and all.

Millie would be the front end of the cow and do the comedy bustle dance with me. The braces on her teeth would add to the comedy effect. None of the new girls could do my sister's ballad about the little dog, but Ruby was to do a contortion dance in place of it. Contortionists didn't have to be pretty, either. Ruby's neck was even longer than Nancy's. Her legs were long and thin with red bumpy knees, like candied apples on a stick. The brassière part of her costume was ruffled to hide the two tiny swellings that embarrassed her when she did her back bends. "She'll fill out all over," Mother said hopefully, "once we get on the road."

Then there was Dorothy, with her big brown eyes and her sweet little singing voice, and Hazel, the only one of the girls with any stage experience. Hazel had appeared in six dancing-school recitals. Besides her Highland fling, she also did a sword dance and a sailor's hornpipe, none of which fitted into the act. She learned June's Russian toe tap dance, minus the more difficult steps. I was to sing "I'm a Hard-boiled Rose" and we could close with the military finale.

The day we left, the parents, relatives and friends all met at Grandpa's house to see us off. Aunt Helma was there, too, as beautiful and gracious as I remembered her. The girls' suitcases were filled with clean warm underwear, long brown stockings, middy blouses, pleated skirts and outing-flannel nightgowns. Mother had given their parents a list of things the girls would need and the items were carefully selected. Their brown oxfords and tweed coats were enough alike to be uniforms. The question of spending money had been discussed and settled; each girl was to bring ten dollars and Mother would keep the money for her, doling it out as she saw fit.

"They'll all learn the true value of money," Mother said to the parents, "I can promise you that." She made many promises, but this was one promise Mother kept.

The parents brought going-away gifts of oranges, gumdrops, sandwiches, sewing kits, blankets and pillows for the car and boxes and boxes of stationery. Each girl had a fountain pen and a Brownie camera with extra rolls of film. There were tears, waving handkerchiefs, and cries of "Don't forget to write every day" as we drove away from Grandpa's house. Even the neighbors, who hadn't been so friendly toward the end, were on hand to wave good-by and wish us luck. The name of the act on the spare tire now read, MADAM ROSE'S DANCING DAUGHTERS and below, in the same old lettering a bit faded, was the word ENROUTE. The dogs settled down on the front seat next to Mother and Woolly Face, the monkey, sat on her shoulder. They seemed as happy as we were to be back on the road again.

Henry scowled at the giggling and chattering of the girls. He had been given strict orders by Mother concerning his conduct with them, but the orders hadn't been necessary. "If I want a girl," he had mumbled, "I can find prettier ones than these."

18

MOTHER, CLUTCHING
the brief case, gaped in horror at the Chinese Theatre. "I don't
believe it," she breathed. "It's against the laws of nature to build a
theatre like this!"

Los Angeles was filled with new frightening wonders since the
last time we had played there. We couldn't believe half of what we
saw. A restaurant like a derby, a cold-drink stand like a pop bottle,
an ice-cream cone twenty feet high, and now this monstrous theatre.
The girls were running out of film for their Brownie cameras.

The gilt and pergolas almost intimidated Mother. She hesitated
a moment, then setting her lips in a smile she held her head high
and walked through the gilded teakwood portals.

It had been a bad day for Mother, starting first thing that morning when she asked the policeman to direct us to the Metropolitan
Vaudeville Theatre. He told her the only vaudeville theatre left
in Los Angeles was the Orpheum. Mother thought he was joking.
"It's the talking pictures," the policeman had said. "They've taken
the place of vaudeville."

"They said the same thing about radio," Mother replied stiffly.
"Vaudeville weathered that storm and we'll weather talking pictures, too. Nothing will ever take the place of flesh."

One of the agents Mother used to know had offered us two days
at the Lyric Theatre in Yuma, Arizona, for $97.50 and Mother had
stalked out of the office in a fury. Now as she walked hurriedly

toward us, her heels clattering on the marble floor, I could see she was angry again and I knew Sid Grauman had nothing to offer us either.

"Put that camera away," she said to Millie. "Ruby, pull up your stockings. Where is Henry? I told him to meet us here in front of the theatre."

I waited until we were in the car and she was quieted down before I spoke. "What did Sid Grauman have to say?" I asked.

"I decided not to see him," Mother replied. "This isn't the right kind of theatre for our little act."

Later that night when we were alone in our hotel room, Mother told me she sent our photographs in to Sid Grauman and the receptionist came back with them and said he was too busy to see her. "Too busy to see *me*, Louise. After the record-breaking business we did for him!"

I tried to remember if it was 1920 or '21 when we worked for him in the *Blue Bird*. It was a Christmas production and there were over a hundred people in the cast. Mother played one of the witches and June was a good fairy. I was a frog. We never got to meet Sid Grauman but we saw him at rehearsals, his sandy-colored hair standing straight up as though charged with electricity, and his high, piercing voice screaming out orders: "I can't hear the frogs! Make those frogs croak louder!" And I had croaked as loud as I could.

"He has a pretty short memory," Mother was saying. "Why, if it hadn't been for June he wouldn't have *had* a show!"

I remembered how I had hated being a frog, but looking back, it didn't seem so awful. I'd been other things in the act I didn't like, a newsboy for instance. And even as a frog, we were at least working.

"We're wasting time here on the Coast," Mother said. "We'll work our way East, where the real show business is, and always has been—and always will be."

The Lyric Theater in Yuma was on our way East, but it hadn't played vaudeville in a long time. There was dust on everything backstage. The battens and traveler tracks had been removed from the flies to make room for the new-type picture screen with the huge sound box behind it. The dressing rooms were filled with old stage equipment, dusty and rusted. One room was filled with crates and crates of dishes that were given away with each admission ticket on Wednesday nights.

The way Mother went at the room, broom in hand, one would never have known she had accepted the date reluctantly. There was something almost joyful in the way she complained. "I'm not going to hang our costumes in a filthy place like this," she said as the dust flew in all directions. "I have a small fortune invested in those costumes and I'm not having them ruined."

"We'll get this all swept up for ya," the stagehand said, "and don't you worry about that scenery. We'll get it hung if we have to nail it to the back wall. Yes, sir, it sure is good to have vaudeville back—even if it is for only two days."

There was a sister team on the bill with us, who sang Scottish songs and played bagpipes, and a man ventriloquist. The featured film was *Slightly Used* with May MacAvoy and Conrad Nagel. There was no question that we were headlining; the name of the act was even up in lights. The girls took picture after picture of themselves standing under the marquee. The admission sign behind them read, "Twenty-five and fifty cents."

The orchestra was a piano, a violin and drums. But for the rehearsal, we had only the pianist, who was also the organist, because the others were busy at their permanent jobs. The violinist was a butcher and his relief man didn't come on until noon, so he couldn't possibly make the rehearsal. The drummer, who was the manager's nephew, was going to high school so he couldn't make it, either.

Mother had expected the girls to be nervous on their opening show, but she wasn't prepared for the total collapse of all six of them. The scenery had, indeed, been nailed to the back wall and that changed our entrances and exits because we couldn't cross behind it. This was all the girls needed to give way to tears and temperament. Eva Tanguay had never, in her most violent moods, carried on the way Little Mary and Nancy did. They stamped their feet and pounded their fists on the side walls. Nancy refused point-blank to go on with the cow number because she didn't want to carry Porky, the baby pig, in her arms. "I won't do it," she screamed, clinging to the scenery as Mother tried to push her on stage. "You never told me I had to have a pig in my specialty, and I won't go on!"

Mother snatched Porky and pushed Nancy on stage. Then Millie, under the cow head, started crying. "I can't see," she cried. "It's dark in here."

Mother showed her the peekholes at the neck of the cow head, and Millie stumbled on stage with Henry following up in the rear. "It smells awful in here," Millie moaned as Henry booted her into position. Then when Ruby was doing her contortion dance with her head between her legs and her dusty feet dangling over her forehead, her shoulder strap broke. It happened too quickly for anyone, besides a small boy in the front row, to see anything, but Ruby unwound herself and ran into the wings crying hysterically.

When the curtain closed in on the finale four girls were on stage, the others cringed in the wings, their faces tear stained, their costumes half on. The backs of our military costumes were supposed to light up in the dark and spell out the name of the act in radium letters, but for that show the backs of the costumes presented a peculiar alphabetical arrangement. The THE was missing, DAN was there, without her gun, and CING, but the DAU and the GHT were standing in the wings. The ERS had forgotten to turn around and stared at the audience as though hypnotized. The electrician hadn't blacked out the lights anyway, so it didn't matter one way or the other. There was a bit of scattered sympathetic applause from the audience, and the girls finally galvanized themselves into taking their bows. Even those in the wings clambered on stage to nod their heads and dip into curtsies.

"You have to expect a few things to go wrong on opening matinees," Mother said as she quieted the girls in the dressing room later. "It'll be better the next show."

After the last show that night the girls and Henry and Mother and I sat in the hotel room with a bottle of milk and a bag of cookies. Each of us had a special problem. Mother made a careful note of the complaints. None of us mentioned the main trouble, but the act was a complete failure and we all knew it.

Porky, the baby pig, rooted at our legs and begged for pieces of cookie. Mother had spied him as we drove past a farmhouse on our way from Seattle. He was the runt of the litter and Mother said he would be wonderful in the cow number, once he learned the act. Right now he wouldn't keep his hat on and he wouldn't follow Nancy anywhere.

"He has to get used to you," Mother said to Nancy. "Give him a piece of your cookie, dear, and pet him so he'll learn to love you."

Nancy stared down malevolently at the baby pig. She hated Porky and Porky knew it. "Why do I have to give him *my* cookie?" she whined. "I don't want him in my specialty. He'll spoil everything. The audience will look at him instead of me. I won't have him. I won't."

Mother overlooked the heresy for the time being. She knew Nancy was on the verge of tears again; besides there were more important things to be settled. The finale for instance. "You have to keep a straight line," Mother said. "The whole effect of the radium finish is ruined if you don't stand close together. . . ."

"Oh, Mother," I said, my patience completely exhausted. "What difference does it make? The act is awful and we all know it. We might as well admit it's a flop. The audience laughed at us, they hooted at us—"

"Make her stop!" Little Mary cried. "Don't let her say such mean things, Madam Rose. She's always saying things to hurt my feelings—" She dropped her cookie on the floor and buried her face in her hands. "She hates me—because she's jealous of me!"

Mother rushed over and put her arms around the weeping girl's shoulders. "Now look what you've done," she said angrily to me. "This poor little thing has been through enough today without you picking on her."

"I've been through it, too," I yelled. "You weren't out there! You didn't see the audience snickering at us. They hated us. We're too big to be doing that silly old walking doll number. We look like freaks!"

I rushed out of the room, slamming the door behind me. Through the door I could hear the girls wailing and Mother trying to comfort them. I was ashamed of my outburst, but I couldn't go back and tell them I was sorry, because I wasn't. Everything I said was true. We *were* too big to be doing that silly walking doll number. We *did* look like freaks. The audience *had* hooted at us.

I sat down on the steps in the hallway and tried to think. If the girls were prettier, if we wore more make-up and fingernail polish and if our hair—our hair! That was it! The idea made me jump to my feet. I tore down the stairs to the lobby. "Is there a drugstore open this late?" I asked the startled desk clerk.

The clerk looked at the wall clock. "The corner drugstore's open to midnight," he said. "You can make it if you hurry."

Ten minutes later I was back in our room. My spending money was gone, but if what I wanted to do worked, it was worth it. "I've got it!" I yelled kicking the door closed behind me. "I've got the answer to what's wrong with the act! And I know what we can do to fix it!"

I put the two bottles on the table and looked around at the girls, who stared at me with their mouths wide open. "Look at us, Mother," I said. "You're pretending we're little girls and that's what's wrong. We aren't little girls any more. We're almost grown-up. Then why not make us look really grown-up? Have us wear make-up and high heels—"

"Stop that shouting and yelling," Mother said. "You'll wake up everybody in the hotel. High heels? Have you lost your mind? High heels, on these *children?*"

"That's just it!" I said, keeping my voice low. "We're not children any more. We're not anything. We have to make ourselves into something. Just think how much better we'd look if we were blondes!"

Mother stifled a horrified gasp; then her expression changed. "The girls might be very pretty as blondes—" she said thoughtfully. "Yes, I'm sure they would. And we could change the name of the act to Madam Rose's Baby Blondes."

"No, Mother," I said firmly. "I have a better idea. We'll change the name to Rose Louise and Her Hollywood Blondes, and I'll be the only brunette."

Mother looked at me for a long moment; then she dropped her eyes. "Yes," she said. "I think that's a very good idea. . . . But no high heels, that's absolutely out!" Quickly, before Mother could change her mind, I opened up the bottles and snatched a towel off the rack over the sink. "You first," I said to Millie, as I tied the towel around her neck and poured the peroxide and ammonia on her head.

19

CHANGING THE GIRLS into blondes didn't help much at first, but is was an improvement. The audience was so surprised at the six towheads, all the same albinolike color, that they didn't look too closely at each girl. Blue eye shadow, dark eyebrows and heavy mascara completed the effect. The girls still weren't pretty, but they were dazzling and their first appearance on stage brought a gasp from the audience.

From Yuma we drove to Phoenix, where Mother booked the Orpheum Theatre on a fifty-fifty basis. It wasn't a real Orpheum Theatre, but the name on the marquee looked mighty good to Mother. It looked good to the girls, too, who didn't know the difference between one theatre and another. Opening night they wrote their parents they were on the Orpheum Circuit and sent along the advertisements from the newspapers to prove it. We cleared $162 on the four days, which was enough to get us to El Paso, Texas, with a little left over for the nest egg.

The Colon Theatre in El Paso was in the Mexican section of the city. It played Spanish-speaking movies and Mexican vaudeville acts. Mother took all of us with her when she went to interview Mr. Calderon, the manager. We watched the show while we waited for him. The theatre smelled of mildew and dirty clothes and bad breaths, but the show was quite spectacular. The costumes were covered with sequins and spangles and there was a lot of loud boisterous music. There were certain salacious bits of business in the acts Mother didn't approve of; one comedian bit the leading lady on her backside, for instance, and another comic had a particularly lewd way of peering down his trousers. But most disturbing, the entire show was in Spanish.

"They'd never get our comedy lines," Mother whispered as we watched the show. "We'd have to learn the act in Spanish."

"The whole act?" I asked.

"Of course not," Mother said. "Just the key words."

Mother booked the theatre for a full week at $35 a day, payable each night, which was the manager's idea. All Mexican acts, he said, insisted on being paid by the day. That was so they could quit if they wanted to. It also helped keep the management honest, but Mr. Calderon didn't mention that.

None of the girls took pictures of the Colon Theatre. It was too dirty looking and the people standing around the entrance didn't make it look any better. Mother tried to think of them as potential customers and smiled majestically as we passed but that was evidently the wrong thing to do. Henry had to punch one of the men in the nose to make him let go of Mother's arm. The alley in back of the theatre was the local red-light district where each prostitute had her own one-room establishment, and the men lounging around in front of the theatre were their customers, not ours.

The hotel where we stayed advertised "Baños," at twenty-five cents, which was puzzling until we learned *baños* meant baths and that most of the houses in the neighborhood, including those in the alley back of the theatre, had no bathrooms and that the hotel did a lively business supplying this service. Saturday there was a line of people waiting with their own towels all the way down the hall. The hotel was shabby and not very clean but it was cheap and it was exciting to live among people who spoke a different language. We learned how to say *Buenas noches,* and *Gracias* and Mother got over the habit of shouting her words, thinking that would make them more understandable.

Before our opening matinee, one of the stage hands who spoke English gave Mother the Spanish words for "Vamp a Little Lady" and "I Have a Cow." He had a bit of trouble translating "I'm a

Hard-boiled Rose" but decided that "Yo soy una gancha" would do. Mother copied down the words phonetically and that matinee when I spoke my line in Spanish the audience howled. There weren't many women in the theatre but those who were there hid their faces and the orchestra leader dropped his baton. I had said, "I am a hooker." For the second show the theatre manager suggested another phrase, less graphic. But even with that slight mistake there was no doubt we were a hit. The act had never gone over so well. The audience screamed at the cow number, Ruby almost stopped the show, and Little Mary had to do two encores for her vamp number.

"If they love us like this in El Paso," Mother said, "can you imagine how we'd go over in Mexico?"

Mother examined the road map. She was surprised to find that Mexico City wasn't much farther than from New York to Chicago, especially if we cut straight through the mountain route into Chihuahua instead of taking the unfinished highway from Laredo. There was a revolution going on in Mexico at the time but nothing that appeared very serious to Mother. She told us they were always having revolutions in Mexico.

"It's their Latin temperament," Mother said.

Mr. Calderon told us a lot about Mexico City. The National Theatre had a revolving stage and an orchestra pit that went up and down. The theatre tickets he said cost five dollars and the audience wore evening clothes.

"Do you think," Mother asked, "they'd like a little act like ours down there?"

Mr. Calderon shrugged, "It's been a long time since I was home," he said. "But Mexicans always like to look at blondes."

That settled it. After a few formalities, such as vaccinations and affidavits proving the girls were all over twenty-five, which was the age limit, we were practically ready to leave. The affidavits took a little time. Mother had to write each one in a different handwriting and it was slow work. Some of them were written backward, which was one of Mother's favorite ways of disguising her penmanship. Having them notarized wasn't difficult. Mother just went to seven different notaries and signed the girls' names seven

different ways. The girls might have done this themselves, but
Mother didn't want them to. "If there's any perjury to be done," she
said, "I'll do it."

The dogs' health papers were outdated so Mother had to make
those too, and also one for Woolly Face and another for Porky, who
was listed as a trained pig, although he still wouldn't keep his hat on.

There were a few things we needed, such as a desert bag for
water and a five-gallon can for extra gasoline. Mr. Calderon suggested a compass and Mother found a lovely one for a dollar and a
half with a chamois case included. Those things, along with a box
of groceries and three cans of Sterno, were the prerequisites of the
trip.

Mother drew a straight line on the road map from Tia Juana
to Torreón, where she hoped to book the act to break our jump.
Chihuahua was on our way, but Mother didn't want to waste so
much time, and Torreón being in a mining region was presumably a
good theatre town. It was about three hundred miles from the
border. "A good day's drive," Mother said.

Henry had been opposed to the trip from the first, and now when
the Mexican immigration authorities began asking us such questions
as "Where are you contracted to work?" and "How much money
have you for the trip?" he refused to go with us. "Them greasers'll
moider us," he said. "If you wan'ta wake up with a shiv in your
back okay, but I'm hitch-hikin' back ta New York."

"Very well," Mother said, "I can't force you to go. If you want
to walk to New York go right ahead. We'll manage—somehow."

"Who else can drive the car," he muttered, sitting on the
running board, breaking matches into tiny pieces.

Mother reminded him I had driven the car for almost a hundred
miles the time she had given him two five-grain veronal tablets
thinking they were aspirin. The sedative had put him to sleep for
five hours and I had, indeed, driven the car. It was on an open
highway with no traffic and I had a lot of trouble when I had to
stop the car and start it again, but I had driven it.

"Louise will drive us," Mother said, her face a mask of tragedy.

Henry got back of the wheel and began calling the girls. "Come
on if you're coming! As long as we're gonna go, let's go!"

It was past eleven o'clock by the time we left Tia Juana. Five miles and one hour later we lost sight of the road. It just ended abruptly. There were deep wagon ruts and Henry drove the car on the top edges of them. Then suddenly even those disappeared. There wasn't a house or even a hut where we could ask directions.

For the first few hours, even though the heat was intense, the excitement of being on our way to Mexico City was enough to keep the girls laughing and happy. We rehearsed the Spanish words we knew and Mother told us over and over of the wonders of Mexico. "Just think, girls," she said, "here we are in a strange country. Think of it, we're *foreigners!*"

Every few miles we would stop in the blazing sun to get our bearings. Each time Mother would consult the compass, then confirm her findings by checking the shadow of the car. She doled out the water as though we were survivors of a shipwreck adrift in a boat with no oars. When the dogs began panting she tied wet handkerchiefs around their heads. Porky was stretched out on the floor of the car with his mouth wide open, gasping for breath. "Nancy," Mother said in an angry voice, "will you please fan that poor little pig?" And Nancy waved a movie magazine back and forth negligently.

For lunch we opened three cans of sardines and ate them on graham crackers. We had two gingersnaps each for dessert. It was too hot to think about food. Mother covered the windows with the road maps and the little breeze we had felt occasionally was shut off. Then we had to stop the car while Millie threw up her sardine sandwiches. The sun was getting lower, but if anything the heat seemed more intense. We had gone less than a hundred miles when the sun dipped behind the horizon and darkness fell.

There was no sun now to direct us, but the windows were down and a cool breeze passed through the car. Mother consulted the map by the light on the dashboard. "There's a little town about fifty miles south of here," she said. "We'll stay there for the night."

It was very dark and the air was turning cold, but even so the motor began heating up. "I think we're climbing," Henry said. "My ears are beginning to pop."

Mother accepted this calmly. "According to the map," she said, "there are a few mountains. We're probably at the foothills." From time to time there was a path for a road, and sometimes we would see a sign. Most of the names written on the signs were for places that didn't appear on Mother's map. We didn't see one sign for Torreón or Chihuahua. Henry was driving very slowly because there were huge boulders along the path and deep holes filled with drifted sagebrush. Several times we had to get out of the car and move large rocks from what appeared to be the road. Mother was very gay and cheerful as she tugged and pulled at the rocks. "What an experience this is for you girls," she said. "Mark my words, you'll never forget this trip as long as you live."

At dinner time, we sat on the running board of the car and ate two cans of cold beans, a can of salmon and more graham crackers. Later when the girls glanced around for a place where they could hide themselves from Henry, he walked up the road a bit, keeping his back to us. As we lifted our skirts Mother called out, "Be careful of snakes, girls, and stay together."

When the girls told him the coast was clear Henry wandered back. "I don't know much about stars," he said, "but isn't that big one the North Star?"

Mother looked up at the sky. She said she was looking for the Big Dipper. Then she told us how to recognize it and we all looked up to help. She said the handle of it pointed to the North Star, but none of us could find anything that looked like a dipper. We could see all sorts of other things though. Millie saw a group of stars that looked like a tent, and Little Mary saw a horse as plain as day. Henry didn't join in the game. After a while he asked Mother for the compass. "If that *is* the North Star," he said, "we're heading in the wrong direction."

Mother snatched the compass from him, and put it back in the chamois case. "We'll stay right here for the night," she said. "We can sleep in the car, and in the morning when the sun comes up we'll settle this question once and for all."

I knew then that Mother couldn't read a compass.

As we settled down in the car Mother gave us our instructions. We were to lock the doors from the inside, leaving the windows down just a bit for air. If anyone had to get up during the night (she directed this mainly to Henry, whom she had accused several times of babying his bladder), they were to stay close to the car. One of us was to keep guard, and for that we would take turns.

I wondered why a guard was necessary. We hadn't seen a living thing since we left Tia Juana, not even a rabbit or a desert rat, but keeping guard was exciting, and no one complained about it. When it was my turn to stay awake, I rolled down the window as far as it would go and leaned out of the car with my head up to the stars. I thought about Mexico and how lucky I was to have been born in show business. Then I thought about my sister and wished she were with us and wondered if she and Bobby would ever get to go to Mexico City. I thought about Stanley, too, and how envious he would be. Later when it was Hazel's turn to keep guard I slept and dreamed about the big stage and the orchestra pit that went up and down on an elevator.

It was hot again when I woke up. The sun was white and it was shining in through the rear window of the car. Mother and Henry had both been wrong. Somewhere in the darkness we had turned toward the west. The scenery had changed, too. Instead of dried clay there was nothing but rocks and mountains. They loomed up before us, their jagged peaks becoming lost in the haze. There was no path at all. Nothing but the rocks and hungry-looking clumps of dried-out vegetation shoving up through them.

Little Mary began to cry softly at first, then in great loud bellows. "We're lost," she cried. "We'll die out here on the desert. I just know it!"

In a moment all the girls were crying. Not only because we were lost but because we were stiff and tired from sleeping crowded up in the car, because we were hungry for a real breakfast, not the stale old gingersnaps, and mostly because we knew somehow that we weren't going to Mexico City after all.

Mother didn't say anything when Henry turned the car around and headed back for Tia Juana. Later that afternoon she began making new plans. We would go to Mexico City from Laredo, she said, and this time we would be prepared. "We'll bring a camp stove and a tent and we'll get a real compass." She added to the plans as we drove through the heat. We would carry an icebox on the running board and each of us would have her own desert bag of water. We would have awnings made for the car and Henry would have a real gun. Listening to Mother talk about it was almost as much fun as going there. By the time we got back to El Paso we all felt as though we had seen enough of Mexico.

Henry suggested we go to Kansas City and Mother agreed. Our vaccinations were good for three years; the affidavits would improve with time. We would go to Mexico some other day.

The agents in Kansas City were impressed with Mother's stories of Mexico. She spoke glowingly of vaudeville conditions there and told them how beautiful the theatres were with their revolving stages and orchestra pits that went up and down on elevators. She sprinkled her conversation with words like *adiós* and *buenos días* and told them how the Mexicans loved our act. "If it weren't for that terrible revolution," she added, "we'd be there right now."

The headline of *Variety* on the agent's desk read: WALL STREET LAYS AN EGG. Mother pushed the trade paper aside as she opened her brief case and took out the contract from the Orpheum Theatre in Phoenix, Arizona. She held it in such a way that the name of the city was concealed. The brief case was shabby but Mother's armor glittered like new. As she told me later, the worst that could happen to us had already happened. From now it had to be clear sailing.

20

HERE WAS NO VAUDE-
ville in Kansas City, either. The Mainstreet, the Orpheum, even
the nearby towns such as Topeka and Sedalia played nothing
but talking pictures. Mother's money bag was getting very flat.
Then when it was empty she dipped into the separate pocket where
she kept the girls' spending money. Before she knew it that pocket
was almost flat, too. When the girls asked her for money for candy
bars and film and movie magazines Mother told them they had
spent it all. "A dime here, a quarter there," she said. "It all adds
up, you know. Next time your parents send you spending money
you must keep notes on how much you spend. In that way you'll
know just where you stand."

Henry became difficult about his money, too. He had learned
to keep notes long ago and he knew where he stood. Mother owed
him $19.40. There was no doubt about it. Mother added the figures
twice to make sure. "It's just goes to show," she said, "how much
money you can save when you're careful."

"I don't need all of it," Henry told her, "but I gotta have three
dollars."

"Three dollars!" Mother exclaimed. "Why in the world do you
need that much money?"

Henry looked down at his feet and refused to answer.

"Look at me, Henry," Mother said firmly. "Now tell me the

truth. Are you playing fast and loose with some girl here in Kansas City?"

"I just want to take her to the movies," Henry muttered.

Mother clucked her tongue. "That's the way it starts," she said ominously. "First it's the movies, then it's a Chinese restaurant and before you know it your money is gone. And so is the girl."

But Henry insisted, so Mother gave him a dollar. "Take her to a matinee," Mother said. "It's cheaper."

A few days later when we were offered two weeks in a night club on the outskirts of the city Mother hesitated. "Things have been bad for us before," she told the agent, "but we've never stooped to *that*."

"It's a nice, quiet little place," the agent said, "and two weeks, Rose, is two weeks."

"Of course," Mother said reconsidering, "we could change our name and play it miscellaneously."

The night club was called the Cuban Gardens. There wasn't anything Cuban about it and it certainly wasn't a garden. The money partner of the owner was involved in a rather shady deal with a local dog track and after the show Tuesday night was shot dead by a rival dog fancier. He had been shot in someone else's night club, but even so it was the end of our job at the Cuban Gardens.

The night we closed was my sixteenth birthday, and a snowstorm that broke a seventy-seven-year record fell on the city, ruining our plans for a celebration Chinese dinner. The streetcars were stalled in their tracks, the highways were blocked for miles in every direction. The fact that we owed two weeks' room rent at the hotel and had exactly $82 in the money bag, including our salary from the Cuban Gardens, might have had something to do with canceling the dinner.

"We'll just have to pull in our belts and retrench," Mother said.

It was a new word for the girls. "Retrench?" Millie asked. "What does that mean?" Mother explained that it meant we would have to cut down on a few luxuries. "Our night lunches, for instance. We've been stuffing ourselves lately. Bananas, cookies, candy bars

—you're all getting much too fat."

That was true. We were getting fat. Mother called it baby fat, but our costumes would hardly hook in the backs. Mine especially. My cheeks were like apples and I was getting a double chin. Little Mary looked like a butter ball. Ruby hadn't exactly filled out but her stomach was rounded and it made her arms and legs look longer and thinner than ever.

We were busily measuring each other when Henry knocked on the door of our hotel room. Mother sang out a cheerful welcome and Henry shuffled in with his head down. Mother knew something was wrong the moment she looked at him.

"What is it, Henry?" she asked, fear making her voice high and shrill. "It isn't anything to do with that girl? Henry, you haven't . . . she isn't—"

"We got married," Henry said. Mother's first reaction was relief, then anger.

"Have you lost your mind?" she said. "What are you going to do with a wife?"

Henry gulped uneasily, and glanced at the door. "She's out in the hall," he said. "I wanted her to meet you."

Millie giggled and Mother shushed her impatiently. "Go over and sit down, all of you, and no laughing. This is serious." Then with a sigh she put the tape measure on the table and told Henry to bring in his wife.

Henry went out and a minute later he came back, leading a girl by the hand. She was small and dark with great brown eyes that darted about the room like a frightened child's.

"This is Sheila," he said, "my wife."

She was wearing high-heeled shoes but she didn't look a bit older than the girls or me. I hoped Mother would notice them, but without looking down she put her arms around the girl and brought her over to a chair near the table. "Sit down, dear," she said. "Take off your coat and have a cookie and some milk with us."

Henry waited at the door, twisting his cap in his hands. He smiled sheepishly at the girls, who gazed at him as though they had never seen him before. In a way that was true; we had looked at him many times, but we had never seen him as a man who might want to get married and have the courage to go ahead and do it without asking Mother's permission.

"There's not a reason in the world why we can't use her in the act," Mother was saying. "Of course, we'll have to bleach this lovely brown hair—"

"We're leaving for Chicago tonight," Henry mumbled. "Sheila's parents live there and they sent us the train fare. We're—that is . . . we're going to do an act together. Me and Sheila."

"An act?" Mother said as though she couldn't believe her ears. "What kind of an act?"

"She's gonna be my dancin' partner. We got it all figgered out. Come on, Honey, we gotta hurry or we'll miss the train."

Sheila got to her feet and smiled around at all of us. "I never danced on the stage," she said, "but I won a Charleston contest once."

Mother shook her head forebodingly. Then, motioning to Henry to turn his head, she opened her kimono and took off her money belt. Holding it in such a way that none of us could see inside, she pulled out a twenty-dollar bill and gave it to Henry. "This isn't a loan," she said, "it's a present. A wedding present from all of us."

She didn't mention the $18.40 she owed him; neither did Henry. She closed his hand over the money and kissed him on both cheeks. "I hope you'll be happy," she said. "You have a dear, sweet little wife, and I hope you'll remember all the things you've learned from me."

"I will, Madam Rose," Henry said solemnly. "I'll never forget you. You've been like a mother to me."

He took Sheila's hand and led her out of the room. Mother looked at the door as it closed after them, then she picked up the tape measure from the table and spread it around Nancy's hips. "Thirty-three inches," she said. "Write that down somebody. We'll keep these notes and measure ourselves once a week."

No one said anything about Henry, but I'm sure we all had the same thought in mind; now that he had left us who was going to drive the car?

"I hope I don't have to be the rear end of the cow," Dorothy said. A hush fell over the room.

"An actress," Mother said, "has to learn everything. Read your contract, dear, it says you will perform as directed."

The following morning the phone rang, and Mother raced to the wall and took down the receiver. "It's Henry," she said. "Something's happened to Henry. . . ."

But it wasn't Henry after all. It was Sam Middleton, our agent.

"Now here's the deal, Rose," the agent was saying on the phone. "They bought some act outta Chicago and on accounta the storm the act can't make it. It's for a full week, right here in the city, two shows a day—"

Mother held the receiver from her ear. The agent's office was six blocks away but with his shrill voice he didn't need a telephone. "What's the money?" she asked.

"Well," he said, "I might as well be frank with ya, it's short money. But you gotta look at it like this, two shows a day, right here in town—"

"What is the salary?" Mother repeated.

"Three hundred," the agent replied.

We'd been asking for five and taking two hundred and fifty. Mother tried to keep the elation out of her voice as she confirmed the date. "As a personal favor to you, Sam, we'll take it."

"Fine. Now write this down. It's the Missouri Theatre, Tenth and Missouri Avenue. Rehearsal twelve noon, sharp. Okay?—Oh, and Rose? Let the girls wear a little make-up will ya? I don't want to scare hell outta the guy. And bring along some photographs for the lobby. I'll meet ya there with the contracts."

Little Mary grabbed up her long underwear and began pulling it on. "I'm glad it isn't another night club," she said, wrapping the leg of the underwear neatly around her ankle and holding it in place while she unrolled the long brown stocking over the fold. "I don't think Mom would like me working in a night club."

"It all comes under the heading of experience," Mother replied with her mind on many other things. "Hazel, you'll take the scenery and the cow head and as many of the suitcases as you can in a taxi. We'll bring the music and make-up, and walk."

At a quarter to twelve we were on our way to the theatre. We all wore scarfs tied twice around our necks and fastened with safety pins. Under them, and pinned to our underwear, was a small bag filled with camphor cubes to ward off pneumonia. The dogs wore two sweaters each. It was very cold and my hand carrying Porky's bag felt almost frozen. I shifted the bag to the other hand and he made an angry oinking noise. His pink snout pressed close to the airhole looked like a rosebud.

Dorothy, carrying the walking dolls, ran up beside me. "Wait for me," she said. "I don't want to walk alone on this awful-looking street."

I hadn't noticed anything unusual until she mentioned it, but then I saw what she meant. It wasn't just the dirtiness of the street; there was something sinister about it. The all-night movie theatre we were passing, for instance, with the lurid pictures out front advertising *Pitfalls of Passion*. A blonde ticket seller sat in the cage, her huge breasts resting on the counter, behind a stack of quarters like a mother pigeon sitting on her eggs. A drunk staggering out of the theatre blinked his eyes as he saw us go past, then, shaking his head as though we were pink elephants, walked uncertainly down the street.

"We'll take a different route home," Mother said, curling her lip at the sight of the red, greasy hot dogs piled high on a griddle in the window of the chili parlor next door to the theatre.

We passed a barbershop with a sign in the window reading, TATTOOING ARTFULLY DONE. Samples of the artist's work decorated the sign. One was of a women clinging to a rock with MOTHER written under it, the other a dagger being thrust through the skin of an arm.

Nancy let out a whoop, "There it is, there's the theatre!" she yelled.

Next door to a hotel advertising beds for fifty cents was the Missouri Theatre. In electric lights was the word BURLESQUE. Mother closed her eyes then opened them, as though in that time the sight ahead might have been altered. A canvas banner hanging from the marquee of the theatre read: 40 GIRLS 40. BURLESQUE AS YOU LIKE IT. 40 GIRLS 40. "Burlesque!" Mother gasped. "Sam wouldn't dare do a thing like this to us."

Mother advanced on the theatre, a steely glint in her eyes. She stopped at the stage-entrance alley and gave Millie the dogs' leashes. "Wait here," she said, "and stay close together. I'm going in to get Hazel." She made it sound as though she were about to rescue Hazel from a burning building, but I knew exactly how she felt. Vaudeville performers looked down on burlesque. For an act to play such a theatre was professional suicide. Mother took a deep breath before she opened the stage door and strode purposefully through it.

While we waited the girls and I watched a man adjust an electric fan under the marquee of the theatre. He was aiming the breeze from it down on a larger than life-sized photograph of a blonde woman who wore nothing but a triangle patch where she should have worn panties and two smaller patches for a brassière. Another man was nailing black silk tassels to the brassière part of the photograph. As he stepped aside the breeze from the fan picked up the tassels and made them spin like windmills.

The girls and I inched closer to the lobby so we could see more. The animated picture of the blonde had silver flittered stars nailed around the head, and above in flittered letters that sparkled like rhinestones was her billing: TESSIE, THE TASSEL TWIRLER.

If that was all the blonde did in the show, it didn't look like much of an act to me, and hardly worth the star billing. Inside the lobby were other life-sized photographs. The women in them were all half naked, each of them peeked out from behind something such as a parasol, a fur muff or a balloon, but the only one with stars around her head was Tessie, the tassel twirler.

Millie, her eyes like saucers, nudged me: "Look at that!" she said pointing to an easel that read: WINE WOMEN AND SONG. BEAUTY! FORM! SHIMMY! At the bottom of a long list of names was Rose Louise and Her Hollywood Blondes. "We're not even headlining," Millie whispered. "Wait'll Madam Rose sees that."

We scooted back to where Mother had told us to wait, and just in time, too. Mother, holding Hazel by the arm, was marching up the stage entrance alley. At the same moment a taxi stopped at the curb and Sam, the agent, got out. "Right on time, eh?" he said cheer-

fully. His yellowish polo coat was soiled; the long belt from it
dragged on the sidewalk behind him. A dark stubble on his face was
partly concealed with white talcum powder; a cold cigar was
clamped in his teeth. "Did ya bring the pictures for the lobby?"

"Pictures?" Mother said, glaring at him. "Do you think for one
minute I'd let these innocent little girls play this filthy dive?"

"Dive?" Sam repeated. "This happens to be one a the cream de la
cream houses on whole burlesque wheel. Plenty of acts'd give their
eye teeth to play this theatre."

"Not our little act!" Mother said dramatically. "Nancy, pick up
those guns. Ruby, get your dancing mat. We're going back to the
hotel!"

"Now wait a minute, Rose," the agent said. "I okayed this deal.
You walk out on me and I'll blacklist you in every theatre in Kansas
City—"

"Don't make me laugh," Mother said. "I'll report you to the
N.V.A."

"You confirmed this date—I got witnesses—"

Little Mary began to cry. She clung to Mother's arm. "What
are we going to do, Madam Rose?" she wailed. "Where can we
go? We're stranded!"

The word *stranded* was all the other girls needed. They weren't
sure what it meant, neither was Little Mary, but it had a terrifying ring to it. "Stranded!" Millie bawled. "That's what we are,
stranded!" Nancy's face screwed up, then she began to blubber,
and they all started. The agent, his polo coat flying behind him,
ran from one girl to the other pleading with them to be quiet.
"Not in front of the theatre," he begged. "If you gotta bawl, for
crissakes bawl inside; we got trouble enough with the cops. Make
'em stop it, Rose."

He tried to ease Mother down the stage alley but she pulled her
arm away. "Don't touch me! There are laws to protect innocent
women and children against fiends like you!"

"Let's go inside and talk it over," he asked soothingly.

"Never!" Mother said. "I'd rather starve first."

"Well, I wouldn't," I said. "I'm tired of starving to death. That's
all we've been doing for years. We have eleven dollars after the

garage and hotel bill is paid. Where can we go on that? The girls
are right, we are stranded."

"Don't say that, Louise," Mother cried. "Something will turn up.
It always has and it always will."

"It already has turned up," I said. "This is it. Nothing better
is ever going to turn up for us. There's no place left for us to work
any more, Mother. There is no more vaudeville. It doesn't exist
any more. If we're going to stay in show business—"

"*If?* What are you saying, Louise? Show business is my whole
life. I've sacrificed everything for it. What is there for me but
show business?" Mother's hands tightened on her brief case, like the
tattoo picture of the woman clinging to the rock. The girls had
stopped crying now, they looked anxiously from Mother to me,
then back to Mother. Their tear-stained faces showed fear and
dread but above all complete confidence. I knew that look very
well. I had always had the same confidence but it was gone now.

"You gotta roll with the punches," Sam was saying. "There's
a lot of dough to be picked up in burlesque, and what the hell,
your life don't go with it."

"Yes, it does," I said. "This is the end for us. But we'll play the
week. We need the money." I walked down the alley to the stage
entrance and I knew Mother and the girls were walking silently
behind me.

"Hey, wait a minute," Sam yelled. "You forgot your dog bag."

I took the bag from him with a weary smile. "It isn't a dog," I
said, "it's our baby pig."

"Baby pig?" I heard him mutter as I opened the stage door.
"What in hell have I let myself *in* for?"

21

THERE WAS A STAR
on the door, but even so it was the dirtiest dressing room I had ever
seen. Greasy make-up towels dragged off the chairs onto the littered floor. Cigarette butts and empty coffee containers and old
newspapers were all kicked together with dirty frayed satin shoes
under the make-up shelf. Gnats swarmed around a half-empty
container of beer, resting on the edge of a filthy sink that was filled
with laundry left overnight to soak. Sticky red lip-rouge smudges
encircled the entire top of the container. Under each lip-rouge
smudge, penciled in with eyebrow pencil, was an initial. The
mirrors were broken; their jagged edges reached out like claws.
Shreds of net and bits of rhinestones and beads hung by thin
strings on nails behind the mirrors.

Mother wrinkled up her nose at the stale, sour odor. "Well,"
she said, "I guess this will have to do for the time being."

I hesitated in the doorway. "The man told us to take one of the
empty rooms," I said.

Mother picked up a make-up towel with two fastidious fingers
and dropped it into an overflowing can that served as a waste-
basket. "I'm not walking up three flights of stairs in any theatre,"
she said. "Not with my asthma. And not, I might add, in a theatre
like this." She sat on the chair and surveyed the untidy make-up
shelf. It was a cluttered mess of powder puffs, empty perfume and

liquor bottles, black dirty cosmetic stoves, lipsticks with no tops, cold-cream and powder cans with no lids and nasty hairbrushes and combs. One comb, with several teeth missing, had been used to stir a container of coffee and it was still in the container, the cold coffee engulfing it.

The girls and I moved a few of the sweat-stained sleazy costumes to make room on the hooks for ours. Nancy lined up the gilded guns beside the wall and I took Porky out of his bag and tied him to a pipe under the sink, along with the dogs.

Ruby held a glittering patch of rhinestones to her thin scrawny neck and gazed at herself in the mirror. "It's kinda big for a necklace," she murmured.

"Put that down!" Mother commanded. "Don't touch anything in this room that doesn't belong to you. You don't know *what* you might catch!"

A blonde woman wearing a black satin dress stood framed in the doorway, her hands on her big, soft-looking hips. "Of all the gawddamned nerve," she said. "The only thing you'll catch around here is a swift kick in the butt if you don't leave my stuff alone!"

Her blond hair stuck out from under a cerise hat; a squirrel coat with the lining torn was flung over her arm. Part of last night's make-up still lingered on her puffy face. She was fatter and older looking than in her picture, but I knew this was Tessie, the tassel twirler.

"Hey, you with the neck," she said to Ruby. "I just paid six bucks for that G string. It's no play toy. Put it down."

Ruby was too frightened to move. The woman strode into the room and snatched the glittering thing from Ruby's hands. "Who told you to come busting in here like it was a public bathhouse?"

"The—door was open," I said. "We've always had the star dressing room and I assumed we'd have—"

"Oh, you did, huh? Well, you can just assume yourselves to hell out. There's two of us in here already. Now go on—get out—all of ya."

"We'll see who gets out," Mother said. "Girls, unpack the make-up!"

The blonde's anger left her like the air sputtering out of a busted balloon. She flopped onto a chair and let her head hang down between her legs. "Ohmigawd," she moaned, "what a hangover I got. I love my drinks, but they sure don't love me. . . . Why I slop up all that gawddamn beer when I know I got a rehearsal the next day I dunno."

She stirred herself and reached for the container of beer on the sink. Turning it around in her hands until she came to the initial T, she peered in at the dull brownish liquid. "Flat," she announced. "But what the hell, so am I." She held the container to her lips and drank.

Mother picked up the music case. "Stand by for rehearsal," she said; then with a slight curl to her lips, she added, "And no talking to strangers."

The blonde gazed up at her sadly and belched. "I wantta apologize," she said when the belch was over. "I didn't mean to chew your heads off like I did—it's just that I got this lousy hangover—then to find a troupe a acrobats sprawled all over my room—"

"We aren't acrobats," Mother said witheringly. "We happen to be a vaudeville act. We were booked into this theatre by mistake."

"Weren't we all!" the blonde exclaimed; then she belched again.

Mother slammed the door loudly as she left. The girls and I cleared a space on the make-up shelf and laid out our make-up: a can of powder, lip rouge, eye shadow and a can of Crisco. "What's that for?" the blonde asked. "Ya do a little cooking between shows?"

"We use it to take off our make-up," I replied. "Mother says it's purer than cold cream."

"Yeah, and a damnsight cheaper," the blonde said. She leaned forward and I made a half-finished gesture to help her. "It's okay, kid, I'm all right." She braced herself with one hand on the make-up shelf and used the other to rummage through a pile of music that was mixed up in the clutter on the floor. With a satisfied grunt, she pulled herself up and stared myopically at the four sheets of music she had salvaged from the pile. She held the music at arm's length, then brought it slowly closer to her face, trying to bring the title into focus. "Does this say 'Digga Digga Doo'?" she asked, shoving the music under my nose. "I can't see a damned thing without my glasses."

It was a lead sheet for "Turn on the Heat." The one she wanted was under it. I lifted it out and gave it to her. She looked at it for a long moment, then she handed it to Dorothy, who was standing closest to the door. "Do me a favor, will ya, kid?" she asked as Dorothy's hand closed over the music. "Give this to Benny, the piano player, and tell him to play me a verse and two choruses and to fake anything he wants for the strip—and tell him to ask that chuckle-headed drummer to kindly pick up my bumps—if it ain't asking too much of him."

Dorothy, clutching the music, ran out of the dressing room.

"Gawd, how I hate these damn rehearsals," Tessie said, reaching for the container of flat beer.

A voice called out in the hallway, "Everybody on stage for the opening number. Step on it. We're late gettin' started."

The hallway began filling up with chorus girls wearing red satin brassières and abbreviated pants to match. The pants were open at the sides and held together with pink elastic straps that cut into the flesh, making their hips look corrugated. Long red satin tails were attached to the backs of the pants. The girls' hair was tucked up under red satin skullcaps with tiny horns at the ears. Each girl carried a spear and, as they ran chattering and complaining toward the stage, they poked one another playfully with the pointed ends. One of the girls stopped and began fumbling with the elastic on her pants.

"Hey, Tessie," she said, sticking her head in the doorway. "You got a safety pin? Look at the size a the pants they gamme." She held out the front to show the gap between the pants and her slender body. "Look, I got room in here for a friend."

She had been looking at Tessie; now her eyes traveled over the girls and me. "Who the hell are you?" she asked.

"It's the new vaudeville act," Tessie replied flatly, handing her a safety pin. The chorus girl took a fold in the elastic and stuck the pin through it. "What'll they book next?" she said, fastening the pin. "First it's female wrestlers, then it's Kiki Roberts, and now it's a troupe a silly virgins." She picked up her spear and joined the others in the hallway. Millie ran after her, "We are not!" she yelled.

In a moment the orchestra played the introduction to "Lucky Little Devil" and the chorus girls pranced lackadaisically on stage singing the lyrics of the song in several different keys. The stagehands yelled even louder than the chorus girls as they gave instructions to one another: "Let that tab in a few inches—okay, now tie it off and bring in the front traveler—not so fast—give the broads a chance to finish the number—"

A big fat woman in a gingham dress waddled past carrying a spear. "Dottie," she shouted, "you forgot your spear."

Tessie bounced up from the chair and pushed us away from the door. "Hey, Fudge, wait a minute—I gotta talk to ya about that G string." She hurried over and grabbed up the glittering thing Ruby had been trying on as a necklace. She and the fat woman she called Fudge began examining the patch as though it were the Kohinoor diamond.

"It ain't weighted right," Tessie was saying. "It just don't bump when I do—and it scratches hell outta me."

Fudge held the glittering thing to her broad stomach and did a bump that sent the beads flying wildly. "Works okay for me," she said. "Maybe there's something wrong with your bumper!" She laughed merrily over her little joke but Tessie wasn't amused. "It's no joke to me," she said. "I'm out there bumpin' my brains out and nothing's happening."

Fudge took the G string and waddled out the door. "I'll line the flap with plush," she said.

After she left Tessie turned to us and smiled fondly. "She's a great old girl. Used to be one a the biggest stars in burlesque—but you gotta watch her like a hawk. She'll fob anything off on ya."

A voice screamed off stage, "Kill that damned red flood—I told ya I wanted a bastard pink on them red costumes!"

"Is it always this exciting on opening days?" Nancy bubbled. "I love all the noise and the people running around—"

Tessie didn't answer her. She had spotted Porky, who woke up from his nap in a bad humor. He pulled on his leash and squealed in fury, kicking out with his hoofs at Nancy, who tried to quiet him. "He's hungry," Nancy explained. The dogs began barking, and she raised her voice above the din. "We use him in the act."

"Gawd help us," the blonde said. "And they wonder what happened to vaudeville."

"We're skipping the posing number!" a man yelled in the hallway. "Change into the 'Under the Sea' ballet costumes—'Under the Sea' next!"

Then we heard our music and Mother's voice as she gave the orchestra leader our cues. I tugged at my long, brown stockings and walked down the hallway to the stage. The girls, staying close together, followed me. Two stagehands watched us as we took our places for the opening number of our act. "*This* is supposed to keep the cops out?" one of them remarked. "Yeah," another one said. "Next week *East Lynne*."

22

THE AGENT SAT IN
the front row of the gloomy theatre with another man who looked
just like him. They both wore canary-yellow polo coats and sweat-
stained felt 'hats on the backs of their heads. They had stubby
cigars in their mouths and they scowled and talked about us as
though we weren't there. "You won't recognize 'em when they get
their make-up on," Sam was saying, to earn his ten per cent. "The
costumes and lights help a lot, too, ya know."

"I hope so," the other man said grimly.

"It's smart thinking on your part, bringing in a legit act now
and then," Sam said. "It gives the show a lot of class." The orchestra leader pounded out our music on the piano and the girls
and I tried to pretend we couldn't hear the men as we went through
our act.

"That big one," the man said, "can she talk?"

"Sure, talks great," Sam replied. "Why? You wanna use her in
a couple scenes?"

"Maybe. I dunno yet. The new comic's giving me a lot of grief.
He won't use a chorus girl in his scene and I'm short a talking
women. Tessie won't do scenes, I got Gladys doing the ballet right
ahead of him, and Flossie's following him with her strip. Think
this one here could handle the illusion scene?"

"Sure," Sam said expansively. "They don't look like much but
they all got a loada talent."

"Hey you," the man yelled suddenly and loudly. "You, the big one on the end." The music stopped and the girls and I looked at one another. Little Mary was on one end of the line. I was on the other. "Do you mean me?" I asked, my voice going funny on the last word.

"Yeah. Lift up your skirts and lemme see your legs."

"Her *what*?" Mother screamed from the wings.

"It's nothing, Rose," Sam yelled reassuringly. "This is Herbie Michaels, the boss. He just wants to see if she's bowlegged or something—"

"Nothing?" Mother said, striding on stage like Mary Queen of Scots. "I heard what he said."

"Look, Rose—he didn't mean anything by it—he's seen so many naked dames in his day a couple legs don't mean a thing to him. You gotta look on him like you would a doctor."

"Rose Louise is not showing her legs and that's final!" Mother said firmly.

"All right, all right," Sam muttered, waving her off into the wings. He turned to Herbie Michaels. "You can take my personal word for it. The legs are okay."

The stagehands were moving a big pink satin-lined sea shell on stage behind us. It was made of canvas and hinged so it would open and close. A girl wearing a black jersey octopus suit waved her tentacles around as she yelled at them, "Down front a little—now over to the right. Okay." Six show girls were posed on the floor. They wore kimonos over their mermaid costumes but I could see their fins sticking out.

The octopus came up to the footlights and spoke to Herbie Michaels. "How much longer is this act gonna take?" she asked over the blare of the orchestra. "We got three more production numbers to run through, ya know."

"Speed it up, will ya?" Sam yelled up to me. Mother ran out on stage with the guns and hurriedly shoved them at us, then called out the directions from the wings as we went through the gun drill and into our finale dance. At the finish we were careful to stand close together so that when we had on our costumes the radium letters would spell out the name of the act which was now changed to THE HOL-LYW-OOD BLO-NDES.

Before we could get off stage the chorus girls were dancing on, dressed as sea sprites; at least, that's what I guessed they were supposed to be, with the green strips of material tacked to their pink tights. We had to fight our way through them to the wings. "Where's Gladys?" someone yelled, and a girl with brassy red hair, wearing a flowered print robe, scurried across the stage and sat herself in the sea shell. The octopus gyrated and danced around the shell and Gladys took her knitting out of a bag and began to count off the stitches. "Knit two, purl two, knit two—"

"Isn't it exciting?" Nancy whispered. "This is what I always dreamed show business would be like."

It wasn't like any show business I'd ever known, but I had to admit it was exciting. I glanced back at the undersea ballet number and turned my head away quickly. Gladys had dropped her knitting and was standing up in the sea shell with nothing on but a string of big fake pearls.

We walked, close together, back to the dressing room. "I'm not going to write home about this," Millie said thoughtfully. "Mom isn't professional enough to understand."

Tessie looked up at us quizzically. She had taken off the black satin dress and wore a brassière and panties of blue chiffon trimmed with black lace. There was a big black-and-blue mark on her hip. Varicose veins stood out like long slender fingers on her legs. "How'd it go?"

"It was wonderful," Nancy said. "How lucky you are to be with a show like this all the time—"

Tessie looked at her with narrowed eyes; then when she saw Nancy meant it, she shrugged her soft, white shoulders, "It's okay, I guess," she said. "Better than slinging hash in some beanery."

Gladys came into the room and threw her knitting bag on the make-up shelf. "There's a helluva draft on that stage," she said. "No wonder I got sciatica." She took off the flowered robe and threw it over the back of a chair. Now that I saw her close to I realized she hadn't been exactly naked. Two triangles of net held her breasts and a patch of pink net completed the costume. "What's all this stuff doing in here?" she said, looking at our costumes and props and at Porky and the dogs under the sink.

"It's ours," I said. "We're just here temporarily—"

"Yeah, like the seven-year itch," she snapped. "One lousy stage dressing room and everybody wants to dress in it. Everybody but me! I'm moving upstairs where I got a little peace and comfort."

She took two flimsy pieces of net from a nail over the mirror and scooped a bit of make-up into her knitting bag; then, digging through the mess on the floor, she chose a pair of gold sandals with the heels run down and a strap broken. Those few things and her flowered robe were evidently all she needed.

"I hope you're not moving on our account," I said. "We're only going to be here for a week."

"It's got nothing to do with you, kid. I gotta get away where it's quiet."

"She writes poetry," Tessie said after the red-haired girl had left. "To be frank with ya, I'm glad she's gone. It gets on my nerves all that spoon, boon, croon stuff. I write poetry myself but I don't go cramming it down people's throats all the time."

She stood up and scratched herself vigorously. "What the hell am I gonna wear this week?" she said, looking at the sleazy costumes hanging on the wall hooks. "Wardrobe sure is a problem working stock like this. I gotta have two new strips a week and Fudge just ain't got the time to make 'em. Not with the stuff she has to make for the chorus numbers. Fifty, sixty bucks a week it costs me—"

By the looks of the costumes on the wall that was a slight exaggeration. In fact, all the costumes put together weren't worth fifty dollars. "Louise makes our costumes," Millie said. "If you paid her, she could make something for you, too."

"You made all this stuff?" Tessie said in a high voice filled with admiration. "All by yourself?" She looked at the hems and the seams of our costumes the way Mother did. "Look at them little stitches. Say, you gotta make me some stuff while you're here. I'll get the materials and give ya—let's see now, I pay Fudge twenty-five bucks. . . . I'll give you twenty, considering you're new in the business."

"Thirty," I said. "I sew better than Fudge does."

"You're a horse trader, but it's a deal. I'll get the material after the matinee. How many yards?"

"Come along, girls," Mother said in the doorway. "They have a room for us across the stage. Get all the things; Ruby get the guns.

Nancy, you take Porky and the dogs—"

"Across the stage?" Tessie said. "You can't dress in that hole in the wall. It's filthy! Besides there ain't room in there for all of ya— you just stay right here. I'll go talk to Michaels myself." She pulled a skimpy kimono over her gaudy underwear and headed for the door. "These stupid slobs don't know how to treat a classy act when they got one."

Mother stood at the door an instant after Tessie had left. "That, girls, is a rough diamond," she said. "A dyed-in-the-wool rough diamond."

There was a program on the wall, which was evidently a rundown of the show, but it might have been written in Sanskrit as far as we were concerned. We did recognize the name of our act sandwiched between an item listed as "Pickle Persuader" and another as "Spec. Tessie strip in one."

"Better get ready, girls," Mother said. "Heaven only knows when we'll be on. I'm going to get a broom to sweep out this hovel."

The girls and I took off our street clothes and hung them on the hooks we had cleared for ourselves. We were busily passing the community powder puff when there was a knock on the door.

"Don't come in," we screamed in a chorus, "we're not dressed."

The door flew open and Herbie Michaels stood there with a man in a funny sailor suit. The girls and I grabbed for make-up towels, kimonos, anything at all to cover our long underwear, but the men didn't appear to be looking at us.

"We want ya to be happy here, Joe," Herbie was saying to the man in the sailor suit. "We just done the 'Dirty Restaurant' or you could do that, but if you wantta do the 'Illusion' scene, okay, we got a fine talking woman to play it with ya. She's that big one over there."

They both looked at me and I tried to shrink so the make-up towel would cover me.

"Will she do?" Herbie Michaels asked.

"Who's got a choice?" the man in the sailor suit replied. His sailor pants were short, almost to his knees, and his legs were covered with fuzzy red hair. His shoes, which were two feet long, curled up at the toes. The hair on his head was red and fuzzy, too,

and stood straight out. He didn't have on a comedy make-up but
he didn't need it.

"Ask Fudge for a hula skirt," Herbie Michaels threw over his
shoulder as he left. The man he called Joe sat down in Tessie's
chair and bent his rubber cigar back and forth.

"Ever done the 'Illusion' scene before?" he asked me.

I shook my head.

"Well, it don't matter," he replied. "I do a rehash on it, anyway.
I don't use none of that Tondelayo dialogue. I go right inta the
switch on the Joe the bartender bit only I use a ukulele instead of
a bull fiddle. And after the yok yok with Stinky, the second banana,
the lights come up and you're lying stage left in front of a grass
hut. I give you a skull, then a slow triple, and you get up and start
giving me the business. You do about four bars a bumps and
grinds while I chew a hunk outta the grass hut, then you read
your lines, 'I'm no illusion,' you say. 'I'm real—here, take my hand—
touch me, feel me.' "

"I'm no illusion," I repeated slowly. "I'm real, here, take my
hand, touch me, feel me."

"Great," the comic said, "you got it already. You scram on the
blackout and I finish the scene with Stinky."

"What finish?" I asked faintly.

"Him and me clinching—the old tried and true. Is it clear?"
Then, without waiting for my answer, he walked out of the room
and left me standing there behind the make-up towel, confused
and bewildered.

"What was he talking about, I wonder?" Millie whispered.

"I'm doing a scene in the show." I tried to make it sound as
though this was the sort of thing that always happened, but inside
a panic gripped me. I remembered too well the last scene I had
played.

"Gee," Nancy said wistfully. "I wish they'd picked me. I'd give
anything to play in a scene."

While I finished putting on my make-up I wondered nervously
what a yok yok was and what he meant when he told me I was
supposed to give him the business.

"I'm no illusion," Nancy murmured. "I'm real—here, take my
hand. . . ."

23

MOTHER WAS DE-
lighted when I told her about the scene but Tessie wasn't. "It
detracts from your prestige," she said. "Look at me, for instance.
I do only two numbers. One in the first half a the show, the other
in the second. In burlesque, you gotta leave 'em hungry for more.
You don't dump the whole roast on the platter."

She didn't approve of the hula skirt, either. I had it hooked on
around my waist, and she pulled it down low on my hips. I tugged
it back up again. "I couldn't wear it down there," I said. "My
navel shows."

"I'll fix that," Tessie said. Rummaging through the mess on the
cluttered make-up shelf, she found a red, pear-shaped jewel and,
putting a bit of glue on the back, she stuck the bauble on my
stomach. "There," she said, "how's that?"

It looked silly, but I didn't want to hurt her feelings, and I
had to admit the skirt was better around my hips; it didn't make
me look so fat that way.

"I like a covered navel," Tessie said. "It's more classy." Then she
looked down at my patent-leather dancing shoes. "You can't wear
those. They make you look like a rube comic. Here—put these on."
She fished out a pair of gold high-heeled sandals from the litter
under the make-up shelf and tossed them over to me. "There's
nothing like high heels to make a dame walk good. Put them on and
walk around so I can look at ya."

I hadn't had on high heels since that time I did the scene with
Fanny Brice. I had the same feeling now as I had then, as though
I were going to fall flat on my face.

"You oughtta see how much better ya look," Tessie said approv-
ingly. "For a kid, you got a lot of sex in your walk."

I hoped Mother wasn't outside the door. If she heard the word
sex, I knew she'd not only make me take off the shoes, but it would
be the end of my appearing in the scene.

"A sexy walk is a pretty good thing to have in this business,"
Tessie said. "Burlesque stars are made on how they walk."

"Just on how they walk?"

"Well," Tessie replied hesitantly, "that and a couple other
things—"

"Like talent, I suppose."

"Talent?" Tessie yelped. "In this business talent don't count for
a hill of beans. I got talent. I can sock hell out of a song. I can
dance, too, but how do you think I got that billing out front? I
got it on *these!*"

Through the kimono I could see her breasts bouncing up and
down. Without moving her shoulders and with no effort at all, she
bounced them, one after the other. Then one was still and the
other one bounced high and stayed up there.

"You do that on *stage?*" I gulped. "In front of an *audience?*"

"Besides me and Carrie Finnell there's nobody else in the business can do it," Tessie said modestly, with just a hint of pride.
"There's a lot of belly rollers, but only two of us."

"Did—did you take lessons to learn it?"

"Nope," Tessie said in a sudden thoughtful mood, "I guess I was
just born with it. Ya know, like being born with a voice, or being
able to wiggle your ears. I been able to do it since I was twelve
years old. In fact, that's how I got expelled from the seventh grade.
Never did go back to school. I joined a burlesque show instead. I
started out in the chorus and one day at rehearsal I flipped one of
'em, just for the hell of it, and by Gawd, the next day I was a star.
I been a star ever since."

She looked down fondly at her breasts. "They're solid gold, these
boozooms of mine," she said. "Solid gold."

"I wish I'd been born with some kind of a talent," I said. "I can't do anything."

"I wouldn't be too sure about that if I was you," Tessie said. "I been watching you. You got a certain class about yourself, in a screwball kind a way. You just got to learn how to handle it."

"Fanny Brice told me that once," I said. "She said I needed experience. We worked with her on the Orpheum Circuit—"

"Oh, for crissake," Tessie said irritably, "you sound like your mother. There ain't no more Orpheum Circuit. It's gone, dead and buried. The quicker you forget what you used to be, the better off you'll be. Start thinkin' about what you're goin' to be tomorrow— not what you were yesterday."

Mother came hurrying into the room. "Hurry, dear," she said gaily. "The 'Illusion' scene is next. My, how nice you look."

Then she looked at me more closely. "Pull up that skirt!" she commanded, as I ran out of the room and down the hallway. "Louise! You come back here and take off those ridiculous shoes and pull up that hula skirt!"

I ran as fast as I could toward the wings. Then I heard Tessie calling Mother, and they were both behind me.

I stood in the wings, nervously waiting for my cue. Mother was right and I knew it. The shabby gold shoes were silly. The red stone glittering in my navel was vulgar and ugly. The lights suddenly blacked out. That was my cue but I couldn't move.

"I can't do it," I cried. "I can't go on!"

"The hell you can't," Tessie said, giving me a shove. "There ain't anything you can't do. You got the world on a string, kid, and don't you forget it."

Peeking around the side of the grass hut I could see Joe and Stinky lying on the mat. "Six long months on this God-forsaken island," Joe was saying. "Six months and not a human being in sight!"

"What am I?" Stinky mumbled. "Chopped liver?"

"There you are, my beautiful darling," Joe cried, throwing his arms around Stinky. "I wanna go home!" Stinky yelled, trying to pull away from him.

"Come to my arms," Joe said. "I've always loved you. I adore

you. I dream of you by night and think of you by day—I can't get
you out of my mind. Your eyes are like burning pools, your lips
are like rubies, your teeth like pearls—are you following me?"

"Following you hell," Stinky chortled. "I'm way ahead of you."

"Kiss me, my darling. . . ."

The lights blacked out and Stinky passed me in the darkness.
"You're on," he whispered, and I found my way to the front of the
hut before the lights came up.

"You *are* real!" Joe cried as he saw me. "You're not an illusion—"

"Louise!" Mother whispered from the wings. "Hold in your
stomach!"

I took a deep breath. "I'm real," I said. "I'm no illusion—here
take my hand, touch me—feel me—"

"There, that wasn't so tough, was it?" Tessie greeted me as I
stumbled into the wings. "It was great, wasn't it?" she asked the
octopus, who stood beside her. The cotton-stuffed tentacles hung
grotesquely from her black jersey suit and the girl's face, peeking
out from the stocking cap, looked disembodied. "It was okay," she
said. "You coulda done a coupla bumps and grinds when he asks
you if you're real, but it was okay anyway."

I looked back at the stage.

Joe, the comic, was embracing Stinky. They were lying down
in front of the grass hut, doing what I presumed was the old tried
and true. "He said he was going to give me a skull," I murmured.
"I guess he forgot."

Tessie and the octopus roared with laughter. "A skull's a take,"
Tessie said. Then, seeing the question in my eyes, she added, "He
gives you a slow look, then he looks away, and looks back again—
that's a take, a skull, see?"

Flossie, the ingénue, rushed up to the wings breathlessly. She
was wearing a newspaper wrapped around her body. A newspaper
bonnet framed her tired, babyish face. "Did Herbie say if we're
supposed to wear full net pants or not?" she asked. "I got 'em on
but they spoil the whole novelty effect."

The octopus picked up her rear tentacles so they wouldn't drag
on the floor. "I'd wear 'em if I were you, Honey," she said.

I hurried back to the dressing room. The girls were already

dressed in their opening-number costumes. They were adjusting the bows in their brittle white hair, and they eyed me disapprovingly as I took off the hula skirt and the high-heeled gold sandals.

"Take that thing out of your navel," Mother said, "before you get an infection."

I picked out the red bauble and laid it on Tessie's place on the make-up shelf. Mother stared down on it as though it were a chunk of brimstone direct from the fires of hell. I put on my cretonne pinafore and my hair bow and snatched up a walking doll.

"I thought you were wonderful," Nancy whispered to me. "They're just jealous."

Mother, leading the way, escorted us on stage.

"Stand by for your cue," she said, counting us as we lined up in the wings.

Flossie was finishing her song, "I'm Looking at The World Through Rose-Colored Glasses," and at the end of each phrase, she crinkled the newspaper provocatively. There didn't seem to be any connection between the song and the costume, but from the occasional hoots of approval from the audience I knew they liked her. I squeezed closer to the wings so I could see better, holding the walking doll tightly in my arms.

I had seen the runway at rehearsal and wondered what it was used for. Now, as Flossie stepped daintily onto it, I knew. It was a narrow strip, with a frosted-glass floor, extending out into the audience over the heads of the men who sat alongside it. As Flossie wiggled the newspaper at a baldheaded man down front, lights came on under the glass floor and made her bluish legs take on a rosy glow. She tore off a strip of the newspaper and tickled the man with it, then with a little cry of girlish abandon she darted toward the wings. Just before she exited, she tore off a larger piece of the paper and her whole backside was bare, except for the pink net pants which hardly showed at all. There was a bit of scattered applause and a lot of hooting and hollering from the audience.

The orchestra played "Whispering" and Flossie came out again, tearing at the newspaper, this time in a slower tempo. As she tore off the strips, she rolled them into balls and threw them into the audience. She danced out onto the runway and asked a man to help

her. "Would ya, Daddy?" she asked in her baby voice. The man
struggled to his feet, holding his overcoat with one arm. He winked
at the men sitting beside him and hauled off and slapped Flossie
on her net-covered bottom. He appeared to be quite pleased with
himself as he sat down. Flossie, squealing like Porky the time he
got his tail stuck in the door, limped off the runway. Just as she
reached the wings, she tore off the last bit of newspaper covering her
front, and rolling it into a ball held up her arms to cover herself.
The audience yelled, "Take it off!" and Flossie obligingly revealed
her breasts cupped in soiled flesh-colored net like two used tea bags.

Someone tapped me on the shoulder and I jumped a foot.
"You're on after the next scene," the man said. It was Herbie
Michaels and he was smiling at me. "You looked great in the hula
skirt."

Flossie was back on stage again. Now the orchestra was playing
"Collegiate" and Flossie covered her undernourished front with a
pennant that had "Harvard" printed on it. A man wearing a
checkered suit pushed me aside as he crowded into the wings. "I
hope she leaves them pants on," he said, looking at Flossie, who
was wiggling her bottom at the audience and yelling, "Oh, Daddy!"

"She'll leave 'em on or she's through," Herbie Michaels said
bluntly, and while he was saying it, Flossie unhooked the side of
her pink net pants and let them drop to the stage. She had nothing
under them but a red heart-shaped patch that must have been
glued on. I heard someone gasp, then I realized it was me. The
girls crowded closer so they could see better. Mother, standing at
the switchboard, had no idea of what was happening on stage.
It was just as well, I thought.

"Black out on her," Herbie Michaels yelled, and the electrician
pushed a buzzer and the spotlight blacked out, leaving Flossie to
struggle off stage in the darkness. The audience jeered and hollered,
but the comic in the checkered suit and the straight man wearing a
policeman's uniform went right on with their scene as though they
had the complete attention of the crowd. When the hooting became so loud they couldn't hear their cues, they began slapping each
other in the face. The audience liked this, so they stopped yelling
for Flossie to come back.

She came tearing around from behind the scenery. "Who dared black out on my specialty?" she screamed.

"I did," Herbie Michaels said evenly. "You're through. Pack your stuff and get out of here."

Flossie, too furious to answer, stalked up the iron stairs to her dressing room, the pennant dragging behind her. One of the stage-hands glanced up at her bare bottom as it swung from side to side. "Put some clothes on."

Flossie looked down at him regally. "I got my hand over it, ain't I?"

"Your hand ain't big enough," the stagehand replied as he went on with his job.

"Stupid fool dame," Herbie Michaels muttered under his breath. "I got troubles enough without her and her novelty numbers."

On stage the comic in the checkered suit looked longingly at the pickle hanging from the end of a piece of string. "You mean all I got to do is wave this under a girl's nose and she'll give me anything I want?"

"That's right, m'boy," the straight man said.

"She'll give me money?"

"Yep."

"She'll give me a kiss?"

"Yep."

"She'll give me—?"

"Yep."

"Look, I gotta have this pickle persuader. I'll give you a hundred dollars for it." He took a roll of stage money from his pocket and gave it to the straight man, who exited.

One of the chorus girls, wearing a street coat over her sea-sprite costume, crossed the stage and the comic waved the pickle under her nose. She snapped her fingers in his face. "Zis for you and zat for you," she said; then she pulled up the back of her coat and waved her bottom at the comic. "And zat for your papa."

"Papa," he said, "gets the best of everything." Throwing the pickle away, he pulled a large cucumber from his coat pocket. "I got a better persuader of my own," he shouted, and the lights blacked out.

The orchestra played the introduction of the "Doll Dance" and a voice blared over the loudspeaker, "Introducing Rose Louise and Her Hollywood Blondes."

There was a surprised silence from the audience as the girls and I walked our dolls on stage in time to the music.

Mother, in the wings, whispered, "Count four, Louise; then start." I counted to myself, then made the doll kick out a chubby leg.

The piano player had a container of beer beside him. He raised it to his lips and took a swig as he played our music with one hand. The girls and I walked the dolls through the routine. "Forte on the last eight bars," Mother hissed and the music swelled as we walked the dolls off the stage.

Ruby pulled off her cretonne dress and stood in the wings, wearing the contortion suit she had under it. Grabbing up her dancing mat, she skipped out on stage and unrolled it. Grinning fatuously, she did her back bends and splits as the orchestra played the "Destiny Waltz."

Then I was on in my "tough" number. "I will now sing a little number entitled 'When your hand itches you're going to get something—when your head itches you got it'—I'm a Hard-boiled Rose. . . ."

Matches flared up here and there in the darkness and I realized the men were lighting cigarettes. The smoke threw a haze around the spotlight.

My eyes became accustomed to the haze and I could make out the figures of the men in the front row. They sat slouched way down in their seats, their feet up on the orchestra railing. Their faces were expressionless as they looked up at me, but there were a few laughs from the balcony.

My number was over and Nancy flew on stage with Porky in her arms. I heard the first lines of her song as I ran toward the dressing room to change into my finale costume. It wasn't so bad, I thought, as I ran down the hallway. There had been a few laughs and a bit of applause. Not the kind of applause Flossie received, but enough anyway.

After the finale Mother helped us hang up our costumes and place the gilded guns along the side of the wall. "The orchestra just about butchered our music," she said, "but all in all I think it was a pretty good opening show."

Sam and Herbie Michaels agreed with Mother. Before the night performance, we had signed to stay on for another week. I was to have a new hula skirt with a higher waistband on it, and the following week, if the scenes were ladylike and met with Mother's approval, I was to appear in several of them.

As Mother said, it all came under the heading of experience. "A lot of big stars worked in burlesque," she said. "There's not a reason in the world why we can't—until vaudeville comes back."

24

ONE OF THE STAGE-hands who knew we needed a driver told us about Murphy. "She drives a car like a man," he said.

"She?" Mother asked. "Murphy?"

"Yeah. She's got the strength of ten men. She's as big as a horse—a real good-natured slob."

"She sounds perfect for the job," Mother murmured.

Bright and early the next morning Murphy appeared at the hotel. She was everything the stagehand said she was and a little more besides. She was bigger and stronger looking than we had expected and, most important, she was willing. Mother liked willingness in a person. "We're just a big, happy family," Mother told her. "When something has to be done, we all pitch in and do it. The laundry, for instance. There's never very much, but if we let it get out of hand it can pile up. Then, there are the dogs to bathe, the car to grease and keep clean and—you know, little things like that." Mother didn't mention the rear end of the cow. I guess she thought that could wait until later.

"I sure need a job," Murphy said in a low, booming voice. "I'm flat broke. About all I have to my name is this suit I have on."

The suit she referred to was a pin stripe like Henry's, only with a skirt instead of trousers. With it she wore a man's shirt and necktie. Her dark, curly hair was cut short like Henry's too, and Mother was pleased to see she wore no make-up, not even lip rouge. Her face was round and shiny. She looked very healthy. If it hadn't been for her huge bust she could have been mistaken for a man, but the bust was a dead giveaway. It was the low, spreading kind. Murphy told us later she developed it from playing basketball.

"Now, about the salary," Mother said. "Henry, the boy who used to drive the car for us, not only managed very nicely on twenty-five dollars a week but he saved a tidy little nest egg."

Murphy's smile faded; she looked doubtfully at Mother. "Gee, I don't know—"

"You can't take a job like this for mercenary reasons," Mother said. "You have to think of the experience you'll get, the places you'll see and the people you'll meet. Try it for a week anyway."

As the girls began wandering in for breakfast Mother introduced them: "This is Murphy, girls, our new driver. She's taking Henry's place. Won't that be lovely?"

While we were fixing breakfast the girls and I kept stealing peeks at the new driver. She stole a few peeks at us, too. Porky was rooting at her thick legs and leaving round wet spots on her stockings from his snout. "Just look at that," Mother exclaimed. "Porky adores her already. He's never made friends that quickly before, has he?"

The girls didn't say anything. Nancy put Henry's coffee cup in front of Murphy. Mother had given him the cup for Christmas and it had PAPA written on it in gold letters. Then we got out the bag of sweet rolls and began to eat. Woolly Face sat on the table picking up crumbs.

During breakfast Murphy told us about herself. She was the only girl in a family of five boys. Her parents were so sure she would be a boy they named her Murphy before she was born and in all the excitement that followed the name was never changed. She was from a small town near Chicago and had held many different jobs, none of them very long. She had been a singing waitress, a taxicab driver, a messenger boy, and for a while had worked as a house painter. As Mother said, she was made to order for our act.

Right after breakfast Murphy dug in and went to work. By matinee time she had done four lines of laundry. They ran the full length of the room. For such a strong-looking person Mother was surprised at how soft her hands were. She wanted to rub some hand lotion on the blisters but Murphy wouldn't think of it. "I won't go around smelling of that perfumed stuff," she said gruffly, sucking her red, swollen knuckles.

Mother put away the hand lotion. "You're as bad as Henry," she said laughingly and Murphy seemed very pleased.

We all sat under the lines of dripping laundry and had a cup of tea before we left for the matinee. "How nice it is not having a man around," Mother said comfortably. "There's no getting away from it, a bunch of girls can have a lot of fun together."

Murphy carried Porky to the theatre. She swung the bag around as though there were no pig in it at all. "I wonder," Mother mused as she looked at the broad rear swaggering down the street ahead of us, "I just wonder how she'd look in a chauffeur's uniform."

Murphy wasn't too happy about being the rear end of the cow. Millie and Dorothy got into the skin before the matinee that day to show her how easy it was. As they were dancing around Mother whispered to Murphy that Dorothy wasn't very good in the number. "With your build," she said, "you'll have it all over her. Besides it's a man's job. Henry was wonderful in it."

Murphy smiled grimly. "If Henry did it," she boomed, "I can do it."

The cow took on a new dimension with Murphy working in the suit. The first show she added all sorts of new things. She had the cow skating and doing a jig and clicking its heels in tango tempo. From time to time her bust got in the way, but that only added to the fun. She made wonderful cowlike noises.

Mother, standing in the wings, was delighted. "She's the best rear end we've ever had!" she exclaimed.

Murphy gave the cow's bag a flip as she danced around the stage. "Moo Moo," she sang in her deep baritone voice, "Moo Moooo—"

We had to change the act for the following week, so we did the same dance routines to different music, which we found in the pile under the make-up shelf, and I made a new set of costumes. The new costumes had pink elastic at the sides of the panties and were quite different from our old ones. Mother wasn't sure she liked them, but she had to admit that by using so much less material the cost was considerably reduced. I also made Tessie's costume: a blue velvet sheath which stripped down the side. Tessie was overjoyed with it. She told me she had never had a costume made with such neat little stitches.

Mother let me keep five dollars of the money Tessie paid us and I bought a pair of high-heeled shoes all my own. I wore them back to the theatre from the shop so they couldn't be exchanged, but Mother wasn't angry about them at all. She had to admit they made me walk more gracefully.

We stayed on at the Missouri Theatre in Kansas City for four weeks, changing the act a bit for each week. I played in many scenes during that time and worked with all the new comics as they came in. I played the wife in "Low Man Again" and the next-door neighbor in "The Pineapple Growers." In other scenes I was the one who said, "Meet me round the corner in a half an hour," and "Quick, hide, my husband." Most of the scenes I thought were silly and pointless and neither Mother nor I could understand why the audience laughed, but I liked doing them. I felt that, in a way, I was acting.

Then suddenly, without any warning at all, the police raided the theatre and we were out of work again.

Tessie called the hotel after the show that night to tell us about it. "It was Ida and those damned monkey-fur pants of hers," she said over the phone. "It's a good thing you'd already left the theatre. But I don't think the cops were looking for you anyway—"

"I should think not," Mother breathed righteously.

"—anyway, Herbie'll be around in a little while with your money, and about your stuff at the theatre—the dressing-room key is in the mailbox. I don't dare show my nose around the place. If they nab me again I'll get ten days, so I'm leaving for Chicago tonight."

Mother wept a bit when she said good-by to Tessie.

As soon as Herbie Michaels left us and we were alone Mother counted our money. We had almost four hundred dollars; the most money we'd had in years. We had a lot of new costumes too, and, as Mother said, a world of experience.

"It was rather interesting in a way," she said. "But it will be good to get back to real show business again."

She decided we should head south. It was warmer there and Mother was sure we would find work. She booked us for two weeks at the Four-Leaf Clover Inn in Louisville. The owner of the club was Barney Duffield, a massive man who wore high-laced shoes and a vest. We dressed in the boiler room, but otherwise it was a very nice club, even though it did have gambling. The stage faced an open archway that led to the gambling room. All during our act we could hear the sound of dice rattling on the green-topped tables and the whirr and clatter of the slot machines. In each corner of the ceiling was a peekhole where armed men sat with their eyes trained on the room.

Opening night Mr. Duffield told us in case of trouble we were to make a bee line for our dressing room and stay there. "Get behind the boiler," he said. "It's the safest place there is."

Mother eyed the boiler suspiciously. Its black, oily bulk and the noise and smell of it had bothered us all day. "What do you mean by trouble?" she asked.

"Oh, every now and then the boys get excited," Mr. Duffield replied casually. "Once in a while we have a stickup—nothing to worry about as long as you stay behind the boiler."

We were making $250 a week and Mother managed to save most of it. Our expenses were low. We had rented a big old partly furnished house with a real kitchen, and the chef at the club had loaned us a few pots and pans. He also gave us all the turkey legs he couldn't serve the customers. We ate turkey legs every day in one form or another. Mother would make turkey leg stew, turkey leg hash, creamed turkey leg and turkey leg on toast. But even with all this she wasn't happy about our job at the Four-Leaf Clover. "I don't like it," she would say. "I have a premonition something is going to happen."

Barney Duffield was very nice to us. On slow nights he would visit us in our boiler room and tell us stories of his old days when he had a Privilege car that was hooked onto a train carrying rich people to Saratoga or Hot Springs. The Privilege car served drinks and sandwiches but specialized in gambling. He told us he was arrested once and had to serve three months in jail. "Best vacation I ever had," he said, reminiscently. "I had a roulette wheel set up in the warden's office and cleared over ten thousand dollars."

"W-who were your customers?" I asked.

"The warden," Barney Duffield replied, as though he had already told me, "and his friends, of course. Great little guy, that warden. He and I really understood each other. He made a neat little pile of dough himself."

Then on Thursday, our second week, Mother's premonition came true. The girls and I were on stage for the finale when there was a loud bang and a flash of light that almost blinded us. Mother screamed from the dressing-room door, "Quick, girls, run for your lives!"

We fell all over each other getting off the stage. Millie fell flat on her face over her own gun and Nancy tried to drag her off by the arm. I grabbed the other arm and pulled as hard as I could. "Head for the boiler!" Mother cried. "They have machine guns back of those peekholes."

She pushed us past her into the boiler room, counting us as we flew by. "Keep together and get Porky and the dogs!"

Murphy was already behind the boiler and her large bulk took up nearly all the room. We pushed her back as far as we could and, holding the animals close, we huddled together and waited in agony for the shooting to continue. There was nothing but the noise of the boiler pumping away, and the heat and smell were almost unbearable. I tried to stretch a leg and Mother grabbed my arm tightly. "Don't move," she said and the urgency in her voice made me freeze. Someone had opened the door of the boiler room. We heard the heavy tread of footsteps and suddenly a voice. "Where's everybody?" Mr. Duffield said. "Why didn't you come back for your bows?"

Mother crawled out from behind the boiler, her face white with fear.

"Bows!" she exclaimed. "They were shooting at the girls!"

Mr. Duffield began to laugh. He laughed so hard he had to lean against the side of the wall. "That was a flashlight picture the dame was taking," he said when he caught his breath. "It's some

new-fangled idea where a girl takes pictures of the customers and
sells 'em to 'em."

The girls began crawling out from behind the boiler one by one.
Murphy was the last to emerge. She was ashen as she brushed off
her pin-striped suit and reset the wave in her short dark hair. "It
sure sounded like machine guns to me," she boomed.

"When they start shooting," Barney Duffield said, "you'll know
it."

Mother was very glad when the engagement was over. There
never was any real shooting and the girls and I were a little disappointed. It had been fun to run for the boiler and we would have
enjoyed it more, we felt, had it been for real.

"I think," Mother said, looking at the road map, "that we'll head
straight for Florida. We've never been there and I'm sure there's a
lot of work for a clean, wholesome little act like ours."

The Club Oasis was in Hialeah County, a few miles from Miami.
We opened there two weeks after closing in Louisville. There was
no gambling at the Oasis but the male customers were all frisked by
the doorman and their guns were checked along with their hats and
coats. The owner of the club had a gun, too, but he wore his in a
leather shoulder strap and it was hardly noticeable unless you knew,
as we did, that it was there. We knew it was there because every
time he got angry at anyone, even a waiter, he would make a sudden
move for it. He never fired it that we knew of, but he had a disturbing habit of swinging it around on his finger.

"There's something unwholesome about this place," Mother said
one night when they carried a customer out feet first. The customer had appeared perfectly all right during the act, but the
moment after he drank his highball he turned green and fell off the
chair. Right during our act the waiters picked him up and carried
him out. The cigarette girl told us the man had been given a
mickey. "He's a bad egg," she said, arranging the cigarettes on her
tray along with the fuzzy dogs and gardenia corsages. "A mickey
won't hurt him any. In fact, a physic every now and then is good
for ya."

Mother shook her head slowly after the girl left the room. "I don't like it," she said. "I can't put my finger on it, but there's something about this place I don't like."

She liked it less on pay night when the owner asked us to wait a few days for our money. He said he had run into a little unexpected trouble. "I had to make a pay-off, but you'll get your dough okay. Just give me a little time.

Our dressing room was upstairs in the club and the window overlooked a papaya grove. We had been sleeping in the dressing room to save money on hotels but the owner didn't know that. We would leave the club after the show at night and sneak back in and up the rear stairway. We used our blankets and pillows from the car to make beds for ourselves on the dressing-room floor. There was an army cot for Mother. It was a large room and as comfortable, once we got used to sleeping on the floor, as most of the hotels we stayed in.

Mother stood in the window the night we didn't get our money and watched three men who were crossing through the papaya grove. Two of them had shovels. Mother held her fingers to her lips and whispered to the girls and me. "Don't let them see your shadows in the window." The lights in the dressing room were out, we always left them out when we sneaked back in, and we could see the men clearly in the moonlight. They seemed to be counting the papaya trees. Then suddenly they stopped and one of them held a flashlight with a cloth wrapped over the end of it to soften the glare while the others began shoveling. They dug for a while; then one of them, stooping over, took a small box out of the dirt and the others hurriedly filled in the hole. Carrying the box and the shovels, they walked silently back toward the club.

"What was all that?" Mother whispered, letting the curtain fall gently over the window. "What do you suppose they were doing?"

Murphy, standing beside her, began to tremble. Her mannish pajamas hung like a tent from her huge, drooping bust. "There's something spooky about it," she said. Mother gave her a sharp look. She had spoken to Murphy several times before about her nervousness. "Show business," Mother had told her, "is no place for weak sisters." Murphy hadn't liked being called a weak sister, but for such a strong-looking person she had a remarkable lack of courage. She was afraid of so many things, such as knives and thunderstorms and firecrackers. From the look of terror on her face right now, I could tell she was also afraid of men with shovels.

"I don't like it," she said gruffly. "They all look like a bunch of gangsters to me."

"That's enough out of you, Murphy," Mother said sternly. "Go to bed, all of you. It's none of our business, whatever it is."

The following night the owner didn't bother with an excuse for not paying us our salary. "Don't bug me," he said. "I don't like it. You'll get your dough when I'm good and ready to give it to ya."

Mother didn't argue with him, but the next morning she told Murphy to drive us into Miami. "I'm going to the police about this," she said. "He owes us the money and I'm going to get it. He's not going to frighten me."

The policeman sat at his desk with a picture of President Hoover on the wall behind him. We had waited a long time and had seen many other policemen before we were led into his office. He was a big, square-jawed man. His jacket hung on the back of his chair and his blue shirt was wet with sweat.

Mother placed a small white packet on his desk. "I think you'll find it's dope," she said.

The man picked up the packet and opened it carefully. He looked at the white powder, then, touching his finger to it, placed it on the tip of his tongue. "Where did you get this?" he asked.

"Back of the Club Oasis in the papaya grove," Mother replied. "I dug it up myself."

She told him about the men with the shovels and how we had watched them from our dressing-room window. She said she waited until the men had left the club, then she had taken the shovel and gone out into the grove herself. The policeman made doodles on a piece of paper as he listened to her. When Mother finished he said, "What makes you think it's dope?"

Mother was surprised at the question. "What else could it be?"

"It could be a lot of things," he said, clearing his throat noisily, "but it happens to be talcum powder."

Mother reached for the packet and the policeman moved it closer to him.

"I'll just keep this right here," he said easily. "But in the future you'd better be more careful about making statements you can't back up."

Mother opened her mouth to say something, then she changed her mind. Picking up her purse she rose and went to the door. "Come along, Louise," she said. "We'll have to fight this thing out by ourselves."

Two things happened at the club that night. A telegram arrived from Sam, the agent in Kansas City, offering us a week at the Gaiety Theatre in Toledo, and the owner of the Club Oasis paid us a visit in our dressing room.

He sauntered in after our last show while we were taking off our make-up and stood at the end of the long shelf, eying us coldly. Mother busied herself hanging up our costumes and arranging our props.

"I hear you took a little drive today," he said softly.

Mother sat a walking doll against the wall. She didn't look at him or answer him, but I could see she was nervous.

"A friend of mine tells me you paid him a little visit," the owner said. "It's not polite to call on people without an invitation." He took his gun from his shoulder holster and examined it carefully as he spoke. Then he broke it in such a way that the barrel which held the bullets popped up. One of them slipped out into his hand and he dropped it on the shelf in front of me. "Next time you go call-ing," he said, "bring that along. It's my calling card." He smiled at Mother and walked out of the room, closing the door behind him.

"Quick, Murphy," Mother said. "Get the car started. We've got to get out of here. Girls, get your coats—hurry."

The girls and I threw ourselves into our clothes. We shoved on our shoes without even bothering to put on our stockings. Snatch-ing up the animals we followed Mother down the back stairs, tip-toeing and holding our breath. The stairs creaked under our weight and Mother whispered to us to be quiet. Then when we were through the back door we ran as fast as we could to the car.

Murphy already had the motor running and she drove like a fury out of the parking lot, the wheels crunching loudly on the gravel.

Mother sat forward in the front seat. "Find a policeman," she said. "That man's a killer."

The club was located in a deserted place off the main highway. The road was dark and there were no other cars on it that late at night. "Faster," Mother said, and Murphy pressed harder on the gas pedal. The girls and I sat looking out through the rear window for the lights of a car or the sight of someone following us.

Then, in front of a small house set back from the road, we saw a sign, HIGHWAY PATROL, and Murphy pulled up before it. Mother ran into the house and came out a few minutes later with two policemen, who jumped on their motorcycles and led us back to the Club Oasis.

We followed them as they pushed open the front door of the club and strode into the lobby. The owner met us.

"What seems to be the trouble?" he asked, every inch the night-club host.

"This lady tells us you owe her some money," the motorcycle policeman said. "We just came along to see she gets it."

The other policeman went with the girls and me while we got our music off the stands and packed our costumes. He even helped us load the trunks and cow head on the car. Mother was putting the salary in her money bag when we had finished. The owner was smiling, a bit grimly now, but he offered the policeman a drink on the house. "No hard feelings, I hope?" he said, a bit hurt when his offer was refused.

"No," Mother replied with a big smile. "None at all. Good-by and good luck," she said, shaking his hand warmly. Mother always believed in leaving an owner with pleasant memories. As she often said, we never knew in our business, when we might run into them again.

She thanked the policemen and the girls and I waved good-by to them as we drove away into the gray dawn. "How nice the police-men were," Mother said. "Of course, they were only doing their duty, but they did it in such a nice way."

"Did you tell them about the dope?" I asked.

"Dope?" Mother said as though she had never heard the word before. "What dope?"

"The packet you dug up in the papaya grove."

"Oh, you mean *that* dope. No—no I didn't. I decided to let sleeping dogs lie. After all it wasn't really any of our business."

Mother never did tell me about the packet she placed on the policeman's desk in Miami. In fact, she didn't want to talk about it at all. She said it was in the past, and that we must look to the future, which was Toledo. "I promise you this," she said. "We've played our last night club. Burlesque may not be everything I'd like it to be, but there's one thing you can say for it. It's in a theatre!"

25

I DON'T KNOW WHERE the money goes," Mother said, adding the figures again. "We had over five hundred dollars when we left Florida and here we are down to a hundred and twenty."

Murphy and the girls were in the room so she didn't mention the two hundred she had tucked away in the separate pocket of her money belt. We all dunked our cookies silently. We had just returned to the hotel from the Gaiety Theatre, where we were to open the following week, and the sight of it had depressed us. It was a dirty, dismal-looking theatre. The lurid photographs out front were gaudy and vulgar, and to make it worse our act was billed at the very bottom of the list.

Mother looked down at the figures. "Of course," she said, "we did make those payments on the car, and we had those two new tires to buy, and there's the money we sent to Grandpa, and Murphy's salary—"

Mother paused and Murphy dropped her eyes guiltily. There was never very much left from her twenty-five dollars a week after Mother had deducted the food and room rent but even so it was more than the rest of us received.

"If we could just keep our heads above water until vaudeville comes back," Mother said. "If we could just cut down somewhere . . ."

No one looked at Murphy. She dunked her cookie and made

a slurping sound as she plopped it into her mouth. The silence was heavy and seemed to hang like a cloud over the dreary room. The bare electric light bulb hanging from the center of the ceiling cast a yellowish glare on our faces. The dogs and Porky were stretched out on the ugly pink bedspread enjoying the spring breeze that blew into the room waving the dirty lace curtains.

Murphy cleared her throat. "If it would help any," she said faintly, "I'll go along on the same deal the girls have."

Mother was too touched to speak right away. She reached over and patted the big, thick arm that bulged under the pin-striped sleeve. "Thank you, Murphy," she whispered. "You're a real trouper."

The cold-water faucet in the corner washbasin dripped with monotonous regularity and Mother looked at it impatiently. "Two dollars and fifty cents a day," she muttered, "for this hole in the wall."

"It's better than our room," Dorothy said. "Your window looks out on something. Ours faces a court!"

Murphy didn't say anything. Her room was at the end of the hall and it was so small she had to walk sideways to get from her bed to the dresser.

"We'd be better off living in a tent," I said bitterly.

"That's it!" Mother exclaimed. "Louise, you've hit the nail on the head. That's exactly what we'll do!"

"What is?" I asked.

"We'll buy a tent!" Mother said. "I don't know why I didn't think of it myself. It's an inspirational idea."

"You mean we can camp out?" Dorothy cried. "All the time?"

The girls began dancing around the room. They were all talking at once and hugging Mother and each other. "We're going to live in a tent!" they yelled. "Won't that be wonderful?"

Mother quieted them with a happy little laugh. "First we have to find out how much a tent will cost," she said. "It might be that we can't afford it."

It was too late to go shopping for a tent that day, but we got up early the next morning and started out in high spirits. By noon we were tired and irritable and disappointed. Mother was surprised at how expensive tents were. She was surprised, too, at how many things one needed aside from the tent. Then, when we had almost given up hope, we found exactly what we wanted in an army and navy store.

The over-all price of $42.50 not only included the secondhand tent, which the salesman assured us was large enough for nine people, but a Coleman two-burner cook stove, guy ropes, stakes and a box of cooking equipment. Mother talked the salesman into adding an army cot for herself to the lot, and, packing everything on the car, we went back to the hotel to check out.

Mother took a last look at the hotel room, then, like the Count of Monte Cristo bidding farewell to his cell, she tucked two hotel towels into her suitcase and snatched up the extra bars of soap. "Tonight," she said, "we sleep under the stars."

Porky sat in the front seat of the car with Murphy and Mother. He had grown so big that he took up almost as much room as Murphy. Mother kept his comedy hat in the glove compartment so when we stopped for a red light or for gasoline she could put it on him. The car and the monkey attracted a lot of attention, but Porky, sitting in the front seat with the hat on his head, stopped traffic. "He's a trained pig," Mother would say as people gathered around. "We're opening at the Gaiety Theatre next week and he's in the act. You must come and see us." Then she would scratch Porky's stomach and he would open his pink mouth and let out a happy oink.

We had been driving for over an hour and were still in the city. None of us realized how large Toledo was until we tried to leave it. Then gradually the factories and warehouses began to thin out and we could see an occasional tree or a clump of grass. We were looking for a camp site not too far from the city, but with a country atmosphere. The girls and I were on the lookout for a place with shade trees and running water.

Mother turned around and smiled at us. "Keep your eyes peeled," she said gaily.

The tent was flattened out on top of the car along with the scenery. The rest of the equipment rode on the running boards with the make-up and suitcases. Mother stretched her arm out of the window and patted the tarpaulin. "Just think, girls," she said, "we have our shelter with us. No more dirty, uncomfortable hotels where we aren't welcome. From now on we can stop where we like, when we like. We'll be like gypsies, breathing in the good fresh air all day, sitting around our campfire at night—"

"It's four thirty," Murphy said interrupting Mother's reverie. "It'll be getting dark soon. We better find a place in a hurry."

"Just what," Mother asked, "do you think we're doing?"

"Oh, look, Madam Rose," Little Mary cried. "Look at that beautiful spot."

She was pointing to a patch of grass behind a welding shop. It was a sort of combination welding-junk shop and the entrance of the shack was covered with automobile hub caps. But back of it was a space that looked quite countrylike, if you closed your eyes to the pile of rusted old automobiles heaped one on top of the other and the smoldering remains of the dump fire nearby.

"That's a willow tree," Mother cried. "Stop the car, Murphy. Where there's a willow there's always water."

Murphy stopped the car on the side of the road and we all got out to investigate. The remains of the dump fire smelled awful, but as Mother said I was standing right in the breeze from it. When I moved to the other side I could hardly smell it at all. Porky and the dogs watched us from the car windows as we walked through the deep weeds until we came to the tree and, sure enough, there was a trickle of water running past. It wasn't exactly a brook, but it was water, and it was almost covered over with grass and pussy willows.

Mother took a deep breath. "Just smell the fresh air," she exclaimed. We all breathed deeply, even Murphy, who had her own opinions about the country, which were quite different from Mother's. It did smell good, now that the breeze from the dump heap had shifted. "God's own fresh air," Mother said.

She stomped her feet a few times, then she kneeled down and put her ear to the ground. "What are you doing?" Nancy asked.

"Listening for water," Mother replied. "We don't want to run into an underground spring when we drive in the stakes."

The stakes were a foot long, and I always thought one had to dig fifty feet or more for water, but I didn't say anything. Mother had a peculiar knowledge about such things as the tides, the moon and the weather. I was almost sure she knew about underground springs, too.

Mother began jumping up and down, "Everybody jump," she said, getting quite red in the face. "We have to see if the ground is firm enough to support the weight of the car." Murphy didn't want to jump up and down with us, but Mother insisted and for a while we jumped and jumped, and the man came out of the welding shop and watched us.

"This is the place," Mother said, and we all stopped jumping up and down. "Bring the car around, Murphy, and be careful of the ditches. Louise, you go with her; you know how nervous she is."

The man in the welding shop kept his eye on us as we got into the car and drove across the road and onto the field. The tires spun in the wet grass and Murphy began to perspire. She told me sharply to mind my own business when I asked her if she wanted me to drive. Shifting into low gear she bobbed and weaved over the lumpy ground, trying to avoid the bits of refuse the dump fire had missed, until Mother waved her to a stop.

Millie and Nancy had once gone on a camping trip with their parents to Mount Rainier and they knew how to set up a tent. It was good they remembered because none of the others of us had any idea of how it was to go. But when we had the tent spread out on the ground and the poles under it, and the guy lines attached and the stakes driven into the ground, it was exciting to see the tent take shape. It looked secure and steady, too, except for one small hole in the roof which was hardly noticeable. Inside there was a good smell of crushed grass and oiled canvas.

The girls and I scouted around for rocks to hold down the side walls while Mother cooked dinner, hot dogs and beans, on the new cook stove. Then we lined up with our new tin plates in hand as Mother dished out the food. It was dark when we finished eating and we had our coffee in the beam of the headlights from the car. The lantern had been too complex with its directions and warnings.

"It's hard to believe we're only a few minutes away from the theatre," Mother said. She was leaning against the running board of the car, the monkey on her shoulder and Porky and the dogs snuggled up at her side.

The stream made a gurgling sound as it trickled past and somewhere a frog croaked. The welding shop was closed now. A small night light gleamed from the back door like a misplaced star. A stillness fell over us and Murphy moved in closer to the group around the headlights. "I'm glad you have that gun," she said to Mother.

The girls sat up straight. "What gun?" Hazel asked. "When did we get a gun?"

Mother told us she bought it in the store where we found the tent. She took it from her purse and showed it to us. "It's an automatic," she said, as though we should all know what that meant. The gun was so small it fitted into the palm of her hand and the box of bullets that went with it were like toys.

"Do you think it could kill a person?" Millie asked.

"Of course not," Mother replied. "But it makes a good loud bang and that's all that's necessary."

We took turns holding the flashlight as we got into our outing-flannel nightgowns and, lifting them high, we walked through the weeds with our toothbrushes and towels to the stream.

With our blankets and pillows from the car we made beds for ourselves alongside Mother's cot in the tent. We lined up close to one another, facing the flap that was left open for air. Porky and the dogs were tied to long leashes and they snuggled up at our feet. Murphy, grumbling about snakes and bugs, made a separate bed for herself at the back of the tent.

"Don't forget to say your prayers," Mother said, and in a little while I went to sleep.

Then suddenly I was wide awake.

Mother was sitting up straight, dead still. The dogs in her arms growled softly and she held her hands over their noses. Then I heard it. It was a crunching noise of someone walking outside the tent. Mother fumbled at her pillow for the gun and I could see the dull blackness of it against the white of her hand.

"Close the flap," she whispered.

I was too frightened to move. My nightgown was wet with sweat that had popped out on me suddenly. "Hurry, Louise," Mother said, and I pushed out of my blanket and crawled between the girls until I was at the flap of the tent. A heavy fog had settled and I could barely see the outline of the car. The flap was tied up with rope and it was slippery from the damp. I couldn't untie the knots. My hands felt as though they had gloves on them.

"Hurry, Louise," Mother whispered.

The footsteps seemed to be coming closer and closer to the tent. Then Murphy was awake and when she saw Mother and me she stifled a sob. "Wake the girls," Mother said. "There's someone out there."

The knots were untied and the flaps fell down and we were in darkness.

"Stop where you are!" Mother shouted. "Stop or I'll shoot!"

For an instant the footsteps stopped. The girls woke up and clung to one another in half-wakeful terror. "Who is it?" they whispered. "What do they want?"

"Get down flat, all of you," Mother said in a low voice, then she yelled, "One step closer and I'll shoot!" The dogs barked and strained at their leashes.

Mother fired the gun right through the side wall of the tent. It didn't make a loud bang at all, more of a singing noise; then she fired again and again and the tent smelled of gunpowder. There was a sound of something heavy falling, and stillness. I had held my breath so long that it escaped with a rush and I felt myself falling. Mother pushed me firmly. "This is no time for fainting," she said in a sharp, clear voice. "There might be more than one of them. Get the flashlight. We're going out there."

I felt under Mother's pillow in the darkness for the flashlight and when I snapped it on she lifted the flap of the tent with the nose of the gun and crawled out. I followed her and I could hear the girls behind me, their nightgowns making swishing noises in the tall weeds.

The car was as we had left it, the tarpaulin and trunks undisturbed. The stove and dishes were exactly as they had been. The frog had stopped croaking. The air was deathly still.

"It was self-defense," mother was saying almost to herself as

she walked through the tall grass that was wet with dew and
sparkled as though it had been dipped in flitter. "I warned him
and warned him—"

Mother followed the gleam of the flashlight, the gun hanging
listlessly from her hand. The girls and I walked behind her, looking down as she was doing for something in the weeds.

Mother stopped suddenly and, dropping the gun, put her hands
to her mouth, "Oh, no—" she cried. "Oh, no—no—" The girls
and I ran up to her and looked where she was looking. There in
the weeds was the prowler, two big brown lifeless eyes staring up
at us. One of the bullets had gone straight between them and
left a small red hole that oozed and dripped down the fur-covered
face.

"Why did I do it?" Mother cried. "Why, why—I didn't mean
to kill anything—I just wanted to frighten him away."

I put my arms around her and led her to the car. "We should
be glad it was just a cow." I said, "and not a man."

"A poor defenseless cow," Mother said. "Oh, why did I do it—"

Then she grabbed my arm and held me very tight. "Where was
its bell?" she asked. "Did you see a cow bell?"

Millie began pumping up the cook stove. "I'm going to make
some coffee," she said, trying to keep her voice steady. We opened
the car door and Mother sat down in the front seat and cried while
we made the coffee. "All cows have to wear a bell," she sobbed.
"It's the law."

Murphy crawled out of the tent. The knees of her pajamas were
grass stained as she got to her feet and sheepishly joined us around
the stove. None of us looked at the brown furry lump we all knew
was lying beside the tent. The dogs had been sniffing at it and we
had tied them up. Then, after I had a cup of coffee, I took the
flashlight and went over to the dead cow to see if there was a bell
around its neck. I had to lift the heavy head and I felt faint and
weak as I touched the fur and felt the still-warm stickiness of the
blood on my hands. I let the head drop back on the grass and went
over to the stream to rinse off the blood. Then I went back to
Mother.

"There was no bell," I said. "There's a broken piece of rope around its neck, but no bell."

"I'll bet we have to pay for the cow," Nancy said. "How much do cows cost, I wonder?"

Mother sipped her coffee and in the dim light from the dashboard I could see where the tears had dried on her face, leaving it shiny and stained. Then she handed me her empty cup and got out of the car. "Get the shovel," she said. "We have to dig a deep hole. Hurry, girls, it will be dawn soon."

I got the shovel off the running board of the car, and we took turns digging the grave while Mother held the flashlight. We dug as close to the dead cow as we could, and when the hole was large enough we tugged and pulled and pushed until the huge body fell into it; then we covered it up with dirt. Dawn was breaking through the fog and we didn't wait for our turns at the shovel but pushed at the dirt with sticks and boards and our hands. There was a lot of dirt left over when the hole was filled in. We spread it evenly over the grave; then, using the back of the shovel, we pounded it level and moved the box with the camp stove on it over the spot.

The sun was up when we finished. Mother, satisfied with the job, examined the grave from every angle, then told us to go back to bed. "If anyone questions you," she said "remember, you slept soundly all night. You heard nothing."

The girls and I nodded our heads, too exhausted to speak. We crawled back in the tent and, rolling ourselves in our blankets, dropped the flap. For a long time I listened for the sound of police cars and people looking for a cow, then I closed my eyes and before I knew it I was asleep.

Sunday morning, two days later, the man from the welding shop came visiting. His wife and little girl were with him. They were all dressed up and I guessed they had been to church. The girls and I were peeling vegetables for dinner. We sat on the grass near the stream and let our bare feet dangle in the water. The man called out a cheerful "good morning" as he approached us.

"We came over to see the pig," he said. "I've been telling my family about you folks and they just had to see for themselves. This is my wife, Mabel, and Gloria, our little girl."

Mother, sticking her head out of the tent, cast a worried eye on the cow's grave, then smiling broadly she came out to greet our guests, who were, in a way, our hosts.

"Welcome," she said, "to our camp site."

"You sure fixed things up nice," the man said appreciatively, peering around at the boxes we used for chairs and the large packing case we had turned into a table. "I've been trying to talk the wife here into taking a camping trip for a long time—"

"I'm so afraid of bugs and things," the woman said. "Aren't you ever nervous or frightened?"

"Of course not," Mother said lightly. "What is there to be nervous or frightened of?"

Gloria, their little girl, went up to Porky and put her arms around him. "Isn't he pretty?" she said. "I think he's the prettiest pig I ever saw."

I could see the germ of an idea growing in Mother's head; the glitter in her eye was a dead giveaway. "He's a trained pig," she said. "He wears a little hat on the stage and does all kinds of tricks."

"Oh, let me see," the little girl cried, clapping her hands together. "Please, Mommy, ask her to make the pig do its tricks."

Mother went over to the car and took Porky's hat from the glove compartment. She put it on him and snapped the elastic under his big pink chin. "Come, Porky," she said, and the pig followed her as she walked back and forth in front of the tent and down to the dump heap and back.

The little girl was fascinated as Porky picked his way daintily through the rubble. "Oh, please, Daddy, buy me a pig like this one." Porky, standing beside her, was almost as big as she was. He rooted at her pink organdie dress and the little girl put her arms around him. Her father watched fondly, then he turned to Mother. "I don't suppose you'd want to sell this pig?"

"Sell him?" Mother said, shocked at the thought. "Porky's one of our family. We wouldn't sell him for all the money in the world." She put her hand on Porky's thick rump and the pig looked up at her and oinked. "—But he's reached the age where he needs a real

home, a back yard to play in and someone like little Gloria to love
him. We'd like you to adopt him and give him the home he's been
denied." Mother dropped her eyes so the man couldn't see the tears
that welled up in them.

Their gratitude was embarrassing. Mother brushed away her
tears and untied Porky's leash from the tent stake; then, snapping
it to his collar, she handed it to the little girl. "Be patient with him,"
she said softly. "He may not do all his tricks for you right away, but
love and kindness will be its own reward."

Porky, with his new family, picked up his hoofs carefully as he
stepped over the tin cans and broken bottles of the dump heap on
the way to their car, which was parked near the welding shop. He
didn't look back once, not even when he was sitting in the front
seat with his chin resting on the window.

"No tears now, from any of you," Mother said to the girls and
me. "We have to think of his happiness. He deserves a real home
after the childhood he's had."

The man at the welding shop, whose name was Walt, became
a good friend of ours. He let us run an extension cord to the back
of his shop so we had real electricity in the tent, and he let us use
his bathroom. But most important, when a man came around asking
if anyone had seen a stray cow, it was Walt who assured him that
no cow had been seen in the neighborhood.

The grave was flattened down, and almost overnight weeds began
growing on it. No one would have guessed a cow was buried under
the place where we had set up our outdoor dining room.

One night when Mother was frying the hamburgers she looked
down at the grave and shook her head sadly. "What a waste," she
said. "We should have cut off a few steaks before we buried him."

26

THE GAIETY THEATRE in Toledo, on opening day, was a scene of chaos. The show "Girls from the Follies" was late getting into town and when they arrived their star, Gladys Clark, was not with them. Closing night in Dayton she had bopped the hotel manager with his own inkwell. He was in the hospital and she was in jail. The show had moved on without her.

The producer, Ed Ryan, was frantic. His star not only did two strip-tease numbers in the show, but she appeared in five scenes and both finales. She was also his wife. Toledo, for them, was the tag end of a long season. This was her third arrest within as many weeks. Once before she had been arrested for opening someone's head with the heel of her shoe, and the other time for biting a policeman who tried to pull her off the back of a chorus girl. Her husband said she was an *artiste* to her finger tips. She was also, he explained later, too fond of her bottle.

"There isn't any show without her," he told the theatre manager. "Where can you find a woman in Toledo who strips, does scenes and plays five musical instruments?"

Mother stepped forward. "My daughter does scenes," she said, and the two men stopped screaming at one another long enough to look at her.

I wanted to hide somewhere. Mother pushed me toward the

two men and I wanted the floor to open up and let me drop quietly
through it. "We've just finished a tour of supper clubs in Florida,"
Mother was saying. "Rose Louise has been playing scenes there
with all the big stars. She's appeared with Fanny Brice on the
Orpheum Circuit—"

"They're part of the vaudeville act I brought in," the theatre
manager said in answer to Ed Ryan's raised eyebrow.

"Does she strip?" Ed Ryan asked.

Mother looked him straight in the eye and said yes.

Later, in our dressing room, Mother began making plans. "Of
course, you won't really strip," she said, "but there's no reason why
you can't walk around the stage in time to music and drop a
shoulder strap at the end. Our act will put us over anyway. Get
your make-up on. I have to buy some material for a couple of
costumes."

It was eleven thirty and the show went on at two forty-five.

Mother rushed out to buy the material and Ed Ryan and the
theatre manager hurried to change the sign on the marquee. The
full importance of what had happened suddenly hit me. I sat down
on a chair in the dressing room and looked at myself in the
wavy, cracked mirror. I was a star. I picked up the lip rouge and
rubbed it on my mouth, then I put my hair behind my ears and
gazed at myself for a long time. I was a *star*.

It was even simpler for me than it had been for Tessie.

I put on my sweater and went out front to see how my name
would look in lights. The theatre didn't seem to be quite so dismal
now. Even the photographs in the lobby appeared less vulgar. The
man was still rearranging the sign and I watched as the name began
to grow "Rose L-o-u—" I wanted to shout up to him, "That's
me! That's my name you're putting in lights," but I didn't. He'd
know soon enough, I decided. Everyone would know—June and
Gordon and Stanley and Grandpa—Grandpa! Suddenly all the
joy was out of it. Grandpa wouldn't like it at all. He didn't even
approve of the Pantages Circuit. What would he think of a theatre
like this?

"Wait a minute," I yelled to the man on the ladder. "That isn't
the right name you're putting up. It's—Rose Lee. Not Rose Louise."

The man took a piece of paper from his overall pocket and looked at it.

"Rose Louise is what I got," he said. "That's the way they gamme it."

"Yes, I know," I told him, "but I've just changed it. Make it— Gypsy Rose Lee."

"I got my orders from the boss, girlie," the man said impatiently. "I put up what he tells me to put up."

"I happen to be the star of this show," I said, "and you'll put up *my* name the way *I* want it put up!"

The man looked at me for a moment, then he began rearranging the letters on the marquee. "Okay," he said, "it's your funeral."

Funeral wasn't exactly the word I would have chosen. I tried to think of the word I had seen in a book recently—renascence? I wasn't sure, but it sounded better than funeral. I was going to use it on the man on the ladder, but I changed my mind. He didn't look like the type who would be impressed. I waited until the three names were up in lights, then I read them out loud and, pleased with the sound of my new name, I went backstage to wait for Mother.

"But why?" Mother asked me. "Why change your name at all?" She put down the bundles on the make-up shelf and took off her hat and fluffed out her soft, curly hair. "Gypsy sounds so cheap."

"I didn't want Grandpa to know about us," I insisted. "Then when I told the man 'Rose Lee' it didn't sound like enough of a name so I just added the Gypsy."

"But why Gypsy?" Mother asked. "And what makes you think Grandpa could hear about us way back in Seattle?"

I didn't answer her, but I knew that everyone was going to hear about us. What was the point of being a star if people didn't know you were one? Mother began unwrapping the bundles she had brought in. She had ten yards of lavender cotton net and four bunches of violets for one costume and ten yards of red net and three red cotton roses for the other.

"You can wear the leotard you wore with the hula skirt under them," Mother said.

I threaded a needle and began sewing the costumes as fast as I

could. They were both made with full, gathered skirts and simple
bodices. I didn't bother with hooks and eyes or hems. The dresses
could be pinned on, and the hems would never show anyway. As I
gathered the net onto a needle I decided I would throw the pins
into the orchestra pit. Mother couldn't complain about that. Throwing away a few pins wasn't really stripping.

Fluffing up my hair, I took one last look at myself in the mirror.
The lavender net was transparent, the violets on my breasts showed
through and I patted them down so I wouldn't look bunched up in
the front. Then I bent one knee, like a real strip teaser and smiled
at my reflection.

"Quick, Louise," Mother said from the dressing-room door.
"You're on next." She followed me down the hallway to the stage.
"Remember now, keep smiling and don't look at your feet."

The orchestra played the introduction of "Little Gypsy Sweetheart" and I opened the center of the curtains and stepped through.
The spotlight blinded me for an instant, then my nervousness was
gone, and I began parading back and forth on the stage as I had
seen the other strip teasers do. I lifted the sides of the full net skirt
and made it swirl around me. Mother was smiling from the wings.
The girls were with her, their white heads glowing in the darkness
like phosphorus.

"Smile, dear," Mother said and her voice carried all over the
theatre. "Hold your stomach in."

I took the pins from the side of my dress and dropped them into
the tuba. They made a plinging sound as they hit the side of the
shiny instrument, and the audience murmured their approval. Then
just as the music came to an end, I dropped the shoulder straps and
the lavender net dress fell to the floor. Wrapping the curtain around
me I disappeared into the wings. I stood there for a long moment
holding on to the scenery and trying to get my breath. I was wet
with sweat, as though I had just finished an acrobatic routine.

The tenor was on stage singing the finale song and the audience
applauded all through it. The louder they applauded, the louder
he sang. That wasn't unusual. In fact, it always happened. I'd been
in burlesque long enough to know that no matter who did the next
to closing strip-tease number the audience always applauded through

the tenor's song. I waited a moment in the wings, then covering myself with the lavender net, I went back to my dressing room, the sound of the applause following me.

Mother and the girls were waiting with my finale costume ready to slip into. I started to close the door and Mother motioned for me to leave it open a crack. "Listen to that applause," she said, a pleased but not too surprised smile on her face. "It's getting louder!"

It *was* getting louder. "It can't be for me," I said. The applause was mixed with shouts and yells and the noise of pop bottles rolling down the aisles. I grabbed up my kimono. "If it is for me I'd better take a bow or something—"

Mother slammed the door shut. "You stay right where you are!" she said. "Get into your finale costume and let on you always go over this way."

"But—"

"No buts about it. Do as I tell you!"

I was the bird of paradise in the finale. Mother lifted down the heavy feathered shoulder piece and fitted it on my back. The girls represented other kinds of birds: Millie was a blue jay, Little Mary was a canary, Ruby was a kingfisher, Nancy was a blackbird, Dorothy was a cockatoo and Hazel was a pink-and-yellow something we couldn't put a name to. The feathers were molting from most of the costumes, and because Gladys Clark was much smaller than I her costume was tight on me; but the wings were huge and I used them to cover the parts of me the costume missed. The girls and I hurried out on stage and waited for our cues. The prima donna, dressed as an egret, was singing with the tenor. I left the girls in the wings while I found my place at the top of the high staircase. Being the star of the show I had a special entrance for the finale. Then when I heard my new name blare out through the annunciator I walked as birdlike as I could down the stairs to the footlights.

The applause was to me unbelievable. I opened the wings and showed the skimpy leotard. It was the least I could do, I thought, to show my appreciation. Then I flapped them shut before Mother could see what I had done. As the curtain began to close in I stepped forward and took the folds and brought them slowly together, smiling out at the audience until the two sides met.

The prima donna glared at me. "We're supposed to hold a straight line," she said.

"You mean *you're* supposed to hold a straight line," I replied gently. "I'm the star. I can do as I please."

The girls and I did our vaudeville act in the middle of the second half, and before the finale I did my second specialty, an audience number, in my red costume. This time when I opened the center of the curtains and stepped through there was a burst of applause. I sang a verse and chorus of "Powder My Back" a number Mother and I copied from the ingénue of the show in Kansas City:

> Oh, won't you powder my back every morning?
> Cause, Honey, there's no one can do it like you.
> Oh, won't you powder my back every morning?
> It makes me feel happy when I'm feeling blue.
> —And if you'll powder my back every morning,
> Then maybe some morning I'll do it for you!

I went down into the audience with a powder puff on a stick as the ingénue had done, and looked around for a baldheaded man. I found one whose head shone in the spotlight like a pink Easter egg. After he had powdered my back I picked up a strand of hair he had carefully combed over the shiny pate and tied a red ribbon to it. "Now stand up and show them how pretty you look," I said, pulling at his coat lapels.

The man didn't want to stand up and the harder I pulled the further he slunk into his jacket. "But, darling," I cried, "I want them to see how pretty you look!" The man was almost hidden by his jacket. I planted a lipstick kiss on the shiny bald head and ran as fast as I could for the wings, while the laugh held.

I didn't strip the red dress. I didn't have to. The applause was as boisterous as it had been for my first-act number. I had heard burlesque audiences applaud for stars like Tessie and Flossie, but I had never heard applause as spontaneous and good-natured as mine. I took three bows, and on the last one I made a half-finished attempt to go after the baldheaded man again and the laughter was even louder than the applause.

I was underdressed for the next finale and, leaving my red net

costume in the wings, I crawled up on the platform and held on to
the ropes while the stagehand pulled me up into the dark, dusty
flies.

Below me, on stage, I could see the tops of the heads of the
tenor and the prima donna, who were singing their duet. The chorus
girls and the other principals were introduced; then slowly the
flyman let in the flittered, heart-shaped platform with me on it,
and I smiled at the audience as the curtains closed.

My first performance as a burlesque star was over! I stepped
off the platform and breathed a grateful sigh. I was pleased and
proud that I had made it. I had no doubts about that. I didn't have
to sing or dance or do anything. I could be a star without any talent
at all, and I had just proved it.

That night, at the end of the first-act finale, a large basket of
flowers was delivered to me over the footlights. I pulled out one rose
and threw it to the orchestra leader as I had seen Olga Petrova do
when we worked with her on the Orpheum Circuit, then I hurried
into my dressing room, eager to read the card tied to the basket.

"You're a lily among weeds," the card read. It was signed, "An
admirer."

Mother looked at it for a long time, then she tucked it into the
frame of the mirror. "An admirer," she murmured. "I wonder who
it can be?"

After the show that night Murphy took the girls home to the
tent and Mother and I had supper with Ed Ryan. He told us he
had a proposition to offer. In the Chinese restaurant he asked us if
we would finish the season with his show. There were four weeks
left to play: a week in Cincinnati, two weeks in Chicago and
Philadelphia. The girls, he said, could work in the chorus and I
would do just two numbers and the finales. The vaudeville act
would be cut.

Mother picked the almonds out of her sub gum chow mein to
save for last. "There would be certain expenses," she said doubtfully.
"Costumes, for instance."

"I'll supply everything," Ed Ryan said. He was a tall thin man
with sparse grayish hair. His long, serious face was dominated by
thick glasses which almost, but not quite, hid the cold blue of his

eyes. A yellowish diamond glittered on his tie; there was a larger one on his finger.

"About the dressing rooms," Mother said. "We'd want it in the contract that we had the star's room—by ourselves."

Ed Ryan nodded his head in agreement. He broke open a Chinese cookie and read the fortune wrapped in it. Then with a cynical smile he crumpled up the slip of paper and dropped it in the ash tray. Mother and I had read our fortunes out loud, as we always did, and I wondered why he had been so secretive about his.

"And about the money," Mother was saying. "The salary we're working for now is ridiculous. I accepted it only as a favor to our agent."

Ed Ryan began writing on the stained tablecloth. Mother looked on with her mouth pursed in a tight smile. When they weren't watching me, I fished out the crumpled fortune from the ash tray and put it in my pocket.

"The six girls will get thirty dollars each," he said. "That's the standard salary for girls who step out of the line with specialties— that's one hundred and eighty—how's about three fifty for the act?"

"I wouldn't even consider it," Mother said firmly. "I have my own expenses, there's Murphy's salary—the very least we could get by on would be four hundred. The contract would of course, be made out in my name."

They talked for a few minutes more, then a contract was drawn up on a piece of paper supplied by the waiter. The salary was to be $375 and Mother was pleased and satisfied with the deal. Ed Ryan bought us a bag of lichee nuts to take back to the girls. While he waited for his change Mother picked up a handful of toothpicks and put them in her purse. "What if Gladys Clark wants to come back with the show?" she asked innocently.

Ed Ryan counted the money the waiter gave him. "She won't," he said. He dropped a quarter on the table and took his hat from the hook. "She's divorcing me."

"Oh," Mother murmured. "That's too bad."

We left him in front of the Chinese restaurant and as we drove away in a taxi I knew he was watching us, but I didn't look back. When we arrived at our camp site Mother asked the taxi driver to wait so we could see our way by his headlights. "But this is the dump yard," he said. "What do ya want out here?"

"Not that it's any of your business," Mother said grandly, "but we happen to live here."

Murphy and the girls were asleep. They had left the electric light on in the tent and Murphy was sleeping with the gun on her chest. Woolly Face snuggled up to her neck. Mother patted the dogs, then she took the flashlight and her toothbrush and walked through the weeds to the stream. When I was sure she was out of sight I took the crumpled slip of paper with Ed Ryan's fortune on it from my pocket and smoothed it out so I could read it. "You find new love." I read it again and had that same feeling I always had when my occult was working. I held it close to me for a second, then quickly I grabbed up my book of sonnets and pressed the yellow slip of paper between the pages.

"Come brush your teeth," Mother whispered loudly from somewhere near the stream. I picked up my toothbrush and a towel and hurried out to meet her.

27

Flowers were sent to me over the footlights every night that week. Each show I threw a rose to the orchestra leader, who stood up from the piano and caught it, then bowed low. The prima donna sniffed in disapproval at what she called "corn," but the gesture, done in the grand manner, pleased the audience. Leaving the basket stage center, I would step forward and take the sides of the curtains and close them in, smiling as though this was a special secret between the leader, the audience and me.

The cards from the flowers were around my make-up mirror. The messages on them varied: "To the fairest of them all," "To stage-land's loveliest," "To my queen," but the signatures were alike, "An admirer."

One night the flowers would arrive in a gilt basket, the next night the basket would be white or blue. They were lavishly trimmed with tinsel and ribbons but the flowers never lasted very long. By matinee time the following day, they would be gone.

"They were faded and dead," Mother would say. "I had the prop man throw them out. It's bad luck to have faded flowers in a dressing room." For the night show fresh ones would arrive so it didn't matter.

The other performers in the company weren't friendly with us. They had been together all season and seemed to resent our coming in on the tag end of it. The prima donna was the most resentful. She was annoyed about many things, but mainly about the dressing rooms. When there was only one stage dressing room, she said she had always shared it with Gladys Clark.

"That may be," Mother told her, "but Gypsy Rose has a room by herself. It's in her contract."

The comics were annoyed that I didn't appear in their scenes as Gladys Clark had. "My daughter doesn't appear in scenes," Mother would say.

"Yeah, I know," Charlie, one of the comics, replied. "It's in her contract."

Mother thought their complaints were petty. She told me to pay no attention to them.

"We can't expect to have friends," she said. "Not when we're on the way up. Once we get up there we'll have all the friends we want."

Closing night in Toledo the basket of flowers arrived as usual. The note attached to the roses read: "To the one and only Gypsy."

Mother read it out loud. "That has a nice ring to it," she said. "I think I'll have them announce you like that in your specialty."

On the last-act finale as I was getting ready to close in the curtains, the prima donna stepped forward. Before I could grab the folds, she clutched one end and closed it with me. My tête-à-tête with the audience was ruined. Her egrets and my bird of paradise were much too big to be crowded that close together. She was smirking at the orchestra leader, who looked up at her warningly. He could see how angry I was, but she was too busy being the personality girl to notice. I waited until she bent over coyly, then bringing up my knee I let her have it. It was a gentle boot, but it caught her unawares and if she hadn't been holding the scenery with a death clutch she would have landed in the orchestra pit.

"Next time you touch that curtain," I said, "you'll wind up in the balcony!"

She threw a robe over her costume and went screaming out front to Ed Ryan, but Mother was there ahead of her. "Just which one is the star?" Mother demanded. "How dare she grab that curtain away from Gypsy Rose!"

The prima donna was in a rage. "Between flapping her wings and shoving that damned basket of flowers around they can't see me in the finale at all!" she sputtered.

Ed Ryan knew the prima donna had a point, but he also knew Mother well enough to know she didn't need one. There were three weeks left to play, and he wanted peace backstage. The prima donna, he decided, would stand on the stairs as the curtains closed in. "In that way," he said, the audience can see you, and Gypsy can still do her bit of business with the curtain."

Opening day in Cincinnati the dressing-room walls shook with the screams of the prima donna. She was barricaded in but her voice carried all over the basement. Everyone in the company knew what had happened. She had received a poison-pen letter. "How dare that woman write me an anonymous letter. I sing like a frog, do I? Well, that fat slob of a daughter of hers can't sing at all!"

Ed Ryan, outside the locked door, tried to comfort her. "You don't know who sent the letter," he said when he could get in a word. "It wasn't signed. You have no proof—it might be a joke."

"Proof!" the prima donna screeched, straining what she often called her golden box. "A joke! You know how she hates me. You saw what she let her daughter do to me on the stage in Toledo—what more proof do you want?"

Mother, listening at the top of the iron circular stairs, clucked her tongue disapprovingly. "These burlesque people," she murmured. "They're so vulgar."

The next show I closed in the finale curtains alone. The prima donna took her pose on the staircase behind me like an ill-natured statue of winged victory, but the audience didn't notice; a few flips of my wings took care of that.

Just before the curtains met an usher came running down the aisle with a basket of flowers. I reached over the footlights for it and dropped a red rose to the startled orchestra leader; then, stepping back, I buried my face in the fragrance of the flowers and smiled at the audience as the curtains closed. The note tied to the basket read: "Cincinnati's gain is Toledo's loss. It was signed "An admirer."

None of the cast said good night to us as we filed out of the

theatre on our way home to the tent, Mother and I in the lead, the
girls behind us and Murphy bringing up the rear. The hostile looks
of those who sided with the prima donna followed us to the stage
door. Then, as we were getting into the car, Ed Ryan leaned in
through the rear window. "I hope you aren't upset about that
disturbance," he said to me. "No one really thinks you had anything
to do with the letter—"

"I don't care what they think," Mother said with a martyred smile.
"But I'm glad you don't believe it."

Our camp site in Cincinnati was provided free of charge by the
city. It was a camp and picnic grounds beyond the river road with
old-fashioned outhouses and a community water faucet. There were
other campers there ahead of us and they had taken all the best sites.
The only spot left for us was on a rocky hill, which I knew was
going to be uncomfortable to sleep on, but even so it was reassuring
to have people nearby.

None of the other campers were living in a tent for fun; they
were all migratory working people who lived there, as we did,
because it was free. Our nearest neighbors were knife sharpeners.
They had a grinding machine on the back of their dilapidated truck
and in the mornings they would make their rounds collecting various
things, such as scissors, knives and tools, to sharpen. Later in the
afternoons the man and his wife would take turns at the grindstone.
The noise was terrible.

Another neighbor was a real Indian. He had on faded overalls
and a bright pink shirt, but we knew he was an Indian from his
long braided hair, that was wrapped around his head like a coronet
and held in place with a hairpin. He made snakeskin belts and
sold them. The empty, scaly skins were nailed to a board near his
tent. He could hunt any time he wanted to without a license and
that first day he brought back a dead furry creature he had killed
with a bow and arrow. He began skinning it at once. Then, while
bits of red flesh still clung to it, he stretched the skin out on the
ground to dry in the sun. The skin gave off a strong, pungent odor
almost as bad as the dump heap back in Toledo.

We had set up our tent before the matinee, and after the show
that night, when we arrived at the camp site the other tenters'

lanterns were all out and it was dark and still. The Indian's dog growled at us as we went past to the water faucet.

Being as quiet as we could we pumped up the gasoline stove and prepared our night lunch: hot cakes and syrup. Night lunch was our favorite meal when we were working. There was never too much time between shows for dinner, and we got up too late for a noonday supper. Six hot cakes each was about our limit, although Murphy could usually put away a few more and Little Mary once ate eleven. When we finished eating we stacked up the tin plates to wash in the morning, and after brushing our teeth in the icy water from the faucet, we rolled up in our blankets and tried to find a comfortable place to sleep on the rocky ground. Camping out wasn't as much fun as we had thought it was going to be.

In the morning, while we were having breakfast, a delegation of campers gathered at our tent. The knife sharpener was their spokesman. The others stood behind him as he approached our tent, his eyes narrow and mean looking, his sweaty undershirt torn and dirty. His trousers were held up with one suspender. Slits cut in his shoes made room for his bunions.

"We want you folks to pack up and get off this here tenting ground," he said. "We don't aim for trouble, but we won't have a bunch of thieving gypsies cleaning us out of house and home when our backs are turned."

"Gypsies?" Mother said. "Are you crazy? We're show people."

The knife sharpener held his ground. "We heard you call that big one Gypsy. You're not putting anything over on us. We're Americans and we won't have a bunch of foreigners crowding us out." The other campers moved closer to their spokesman and added their voices to his.

Mother picked up a tent stake. "If any one of you moves an inch," she said, "I'll wrap this stake around his neck. Gypsy, get the brief case."

I dashed into the tent, almost knocking down Murphy who was crouched in the entrance, peering out through the flap. Mother, handing me the tent stake, snatched the brief case and took out our photographs. "There," she said, passing them around to the campers. "Those ought to prove we're show people."

The knife sharpener looked hard at the photographs, then handed them back to Mother, keeping as far from her as he could. "Actors," he announced, "are worse than gypsies. I move we put 'em out!"

The girls and I stood close together, waiting for our cue. We were outnumbered but we had Mother on our side. There was something fierce and magnificent in the pose she took as she defended the tent. Her blue eyes glared at the ragged, unshaven group of men and their pathetic-looking wives. "This is our home," Mother said, "and we're staying."

The knife sharpener's wife held his arm. "Now, Fred," she whined, "don't go flying off the handle—there's enough of us here to see they don't steal nothing—"

"You dare call yourselves Americans," Mother said. "You're nothing but a bunch of ignorant, stupid blobs of humanity. You're cowards, all of you, picking on a defenseless woman and her little girls—go on, get off our property, *move!*"

The delegation stepped back, their feet shuffling through the dusty ground. They didn't look at one another as they went back to their tents, silent and ashamed. Mother watched them for a moment, then she turned to the girls and me. "Come along, girls," she said very businesslike. "There's work to be done. Don't just stand there with your mouths open. Tighten down those guy lines and cover up the cook stove. My big toe hurts; I think a storm's coming up."

The storm broke while we were playing the matinee. The thunder shook the theatre and rain dripped through the cracks in the roof onto the scenery and the stage. But with all the fury of the storm the voice of the prima donna was louder. She kicked open my dressing-room door with a moccasin-covered foot and thrust a note under my nose. "Don't try to tell me you or your Mother didn't write this!" she screamed. I looked down at the piece of paper. "Why don't you wise up and get out of the business?" the note read. It was signed: "A well wisher."

"I suppose you never saw that before," the prima donna said, hitching up her Indian feathers.

I shook my head. I had never seen the note but I recognized the handwriting. It was the same handwriting as that on the cards around my mirror, the cards which had been attached to the baskets of flowers.

"I never saw the letter before in my life," I said, handing it back to the angry prima donna. "But I have a funny feeling it's the last one you'll receive."

She looked at me suspiciously.

"I was born with two veils," I explained. "I have occult powers."

"Occult, my behind!" she snorted. "You go tell that mother of yours to stop sending me those letters or I'll call a cop!"

I found Mother in the furnace room. The flowers, taken from their container, were lying on a wet newspaper and Mother, with a practiced hand, was dabbing gold paint on the white wicker basket I had just received over the footlights. A roll of silver ribbon and a few fresh flowers were nearby. A card, bearing the familiar handwriting, was lying face up on the improvised work bench: "Always Ahead and Onward." It was signed, "An admirer."

"Mother!"

She let out a startled gasp. "Oh," she said, "it's you. I wish you wouldn't pussyfoot up on me like that. You know it's bad for my asthma."

"You've been sending them all the time. You're the unknown admirer!" I was disappointed and angry and most of all I was embarrassed.

"I'm glad you found out," Mother replied irritably, wiping off a bit of gold paint from her elbow. "I'm sick and tired of doing it all by myself. Get that ribbon and help me tie it around the handle. We have to work fast or the paint will never dry in time for the night show."

I snatched up the ribbon and made a florist's bow. "You should have told me," I said. "It makes me feel like a fool—and unless you want to wind up in jail you'd better stop writing those letters, too. There's a law against that."

"Law?" Mother said. "Don't make me laugh. A mother's love knows no law!"

As soon as we were dressed we piled in the car and headed for the camp site. The storm was over, but the sky was still gray and the roads were wet and slippery. "Thank God for my big toe,"

Mother said as we sped along. "We would have been washed out if we hadn't battened down everything."

It wasn't Mother's big toe, or any of our precautions that saved the tent. It was the other campers. They were still digging away at the trench around the sides of the front flap when we drove up. The knife sharpener was busily hammering in a stake and his wife was shaking rain water off our cooking equipment. "How long have you folks been tenting?" she asked peevishly. "Anybody with a lick of sense oughtta know you can't keep a tent dry if you don't dig a trench around it."

"And whoever drove in these stakes oughtta have their heads examined," her husband added. "You gotta angle 'em away from the tension—any fool knows that."

The Indian and another man were tightening the guy lines. Mother couldn't believe her eyes. "I don't know how we can repay you for your kindness," she said, checking the tent to see that everything was still there. Then, with a big smile, "How would you all like passes to see the show?"

The knife sharpener's wife dropped the piece of wet canvas as though it were a red-hot stove. She straightened up and faced Mother with angry pride. "We may be poor folk," she said, "but we're respectable. Fred and I'd roast in hell before we'd step a foot into a burleycue theyter!"

28

MURPHY TOYED WITH
her food. Her eyes, as she chewed, held a faraway wistful expression
of infinite sadness. It was a boiled-ham dinner, a favorite of hers,
and usually she went at it until sparks flew from her knife and fork.
She prodded a potato negligently; then with a sigh that made the
newspaper tablecloth flutter as though a north wind had suddenly
blown up, she pushed away from the camp table and went over
and sat down behind the tent.

Mother watched her with a puzzled frown on her face. Murphy
had been acting strangely for several days. Mother had spoken about
it to me before. "I don't know what's got into her," she said. "She's
unhappy about something but when I try to talk to her she just
looks at me like a sick bull moose. It's getting on my nerves."

I tried to remember when it had started. Murphy had been
perfectly all right when we opened in Toledo. She was nervous
about the cow being shot, but not unhappy. I remembered she was
all right opening day, too.

"It was the second day in Toledo," I said. "Remember when
you told everybody we were going to stay on with the show?
Remember how funny she acted?"

"No, I don't" Mother said. "She was pleased as the girls were.
Why they almost knocked me down in the excitement."

"Not then, but later . . . Remember how she acted when you mentioned Chicago?"

Mother thought real hard for a moment. Then it came back to her. "It was Chicago that did it!" she exclaimed. "But why, I wonder?"

"It might be about money," I said, and Mother gave me a sharp look.

"Don't go putting ideas into her head," she snapped.

In the dressing room between acts that night Murphy spoke to Mother about what was on her mind. I was lying down on the cot and I guess she thought I was asleep because she talked as though I wasn't there.

"I can't go to Chicago with you," she said suddenly.

"But we're going next week," Mother said. "You mean you're leaving us with no notice, no time to get someone else?"

"Louise can drive the car," Murphy muttered. "I can't face it, that's all, Madam Rose. I don't want to talk about it. I just want to stay right here in Cincinnati."

Mother began to stutter, "B-but why, Murphy? You've been so happy. You told me yourself you'd never been so happy before in all your life. We've done everything in the world for you, Murphy. You've shared and shared alike with Louise and the girls and me."

"It isn't that," Murphy said miserably and the chair creaked and groaned under her weight. "I *have* been happy. I *have* loved it. You've been wonderful to me and I'll never forget it . . . that's just it. I can't bear to have a lot of people tell you things about me—things that—that—"

Mother interrupted her impatiently. "I never listen to gossip, Murphy. You should know that by now. I accept people as I find them. What you used to be has nothing to do with it. It's what you are now that counts."

"But that's just it," Murphy said, and her voice dropped so low I could hardly hear. "They know me in Chicago. . . . What they'll tell you is true. I'm a—a Lesbian."

"Oh, for goodness' sake, Murphy," Mother said with a relieved sigh. "What a big fuss about nothing. You know how I am about things like that. Live and let live is what I always say. You go to your church and I'll go to mine."

Murphy threw her head down on the make-up shelf and cried. Her massive bulk heaved and shook with her sobs and the chair creaked warningly. With a strangled sob she got to her feet and lumbered out of the room. Mother looked at the door after it had slammed. "Who would ever have suspected it!" she murmured. "She's the last person in the world I would have thought was a religious fanatic."

❀❀

Murphy wept when she said good-by to us in Cincinnati, but her mind was made up. She would never, she said, go back to Chicago. Mother didn't urge her. We had looked up the word "Lesbian" in a dictionary and Mother was a bit annoyed with Murphy. Mother hated deceitfulness.

I drove the car to Chicago. We had all day Sunday to make the trip but we left after the show Saturday night to save room rent. Besides, I had to drive slowly because I didn't have a license. Eighteen was the age limit for licenses and I was sixteen and a half. That, by itself, wouldn't have stopped Mother, but I would have had to take a driver's test and she knew I didn't drive well enough to pass it.

"It's only three hundred miles," she said, "and I'm right here beside you." The car was falling apart. Among other things one headlight was burned out and the brakes needed relining. Mother had been meaning to get the brakes fixed; she bought a garnet brooch in a pawnshop in Toledo for that very purpose, but she didn't want to waste it on such a small repair job. She was waiting until something else went wrong with the car so everything could be fixed at once. "Just take it easy," she said. "God is love. We'll make it."

The girls were quiet and thoughtful on the trip. They whispered a lot among themselves and when Mother asked them what they were whispering about they wouldn't answer. That annoyed Mother, too. She hated secrets even more than deceitfulness.

We made it to the Rialto Theatre just in time for the opening matinee. I was tired from driving all day and night but the sight of the theatre nestled behind the elevated tracks made me forget my weariness. My name was up in lights and splashed in big red letters on the canvas banner stretched across the marquee. Below, it said WRESTLING TUESDAY NITES. Mother was delighted with the billing. "Quick, Millie," she said. "Get out and take a picture of it."

Millie refused to budge. "I won't," she mumbled. "It isn't my name. Why should I waste my film?"

"What an unprofessional attitude!" Mother exclaimed. "I'm surprised at you, Millie. I hope you aren't jealous of Gypsy's success. You should be glad and grateful. Why, if it weren't for her you wouldn't be here."

Millie took her time getting out of the car and the girls followed her sullenly. "I could always get a job in a show like this," she said. "And I'd be getting paid thirty dollars a week, too."

"Who told you that?" Mother demanded.

"The chorus girls told us," Millie said, "and we're all sick and tired of working for nothing."

Mother was furious. "That's enough sass out of you, young lady. Your parents are going to hear about this!"

"They already have," Millie replied. "I wrote them about it last week." The girls, their noses in the air, followed her into the theatre.

"Well," Mother said as the stage door slammed behind them. "What do you think of that for gratitude?"

I didn't blame the girls for wanting money of their own; I would have liked to have some myself, but I didn't tell Mother that. She was too angry. "Go get a stagehand to help us," she said, unsnapping the tarpaulin and tossing the luggage out on the sidewalk. "Don't just stand there, go on!"

I started toward the stage door, then I changed my mind. Walking over to the lobby I went in through the front door the way Gordon used to do on opening days. Standing in the back of the dark theatre, I hesitated an instant, then making myself tall, I said, "House lights! Gypsy Rose Lee is here." When the lights went on I marched down the aisle and up the steps leading to the stage. "Where," I asked, "is the star's dressing room?"

The dressing rooms were in the basement but they were bright and cheerful and I was pleased to see there was a silver star on mine. We trouped a star of our own along with a few thumb tacks, but I was glad we didn't have to use it. It embarrassed me to put up my own star.

The audience was wonderful. I stopped the show with both my specialties and during the finale, when the basket of flowers was delivered over the footlights, the applause was like music to me. I threw a rose to the orchestra leader and slowly closed in the curtains. I didn't bother to look in the white envelope attached to the basket. I knew it would be empty.

There was no poison-pen letter for the prima donna either, but during both her big numbers she was booed. The booing began in the balcony, where all the noise and trouble starts in a burlesque theatre, and by the time she was ready to hit her high note in "Indian Love Call," the hooting and catcalls shook the theatre. The prima donna tore off the stage in a fury, the Indian feathers quivering with her rage. Mother couldn't have been more sympathetic. "It's disgraceful," she said. "One unruly boy can get a whole audience in an uproar—"

The prima donna eyed her coldly. "It's mighty damn funny," she said, "none of these things happened until you joined the show."

Mother smiled blandly. "The long arm of coincidence," she murmured on her way downstairs to the dressing room.

Mother was annoyed when she saw the young man waiting in front of our door. "I told you to stay away from backstage," she whispered, shoving a dollar bill and a pink balcony ticket into his hand. "Now get out front where you belong, and make it good and loud for the night show." The young man waited until the coast was clear, then he ran up the hall to the stairs.

"Who was that?" I asked, following Mother into the room. "Why did you give him a ticket and money?"

Mother busied herself hanging up my costumes. "You mean that boy I was just talking to? He's a claque for you, dear. All big stars have claques. They start the applause for you and keep it going. You know, like they do in grand opera."

"Is that all he does?" I asked pointedly.

Mother's eyes widened in innocence. "For a dollar a day what else should he do?" Then she became very businesslike. "I've just had a long talk with Millie and the girls. She tells me they refuse point-blank to live in the tent. What's worse, they insist on being paid! We can thank your friend Ed Ryan for that. He's behind this mutiny and I know it—"

"He wouldn't do such a thing—"

Mother's eyebrows shot up. "Oh no? Well, what would you say if I told you I caught him kissing Nancy!"

"I wouldn't believe it!" I blurted out. I had no reason to be sure. He had never spoken to me alone, and since that first night in the Chinese restaurant we had never been out with him, but I still had his fortune pressed in my book of sonnets and I had read it over and over. In front of my dressing-room mirror I had rehearsed the scene and knew just what I would say when he told me he was in love with me. I would look at him with compassion and tell him how fond of him I was, but that my career came first.

"I saw them with my own eyes," Mother was saying. "He can't get girls for next season so he's after ours. It's as plain as the hand-painting on the wall. Well, as far as I'm concerned he can have them. We can be glad we found him out in time."

"Mail," the stage manager said, shoving some envelopes and a postcard under the door. There were a letter from Grandpa and a note from Big Lady. The postcard was from San Francisco, and had a picture of a blonde girl and a young boy. They were in a dancing pose but both of them appeared to be asleep on their feet. They leaned against one another, the girl holding the boy's arms on her shoulders. Her hair fell over her face in uncombed curls; a pair of dark glasses hung from her ear. Printed below was "Jean and Bobby, the favorite brother and sister team, who have been dancing for five hundred hours at Connely's Arena. Excitement! Endurance! Thrills! Come and bet on your favorite team."

The blonde was June. I had to look at the picture twice to make sure, but it was really my sister, and the boy with her was Bobby, the one she had eloped with. I turned the card over and read the message scrawled on back, "How could you ever stoop to Burlesque! You have disgraced all of us." It was signed "June."

Mother snatched the postcard from me. An anguished cry came from her as she stared at it. "A marathon dancer! Dancing in a marathon after all I sacrificed for her!" She let the card drop as she clung, sobbing, to the back of a chair.

The card had been addressed to me, to my new name at the Rialto Theatre. "How did she know?" I asked.

Mother faced me angrily. "I wrote her, that's how, in care of *Billboard*. I told her you were a star with your own show, that your name was up in electric lights! I wanted her to know what she gave up, what she missed out on."

The stage manager called out half hour, and there was a tap on my door. "Full net pants on all you strippers for the matinee," he said loudly. "The censors are catching the show. Keep your navel covered." In a moment I heard him giving the same orders next door. "Full net pants—no bumps or grinds—"

Mother reached down and picked up the postcard and smoothed it out. "She could have been a big star," she said. "If only she'd listened to me. If only she'd waited. I could have done for her what I've done for you."

Closing night Mother counted the money Ed Ryan gave her. It was short $180. "I paid the girls myself," he said. "Here's the receipt." Mother looked up at him; as their eyes met I could see the effort she made to hold back her anger. She closed the door behind him and counted the money again. "The treachery of it," she said, shoving the bills into her money belt. "But he won't get away with it. I'll get even with him if it's the last thing I do."

The girls didn't travel in the car with us to Philadelphia. They went on the train with the rest of the company. I missed their chattering and giggling, and in a way I envied them. I would never have had the courage to defy Mother the way they had.

It was almost seven hundred miles to Philadelphia. I still didn't have a driver's license, but as much as Mother hated parting with the garnet brooch, the brakes had been relined and the burned-out headlight replaced. With a seven-hundred-mile jump there was no time to waste on roadside repairs; there was no time to stop for anything. We made it, but just in time for the matinee.

The critic from *Zit's* theatrical weekly caught the opening show and wrote that I was a big hit in both my numbers. He said I was like a breath of spring and predicted I would go far in the business. Mother thought, considering how completely I'd stopped the show,

he might have said a bit more, but she bought ten copies of the
paper anyway.

Then on our third day a telegram arrived from New York.

Mother tore into the dressing room, waving it in the air. "It's
from Billy Minsky!" she cried. "He wants us! This is it, Louise.
This is the break we've been waiting for!"

"I don't want to play his theatre," I said, and I was surprised
when I heard myself. Mother stared at me as though I'd lost my
mind. "I mean it," I said. "When we close here we're through with
burlesque. You were right. We don't belong here at all."

"But—but that was a long time ago," Mother said irritably,
"before you were a star. Things have changed now, dear. He's offering us top money, star billing, a dressing room by ourselves, anythink we want."

"It's still burlesque."

"You sound like your sister," Mother snapped. "The Republic
Theatre is the showcase of Broadway. Billy Minsky said so himself.
All the big producers will see you. Why, it's the chance of a life-
time. Now you just listen to me. I know what I'm doing. We open
the Mondey after we close here. I okayed it for four weeks."

Closing night Mother was the busiest woman in the theatre. She
made trip after trip from the stage door to the car. She was all over:
in the prop room, the orchestra pit, the wardrobe room. The
tarpaulin was stretched so tightly over the top of the car we could
hardly manage to snap it down.

Ed Ryan, with the girls behind him, watched us coldly as we
crossed the bare, gloomy stage, our arms loaded with music and
costumes, the dogs pulling on their leashes. "Good-by everybody!"
Mother sang out. "Good luck and thanks for everything!"

When the door closed behind us Mother's smile faded. "I'm
getting so damned tired of fighting for what's coming to us," she
said. "I hope it will be different at Minsky's."

I had been hoping the same thing. All my life it seemed we had
been going from city to city waving good-by to angry people. I
wanted to say good-by to someone, just once, who was sorry to see
us leave.

Mother settled herself in the front seat and tucked the blanket around her legs. "I have a feeling we've come to a turning point in our lives."

"I hope so," I said, and I meant it with all my heart.

It was almost dawn when we stopped at the side of the road and ate the sandwiches we had brought along for the trip and sipped the scalding-hot coffee from our thermos cups. Mother broke off a piece of her ham sandwich and fed it to Woolly Face and the dogs. "I wonder," she said thoughtfully. "I just wonder how an Indian strip tease would go over at Billy Minsky's."

I spilled the hot coffee down the front of my neck. "Mother! You didn't—you haven't—"

"I certainly did," Mother said triumphantly. "It's all under the tarpaulin. Everything from the head feathers to the moccasins! He'll think twice before he cheats another innocent woman alone in the world with a child to support."

For the second act
I made a red net skirt
with a velvet jacket.
The hat was red velvet,
too, pasted on cardboard.

Underneath I wore
a pink velvet
"tease" costume.

Murray Korman

The muff was to
hide behind
on my last encore.

Photos by De Bellis

Newspapers seemed interested in my private life.

"Big eyes, dear," Mother said.

When the big producers
caught the show
I wanted to be ready for them.

Bruno of H

Woolly Face
added to the
hula effect.

Strand

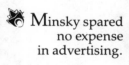
Minsky spared
no expense
in advertising.

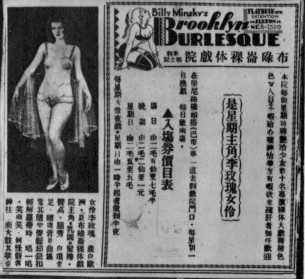

29

BILLY MINSKY'S RE-
public was the most elegant burlesque theatre I had played. The
doorman was garbed as a French gendarme, complete with mustache
and red-lined cape. The girl ushers, wearing French-type maids'
costumes with frilly skirts and long, black silk stockings, squirted
perfume on the customers as they came in. For the ladies there were
gardenia corsages. Velvet draperies framed the combination hotdog-
popcorn stand. The name of the show was in lights on the marquee:
YETTA LOSTIT FROM BOWLING starring Gypsy Rose Lee.

Billy Minsky met us at the stage door and showed us to our
dressing room. It was up a flight of iron stairs, and although it
wasn't the star's room—four women were dressing in that one—it
commanded a view of the stage.

"Where is the green room?" Mother asked grandly.

"Green room?" Billy Minsky said. "What's that?" Mother didn't
pursue it. She had managed to put him on the defensive and for the
moment she was satisfied.

Billy Minsky was a short man and had to look up at both Mother
and me when he spoke. His eyes, behind their glasses, were thoughtful. "How old are you?" he asked.

I hesitated and Mother answered for me. "Just eighteen," she
said. I wasn't seventeen yet, but Mother had gotten into a habit of
lying about ages.

"That's all right then," he said. "I can't take any chances with minors."

I was wearing a new tweed coat Mother bought me in Philadelphia and a rust-colored dress with a white Peter Pan collar. My hair was fluffed out under a gray felt hat; fuzzy curls hung almost to my shoulders. I closed my hand so Billy Minsky couldn't see the mended fingers of my glove.

"Do you wear your hair like that on stage?" he asked.

"Of course she does," Mother replied a bit testily. "Didn't you see her work in Philadelphia?"

Billy Minsky didn't answer her. He pulled a chair away from the make-up shelf and motioned for me to sit down. Then he took off my hat and held my hair down flat, leaving just the bangs curled up around my face. "Wear your hair like that," he said. "It's more ladylike." He went to the door, then turned back to Mother. "Remember now, anything you need just come to me."

I wasn't sure I liked my hair flattened down. It made me look too much like Rose Louise, but for that first show I wore it the way Billy Minsky asked me to because I wanted to please him.

From the platform outside our dressing-room door Mother and I could watch most of the show. The wings and lights hid part of the full stage sets, but we could still see how elaborate they were. The chorus girls' costumes were more ornate than the principals had worn in Ed Ryan's show, and the scenery was lavish. It was a small stage; the Republic had been a legitimate theatre until Billy Minsky took it over, and there wasn't room for the big productions he staged. The scenery was stacked against the walls and the prop room was loaded with lamps, tables, dishes and round balloonlike things we later learned were dried, blown-up turkey bladders used by the comics to hit one another over the head with. Potted palms, flittered staircases, tree stumps, park benches, imitation flowers, gladiators' shields, swords and all sorts of things were crowded into the room that was up a ramp from the stage. Prop rooms had always intrigued me, but the prop room at the Republic Theatre was a glory hole.

Mother and I stood on the platform outside our dressing room and looked down on the stage as the cowboy production number got under way. The chorus girls were dressed as cow girls and

Indians with bows and paper arrows and pop guns that shot cotton
balls out into the audience. For the big finish, the curtains opened
and two white horses raced madly on treadmills that revolved on
the stage. Two of the show girls, naked from their waists up, rode
the horses. The treadmill made a loud grating noise and that, along
with the clatter of horses' hoofs and the chorus girls letting out war
whoops and firing the cotton bullets and paper arrows at the audience, made a spectacular production number. The audience,
apathetic until then, applauded enthusiastically until one of the
horses had an accident, then they began to laugh. They thought it
was very funny while the treadmill faced the wings, but when it
faced upstage and the horses began kicking the manure all over
the first five rows of the theatre, they stopped laughing and ducked
behind the seats. The man from the Ben Hur Stables who owned
the horses was tearing his hair. "Stop the treadmills," he shouted,
but no one paid any attention to him. The half-naked show girls
clung to the galloping animals for dear life. "Close in the curtains,"
Mother screamed from the platform. "Those poor horses will hurt
themselves!"

Finally the curtains closed and the hysterical show girls were
helped to their dressing room. The man from the stables led the
horses away. "For the night show I'll bring in a pair that isn't gun
shy," he said.

At the end of my first number I didn't wait to hear how loud the
applause was; I didn't have to. The noise of it followed me across
the stage as I gathered up the lavender net and started for my
dressing room. The tenor was singing "The Bells of St. Mary's,"
and trying hard to be heard over the clapping and shouting of the
audience. A stagehand, in the wings, was hitting a group of hollow
pipes with a mallet to represent the sound of churchbells. I glanced
on stage just in time to see the curtain open on a tableau depicting
the "Angelus." The straight man, his head bowed in prayer, was
the farmer. Chorus girls, wearing robes and carrying rakes and
hoes were the others in Minsky's version of the famous painting.

The applause for my specialty stopped short and a hush fell over
the audience as the scene of the "Angelus" faded and the curtain
behind it was raised. Sixteen chorus girls, dressed as angels with

silver wings and glittering G strings, posed on the flittered parallels. Mother met me on the platform outside my dressing room. "What happened to your applause?" she asked. "It stopped so suddenly."

"Look!" I said, pointing to the stage below. The chorus girls, their arms crossed and their eyes turned upward in saintly solemnity, had removed their brassières. Their breasts, all shapes and sizes, were completely bare.

"I'll put an end to that," Mother said, racing down the stairs. "I'll go straight to Billy Minsky. No religious act is following your specialty."

Ten minutes later she was back. "I'm beginning to understand why performers don't like the Minsky's," she said. "He absolutely refused to take out the number. I even threatened to quit and he refused." She began tidying up the room as she always did when she was angry or frustrated; then suddenly she stopped, a sly smile on her face. "I know what we'll do," she said. "We'll call Walter Winchell. We won't tell him who we are. We'll let on we're outraged churchgoers—that'll fix the Minskys."

The next day Winchell, after checking the story, ran the item in his column and that night the number was out of the show. "You see how easy it is," Mother said as she pasted the clipping in my scrapbook. "Make sure you're right, then go ahead."

Sunday before we opened we had explored the possibility of pitching our tent at the Bronx tourist park, but it was much too far from the theatre and, with just two of us left, it didn't seem worth while to live in a tent. So we took a room at the Cameo apartments across the street from the Republic Theatre.

There was an exciting flamboyance to Forty-second Street that early summer of 1931. Legitimate theatres were sandwiched between Hubert's Museum, hot-dog stands and burlesque houses. Fred and Adele Astaire were starring in *The Bandwagon* at the New Amsterdam. *Private Lives* was playing next door to Minsky's Republic. The Eltinge Burlesque, with a four-a-day grind policy faced *The House Beautiful* at the Apollo. Upstairs, a beauty salon advertised three items, shampoo, finger wave and manicure, for one dollar.

The Cameo before Prohibition days was known as Murray's, a

gay, expensive supper club with a rather racy reputation. There were still traces of its past grandeur in the faded silk brocade on the walls and the water-stained mirrors in the dark, smelly halls.

What used to be known as the Garden Room was now a storage space filled with bed springs, mattresses, old awnings and boxes and trunks belonging to the tenants past and present. Our scenery and costumes were stored here along with the tent and the cow head, the walking dolls and the gilded guns. "We could put the act together in five minutes," Mother said, shoving our trunks against the wall. "The moment vaudeville comes back we'll be ready for it."

Our apartment was one room with what was called a kitchenette, but was actually a metal cabinet containing an electric hot plate and a few pots and pans. The dishes were washed in the bathroom sink. Our rent was twelve fifty a week. Downstairs was a Nedick's and a huge hot-dog and hamburger bar that sold near beer. The smells wafting up from the street below and the noise of the traffic gave a Coney Island atmosphere to our apartment, but the nicest part about it was that we could look out our window at my billing on the theatre across the street. The name of the show was changed each week: *Ada Onion from Bermuda, Lotta Schmaltz from Greece, Iva Schnozzle from Red Hook,* but my name was always on top. When Mother and I worried about the future, and we worried a lot, we would look out the window and be reassured.

My scrapbook was getting fatter, and so was the money belt, but the Republic Theatre didn't seem to be quite the showcase Billy Minsky had said it was. We had been there five weeks and no big producers had been in. Louis Sobel had mentioned me in his column, Walter Winchell had recommended me to diversion seekers, *The New Yorker* magazine wrote that I was a must for those who felt better with their eyebrows raised, but Flo Ziegfeld hadn't been in to see me; neither had Earl Carroll or George White. "Give them time," Mother would say. "Beauty like yours won't stay hidden behind a bushel."

I tried every reducing diet I heard about. For days I ate nothing but lamb chops and pineapple, or bananas, or sauerkraut juice and lettuce. I kept my thumb pressed against my teeth whenever I could; Mother said that would help straighten them. When the big producer did come in to see me, I was going to be ready.

Before we opened at the Republic Theatre, Mother and I had been under the impression the Minsky brothers were loved by the performers who worked for them. It came as a shock to us to learn this wasn't true. The first inkling we had was when one of the comics showed us a trick he had taught his dog. Hanging an old coat on the wall, he would say, "Minsky!" and the dog, leaping at it, would tear it down from the wall and rip it with his teeth.

The small salaries and long hours might have accounted for some of the unrest backstage. The chorus girls put in an eighty-hour week, including rehearsals and midnight shows on Saturdays, for twenty-one dollars. They supplied their own G strings. If they stepped out of the line to do a strip tease they supplied their music and costumes. For that they were paid five dollars extra. It was pointed out to them by the Minskys that most of the big burlesque stars began in the chorus.

Billy Minsky liked to have people know the chorus girls who worked for him were "good girls." One of them told me they were too tired to be anything else. "It takes time to be bad," she said, "and who the hell's got time?"

Abbott and Costello were featured in the show, along with Jimmy Dugan, Joey Faye and Jack Diamond. Besides the comics there were three straight men, talking women, a prima donna and eleven strip teasers.

Lou Costello and Bud Abbott had been playing a continued pinochle game in their dressing room for months. They kept score on the cardboards the laundry sent back in their shirts but the shirts weren't laundered frequently enough to keep up with the game, so they had begun keeping score on the dressing-room walls. By the time I joined the show the pinochle scores covered the walls and extended out into the hallway. There was a lot of time for pinochle between strip-tease numbers.

There were three, sometimes four talking women. Inez Worth was one of them. She also sang. Inez looked as though she might have belonged to a Long Island garden club, but when she was mad she sounded like a longshoreman. I knew a lot of swear words but Inez added flourishes to hers that made the stagehands blush.

Her mother, Myrtle, and my mother almost went into business to-gether but when they learned the local gangsters frowned on ladies selling home-made gin, even though it was direct from their own bathtubs, they went into the panoche fudge business instead. Mother was sure gangsters wouldn't muscle in on that; there was too little profit in it. In fact, there was so little profit in it that Myrtle and Mother dissolved partnership.

Mae Dix was a featured talking woman but she also did strips. She had been one of the biggest stars on the old Columbia wheel. At the height of her career, she told me, she gave it up and married an undertaker. Mae was bitter about those memories. "Three years it took me to learn his business," she said, "then the sonovabitch gets jealous because I'm a better embalmer than he is." She had divorced him and come back to burlesque. In her less bitter moments she was more philosophical. "The way things are in this business," she often said, "it's not a bad idea to have a sideline."

Nudina was the exotic dancer on the show. She danced with fans, balloons, doves or cockatoos, but her big specialty was the snake dance. The snake, a boa constrictor about six feet long, slept curled up in a washtub under the sink in the women's dressing room.

Nudina loved her snake. After the shows at night she took it to the hotel with her, where it slept on the foot of her bed. She took it with her in a box when she went to restaurants, too, and once when she was arrested at a stag party in Cleveland, she brought it into the courtroom with her. Two women spectators fainted dead away and the judge turned green, but the case was dismissed and Nudina always thought it was because the judge was an animal lover.

Mother didn't believe in fraternizing with performers on the bill. Making a few costumes for them from time to time was all right—the extra money came in handy—but Mother disapproved of back-stage friendships. Myrtle wasn't actually in the show so she didn't count. Inez was a real lady so she didn't count either, but Mother didn't trust the others. "And you know," she would say, "I'm a good judge of character.

I wasn't a good judge of character at all, but the moment Mother walked into the dressing room with Mr. Stephanus I felt uneasy.

He bowed low from his waist, then, with a quick click of his heels, raised my hand to his lips. Over his dark, sleek head, I looked questioningly at Mother; she usually discouraged that sort of thing, especially when the man was young and handsome. "Mr. Stephanus is a Rumanian," she said, as though that explained it. She cleared a chair for him near the make-up shelf and he sat down without taking his eyes from me.

I decided he was a painter. Mother had once brought another painter, Tade Styka, to the dressing room and he had looked at me in the same disturbing way. I hoped Mr. Stephanus didn't want me to pose in the nude as Tade Styka had. Mother had made such a scene that time three stagehands rushed in to throw the artist out.

"Mr. Stephanus came all the way from Rumania to find someone like you," Mother was saying. "He just caught the show and he couldn't believe his luck to find you on his first day in New York." The man nodded gravely, still gazing at me as Mother went on. "He was waiting for you in the alley. One word led to another and here he is!"

The dogs growled as the man jumped suddenly to his feet. "I am Lieutenant Stephanus in the personal guard of King Carol."

Mother acknowledged his bow, then motioned for him to sit down. "He wants us to go back to Rumania with him right away. He has pictures of the boat and everything."

With that Mr. Stephanus whipped a folder of the S.S. *Ile de France* from his inside pocket and, opening it up, spread it out on the dressing-room floor. "This," he said, pointing to a cabin on A deck, "will be your stateroom." He and Mother both studied the ship's plan for a moment, then, scooping up the folder and tucking it away in her purse as though it were a contract for the Roxy Theatre, Mother eased our guest to the door. "Wait for us out on the fire escape," she said. "Gypsy will get dressed and we'll go someplace and talk."

Mother decided the Chinese restaurant would be a good place. There were booths there and it was quiet. Besides she thought Mr. Stephanus, being a foreigner, would like the food. She ordered for all three of us; sub gum chow mein, fried rice and roast pork, then, giving the waiter the menu, she settled back comfortably in the yellow leatherette seat. "Now," she said, her eyes glittering with excitement, "tell Gypsy the plan just like you told it to me in the alley."

Mr. Stephanus cleared his throat and began, "We will sail the twelfth of July, four days from tomorrow. You must have all your papers proving you are American citizens. This is very important—" Mother tapped her fingers impatiently on the tablecloth; important papers were an old story to her.

"From France we will go directly to the King's summer palace near Bucharest. There will be rooms there for you and your mother. For several days you will be seen in the gardens, at the receptions, in the ballroom—"

"What kind of a show is it going to be?" I asked.

"It's not going to be a show," Mother said. "Don't interrupt. Let him tell it in his own way."

"In the evenings you will dance with the handsomest of all the King's guards. You will have lovely gowns, furs, jewels. . . . In this pocket," he said, patting his chest, "I have unlimited funds to buy you the loveliest frocks in all America. Everything like a bride—" He paused, then with a deep sigh went on. "How you will love the summer palace. Swans on the lake, trees with their branches trailing into the water, flowers everywhere, and the music—"

Mother interrupted him impatiently. "We don't care about all that," she said. "Get down to the exciting part."

"One night when you are dancing you will be introduced, informally, to the King. This does not have to be arranged. Once he sees you, a beautiful young American girl, he will insist on it. Then when you are dancing with him you will ask to see the garden by moonlight. He will take you through the garden doors and I shall be there to lead you to the car that will drive you across the border. In a week you will be back in New York."

"With five hundred dollars," Mother added, "and all those lovely clothes."

Somewhere along the line I had lost the point of the story. It was clear to me, in a way, up to where the King and I went into the garden but from there on I was confused. "What happens to the King?" I asked.

"The King," Mr. Stephanus replied, "will be dead." The table-cloth muffled the sound of the heel click, but there was nothing to hide the wild gleam in his eyes. "I shall kill him with my own hands. My country shall be free!"

The Chinese waiter placed the tray of food on the edge of the table and Mother helped him uncover the dishes. "You should hear some of the terrible things that King has done," she said, breathing in the aroma of the fried rice.

Mr. Stephanus, with a worried glance toward the waiter, warned Mother to keep her voice down. "There are spies everywhere," he said.

Mother smile at him indulgently. "They wouldn't dare bother an American citizen," she said. "You told me that yourself,"

"That is in Rumania," he replied. "Here, I cannot be sure."

Mother spooned out the food, dividing it equally on the three plates. For a few minutes we ate silently, then suddenly, with a worried frown, her fork in mid-air, Mother stopped eating. "Tell me," she asked, "does the King speak English?"

"Of course," Mr. Stephanus replied.

Mother sighed with relief. "I was a little worried," she said. "You see, Gypsy and I don't speak a word of Rumanian."

Mr. Stephanus walked back to the Cameo apartments with us. At the door, he bowed low and kissed Mother's hand, then mine. "Until tomorrow morning at nine," he said. "I shall pick you up and we'll go for your passports."

Mother and I were dressed and ready to leave at eight thirty the next morning, but Mr. Stephanus never appeared. We waited until matinee time, then we walked across the street to the theatre. "It's a good thing we didn't hand in our notice," Mother said as we walked up the stairs to the dressing room. "But I had a peculiar feeling about that plan of his. It was too good to be true."

After the show that night Inez was waiting for us at the foot of the stairs. She wore a black maline hat with pink roses on it and a black velvet dress cut very low in front. A pair of silver foxes were draped over her arm. She looked questioningly at my rust-colored dress with the Peter Pan collar and at Mother's knitted bouclé suit. "Did you forget about the party?"

"Of course not," Mother replied. "We've been looking forward to it."

Inez hesitated, then shrugging her bare shoulders walked a bit ahead of us down the street toward Eighth Avenue, trailing a scent of Black Narcissus. After a few blocks Inez slowed down, and waited until Mother and I caught up with her. Motioning for us to follow, she scooted into a dark entranceway and up a flight of stairs to a door with a peekhole in it.

The peekhole opened and a man's eye peered out at us. "We're friends of Tony's from the Republic," Inez said to the eye. "We've been invited to the beefsteak supper." The peekhole closed with a snap and the door opened just wide enough for us to squeeze through. Staying close to Inez, Mother and I walked into the brightly lighted restaurant, our eyes darting from side to side, our purses held close.

"So this is a speakeasy," Mother whispered, and I knew she was disappointed. So was I. A speakeasy sounded dangerous and exciting and this was an ordinary restaurant with checkered cloths and imitation flowers in glass vases on the tables. The people sitting around looked ordinary too. "Which ones are the gangsters and their molls?" I asked Inez, but she didn't hear me. She was heading for a long table at the end of the room where the burlesque performers sat. "The beer's flowing like water," Moey, the candy butcher, said, holding out a clear pitcher filled to the brim, froth spilling over the sides. "Pull up a rock and make yourselves at home!"

This was the first burlesque party Mother and I had been invited to. Every Saturday, between shows, there was a party in the dressing room on the other side of the stage: a pizza pie feast, or a Chinese supper washed down with containers of beer or gin and Nedick's pineapple juice. We could hear them all laughing and joking but we had never been asked to join them. If this was a typical party I didn't feel so badly about missing the others. There was a lot of laughing and joking, but it was a frenzied sort of laughter, and the jokes were mostly old burlesque bits.

Inez leaned over to Mother. "Don't look now," she said out of the corner of her mouth, "but Waxey Gordon just came in."

Mother looked where she was looking then back to Inez again. "Who's Waxey Gordon?" she asked.

"You never heard of him!" Inez exclaimed. "Why, he's one of the biggest racketeers in the country. He practically controls the whole state of Jersey. His beer goes through special pipelines in the sewers—"

Mother looked at the man again, this time with a bit more interest. I looked, too. There were five men sitting at the table, all of them but one wearing green fedoras pulled down over their eyes, and diamond-studded wrist watches. "Which one is he?" I asked.

"The short, fat one," Inez said without moving her lips.

I had seen gangsters before in Florida and others had been pointed out to me from time to time in the audience, but none of them looked like this one. If I had seen him behind a desk with telephones on it I would have thought he was a booking agent.

"He's one of the sweetest guys in the world," Inez was saying. "You can't imagine the charity he does—always helping somebody out—"

"I can imagine," Mother murmured.

"—and there he sits with four bodyguards, afraid somebody'll put a blast on him. . . ."

The waiter brought over four bottles of champagne and placed them on our table. "Compliments of Mr. W.," he said, and other waiters came running up with glasses and ice-filled buckets. "See?" Inez said. "What did I tell you? He's the biggest-hearted guy in the world."

Mother and I sipped the champagne and peeked from the corners of our eyes at the man with his bodyguards. He was looking at us, too, and after a while he got up and came over to our table. The four men followed him closely, their hands shoved in their coat pockets. When Waxey Gordon sat down with us they leaned against the wall, their eyes on the door.

"How's Myrtle?" Waxey Gordon asked Inez.

Using the edge of the tablecloth, she wiped a bit of rouge off one of the glasses and filled it with champagne. "Mother's just fine," she said, offering him the wine, which he refused. "I sell it," he said. "I don't drink it." Then Inez caught his look and added, "I'd like you to meet some friends of mine, Gypsy Rose Lee and her mother."

I tried to put feeling into my smile, but it wasn't easy. The body-guards with the bulging pockets made me too uncomfortable. "Thank you for the champagne," I managed to say. "I—I never tasted it before."

Waxey looked down at the diamond-and-ruby-studded watch on his wrist, then he crooked a finger at one of the waiters. "Give my friends here anything they want," he said. In a cloud of cigar smoke he got up and the bodyguards closed in around him. "Eat hearty," he told us. "You can't tell when you'll run into me again." The four men followed him across the room and out the door, their hands still in their pockets.

"Isn't he the sweetest guy you ever met?" Inez said.

The next morning our phone rang early. Half awake, I answered it. The voice was muffled. "No names," it said. "I'm calling for the friend you met last night. He wants you to go see Doc Kraus—got a pencil? Write this down, Sam Kraus at 1605 Broadway. You got an appointment there at ten thirty this morning to get your teeth straightened."

The phoned clicked in my ear and I looked over at Mother, who was sitting up in bed.

"Did you hear him?" I asked. "He wants me to go to a dentist."

"A dentist?" Mother said. "Who wants you to go? What dentist? I never heard of such a thing."

After the show that night the same man called again. "What happened?" he asked. "You didn't show up!" Mother took the receiver from me. "Now, just a moment," she said. "I don't understand this, but I don't like it. My daughter isn't going to any dentist we never heard of and can't afford to pay—"

"Who said anything about pay?" the man replied. I leaned over Mother's shoulder and listened as he went on. "This doc owes the boss plenty and if the boss wants you to get her teeth straightened you get 'em straightened if you know what's good for ya." The phone made an angry sound as it was slammed down on the other side. Mother waited a moment, then she placed the receiver back on the hook. "What did we do with the address of that dentist?" she said.

Doctor Kraus was expecting us. He was polite, but he was nervous, too, at first. Then, a few days later when he was drilling down my front teeth to make them fit under the porcelain jackets, he told us about Waxey Gordon. The grinding noise of the drill made his voice sound distant, but there was no mistaking the note of gratitude in it. "If it wasn't for Irving I wouldn't be practicing," he said.

"Irving?" Mother asked.

"That's his real name. We gave him the name Waxey when he was a kid on our block. He used to put wax on the end of a stick and poke it down the subway grills. There were always a lot of nickels and dimes down there and they'd stick to the wax—"

"Chewing gum is better," Mother said.

"He sent me through dental college. Paid everything—"

"Very interesting," Mother murmured. She leaned closer to him to make sure he knew what he was doing. His mention of college had disturbed her. Mother distrusted too much education. The dentist stopped drilling to change disks and Mother examined the new sandpaper wafer before he attached it to the machine.

"How much would a job like this cost?" she asked, pointing to my teeth. "Under different circumstances," I mean.

"Oh, about four hundred dollars," he replied. "Why?"

"I was just wondering." She handed me a paper cup filled with pink water. "Rinse, dear," she said.

Two weeks later the job was finished. My four new jackets looked exactly like real teeth. I couldn't eat corn on the cob with them, but, as Mother said, that was a small sacrifice to make for anything so lovely.

Inez was the first one backstage to notice my teeth. Before I had a chance to tell her how Waxey Gordon had arranged for the dentist, Mother interrupted with an explanation of her own. It was a pretty good explanation, considering how quickly she thought it up. In a way, the story was almost true, only in Mother's version it was Grandpa who put the dentist through college. "People," she said to me later, "can misconstrue an act of generosity."

30

THE BLUEPRINTS FOR the house in Rego Park, Long Island, were spread out on the dressing-room floor, and Mother was busily explaining them to me. "That half circle over there," she said, "is the entrance to the dining room—no, I guess that's the front door. Anyway, of all the houses I've seen—and you know, Louise, I've seen them all—this one is a steal. We pay only five hundred dollars down and the rest each month, like rent. The mortgage, carrying charges, everything, comes to about sixty-two dollars and seventy-eight cents a month. Just a few dollars more than we're paying for one room at the Cameo—besides, now that you're a star, you should live like one."

The kitchen, she said, was white Tilene, which was far superior to ordinary tile. A dinette table and four chairs went with the house. Upstairs there were three bedrooms and a lavender-and-sea-green bathroom, with a glassed-in shower. "You've never seen anything so luxurious," Mother said. "The tub, sink, even the toilet is green!"

"How much is it?" I asked.

Mother fumbled around through the blueprints and brochures until she found a photograph of a string of houses all identical and attached. "It's the end house," she said. "That's why it costs more than the others."

"What does it cost?" I repeated.

"Eight thousand, eight hundred and eighty-eight dollars, but we have twenty years to pay for it—all we really pay is sixty-two—"

"You've already bought it, haven't you, Mother?"

"Well, yes, I have. We can move in next week. You'll love it, dear. As the man said, it's the key to gracious living."

We had no furnishings besides a few hotel towels and the camping equipment, but the real-estate agent was taking care of that. He had a friend in the business who was going to get us everything at wholesale prices. In the meantime Mother slept on the army cot and I slept on blankets on the floor. Mother took the big front room—she explained it would be too noisy for me—and I moved into the one in back. The third bedroom she said would come in handy if Grandpa or Big Lady should visit us. Even though Mother didn't say it, I knew she meant that room for June.

Our wardrobe trunks were opened against the walls. Apple boxes served as bedside tables. We had the tins cups and plates from our camping equipment and the car blankets for our beds. As Mother said, we had the necessities. The luxuries would come later.

The first luxury was a grandfather's clock with a radio in it. Mother put it cater-cornered in the dining room, where we had moved the dinette set, so she could listen to Myrt and Marge without interrupting dinner. Next she bought a large white numdah rug with flowers profusely embroidered on it for the living room. The flowers would help hide the dog stains. My books, which had always seemed so many to me, filled only one shelf of the built-in bookcase. They were held together with two plaster figures of sleeping Mexicans. A sofa and an end table with a lamp on it completed the living room.

Mother planted grass seed on the lumpy dry dirt surrounding the house, and we moved our scenery and the cow head and the walking dolls and gilded guns into the unfinished basement. "At last," Mother said, "we have a home of our own!"

Mother found a bed for my room in a big furniture store. From her description it was exactly what I wanted: maple, and with a canopy. It was twenty-five dollars without springs or a mattress, which seemed expensive until Mother explained that it was an antique. "The salesman assured me it was," she said. "He told me it had been in the store when he first went to work there and that was over seven years ago."

Anything that hadn't been made that week was an antique to Mother, but we bought the bed anyway. That is, we paid five dollars down on it and agreed to pay the balance in easy installments.

Being home owners had its disadvantages. The most unpleasant one had to do with taxes. The man came to see us before we had time to unpack. He was polite but firm. He wanted proof we had paid our income tax. "Income tax?" Mother said. "What's that?"

The man looked at Mother for a moment, then decided she was serious. Pulling a sheaf of papers from his brief case, he began explaining how we were to fill out the forms.

Mother was losing her patience with him. There was a lot of unpacking to do and not much time before we had to leave for the matinee. "I've never heard of income tax," she said, "and I have no intentions of paying anything. My daughter and I have trouble enough keeping our heads above water without paying for a lot of things we don't need."

She helped the momentarily bewildered man put away the forms, and, taking his arm, led him toward the kitchen door. "It's very kind of you to try and help us," she said, "and believe me, if I ever go in for that sort of thing I'll get in touch with you."

"You mean you've never paid income tax?" the man said. "*Never?*"

Mother had the kitchen door open now, and stood beside it tapping her foot. "I don't believe in taxes for show people," she said. "What chance do we have to use the schools or things they build with the money? Right is right. And if you're smart you'll get out of this tax-collecting business. There's no future in it." She eased him through the door, then just before closing it in his face she added, "Remember the Boston tea party!"

"He'll be back," I said.

Mother went on hanging up the tin cups in the cupboard. "Maybe," she agreed, "but I'll be ready for him." She placed a hotel towel on a rack near the sink. "The nerve of him," she said. "Next thing you know they'll expect us to vote."

We were more careful in the future when we opened the door to strangers. A few days later when the bell rang, Mother stopped me with an imperious hand. But it wasn't the tax man after all. It was Western Union with a two-page telegram asking me to play a benefit. Mother read it, then handed it to me.

"I have no objections to playing a benefit," she said, "but a benefit in a prison—for convicts—I'm not sure they'd appreciate your work."

"Your presence," I read, "is urgently requested to make this benefit for the inmates of Comstock Prison an outstanding show for a most worthy cause. Among those who have kindly consented to appear are Jimmy Durante, Al Jolson, Lupe Velez, Bill Robinson, Jack Osterman, Mark Hellinger. . . ." It was the last name on the list that interested me most: Florenz Ziegfeld. The signature on the telegram was interesting, too, but in a different way. It was signed "W."

"He must be putting on the show," Mother said with a puzzled frown. "You'd think in his business he'd stay as far from prisons as he could." Then she read the telegram again and looked very hard at the name Florenz Ziegfeld. "We'll play it," she said. "You can do your audience number. I'm sure none of those other acts will do anything like that."

We were to leave the following Monday at midnight. Private cars would be attached to the train that would take us upstate and wait to bring us back. It meant missing a matinee and night performance but Mother was sure Billy Minsky would understand.

She bought me a red velvet dress for the occasion. It had a jacket to match, with a narrow band of ermine around the collar. Red velvet streamers tied in a bow at the neck. Mother wore her bouclé knitted suit and a fur cape, cut down from the old beaver coat.

Monday night, after the show, a black sedan picked us up at Minsky's and took us to the station. From there we were directed to a dining car, which had been hooked onto the train especially for our group. A buffet table was heaped with flowers and food: glazed hams, turkeys, bright red lobsters, bowls of fruit and salad and olives. Silver buckets held the largest bottles of champagne I had ever seen. At the far end of the car an orchestra played loudly. It was as though the dining car had been transformed into a night club.

Mother and I, with my music and costume in our arms, squeezed through the crowd and found ourselves a place near the glazed turkeys. No one had started eating yet, but when they did we wanted to be close by.

The dining car smelled of flowers and food and expensive perfume and cigars. Mink- and silver-fox-clad women waved diamond-studded arms at one another and laughed shrilly at nothing. Everyone it seemed, knew everyone else. But Mother and I couldn't recognize any of the stars we expected to see. Men in polo coats and striped suits brushed against others in tuxedos. There was an anxiety in their faces that reminded me of Woolly Face when he saw a banana. The train began to move and a hush fell. Four men, their hats pulled down over their faces, hands shoved in their pockets, pushed open the door and cleared a path for Waxey Gordon. The orchestra stopped in the middle of "You're Blasé" and went into a chorus of "He's a Jolly Good Fellow." A few uncertain voices sang the lyrics.

Smiling over his cigar, and surrounded by bodyguards, Waxey Gordon walked the length of the diner. Mother waved at him. "Here we are!" she sang out. "Right on time!"

"Well," he said to me, "I see you have a bodyguard, too."

Mother gave me a little shove. "Smile, dear," she said, "and show him how nice your teeth look."

Burning with embarrassment, I stood there grimacing while he examined the four porcelain jackets. "Keep 'em brushed good," he said, then he disappeared in the crowd.

"What a sweetheart of a guy," someone whispered loudly. "This junket'll probably cost him twenty gees."

"I'll gladly take ten per cent of what it costs him *over* that," another voice answered. "And what do you wantta bet there won't be a word about it in the papers? That's the kind of a guy he is."

A waiter began carving one of the turkeys and Mother pushed her way closer to the table. Holding my costume over her arm, she balanced two plates while a waiter filled them with food. Later, when the waiter wasn't looking, she slid a few slices of turkey into a napkin for the dogs. We had left them alone with the monkey in the new house and I knew she was worried about them. She was worried about the benefit the next day, too, and so was I. "Powder My Back" didn't seem quite the number for me to do on a bill with stars like these.

"It will be all right," she said when I mentioned it to her. "We've had tough competition before and we've come out on top. Mark my words, you'll be the hit of the show."

At the prison the next day we followed the crowd to the auditorium, where dressing rooms were assigned to us. The stage was well equipped with scenery and lights, and I was relieved to see there were steps leading into the audience. I unpacked my make-up and the prop powder puff and Mother hung up my red net costume. Considering how crowded it was backstage there was order of a sort. The stage manager, who was a trusty, had made up the program and, glancing down the list of names, I looked to see where I was on the bill. My name wasn't there. I looked again to make sure. "There must be some mistake," I said to the trusty. "My name isn't on the list." He whipped a pencil from his pocket while he was apologizing. "There were so many—"

"It's quite all right," I said. "The name is Gypsy Rose Lee."

He began writing, then stopped. An embarrassed flush covered his face. "But you—that is—didn't they tell you?"

"Tell us what?" Mother asked, joining us in the hallway outside the dressing room.

"The warden, he—well, he figured a burlesque dancer wasn't exactly—" He was backing away from us, and I knew when he could he would make a break for it and run. Mother reached out and held him by the shirt. "Are you trying to tell me they don't want my daughter to go on?" she demanded.

"It's the men," he said, trying to free himself. "You see they aren't used to seeing strip dancers and—"

"Strip dancers!" Mother shrieked. "My daughter has never danced a step in her life! She's a star! Let that warden tell me to my face that he won't allow us to go on! I'll sue him for every cent he owns. Where is he? He won't get away with this."

The other dressing-room doors were opening and people were sticking their heads out. I grabbed Mother's arm and made her let go of the trusty, who ran as fast as he could down the hall; then I tried to urge her back into our room.

"Please come inside, Mother. If you'll just be quiet, they won't even miss us, but if you make it a scene everyone will know."

Mother shook her fist at the empty hall. "Someday," she said dramatically, "someday they'll beg you to play a benefit for them."

Later, when she calmed down, Mother tried to look at it from the warden's point of view. "In a way, I guess he's right," she admitted. "He doesn't want to waste all that stuff they keep putting in the prisoners' food."

Wearing my red net costume I waited in the wings as though ready to go on. Mother, holding the powder puff, stood by. I had been right. No one missed us at all. When the show had been running for over three hours, the warden decided the prisoners had been entertained enough. Someone blew a whistle and I was pushed on stage with fifty other performers, many like me who hadn't been on either. The orchestra played "Auld Lang Syne" and we all bowed to the gray-clad audience with the numbers on their shirts. Mother told me later it was the saddest thing she ever saw. "They cried, Louise," she said. "Hardened criminals and they cried like babies."

The train trip back to New York was less festive. The buffet was as lavish, the champagne as plentiful and the orchestra as loud, but the gaiety was gone. The guests were quiet and thoughtful and rather ill at ease. I knew exactly how they felt. The audience had done it to us. Not that they hadn't been enthusiastic; in fact, I hadn't heard such applause since the time at Minsky's when we played a show for the pile drivers' convention, but this had been different. It was a defiant, sullen applause. During the finale I had looked out at their faces and wondered what they had done to be there. I knew there were thieves, murderers, kidnapers among them and suddenly I was afraid and I was so very glad I hadn't done "Powder My Back."

"Never again," Mother breathed. "The next time we play a benefit we'll be paid for it." The dining car had emptied out early and she was busily scooping up bits of left-over food from the platters. The waiters were too weary to protest as she wrapped up slices of ham and turkey in the napkins and shoved them into the music case.

"That's enough, Mother," I said. "The dogs will never be able to eat all that!"

"Dogs nothing," she said. "This is for us."

She was reaching for a lobster claw when Waxey Gordon walked in with a group of men, his bodyguards behind them. The train lurched and as it did the claw dropped from Mother's hand into a bowl of olives. I made a frantic wish that she would leave it there, but smiling gaily she dipped into the bowl and retrieved the claw. "The dogs adore lobster," she said, adding it to her collection in the napkin.

"It was the greatest show I ever saw," one of the men said to Waxey Gordon. "You oughtta produce it on Broadway." Waxey shrugged. "I'll invest in 'em," he said, "but I won't produce 'em."

He clapped his hands at a waiter, who came scurrying over. "Champagne for everyone," he ordered, "and a bottle of Perrier for me." Then he turned to one of the men. "How about using Gypsy in your show?" Five pairs of eyes looked at me. "She's as good looking as some of the other dames you got." He added, "besides, she's a friend of mine."

I held my breath as the man he was talking to looked me over. He was shorter than I; his cigar came to my shoulder. He wore a cocoa-brown suit that looked soft and expensive and a shirt with a pleated front. "Eleven o'clock tomorrow morning at the Ziegfeld Theatre," he said. "Bring your bathing suit."

"Are you—Flo Ziegfeld?" Mother whispered.

"He's Lew Brown, the song writer," Waxey Gordon said. "Don't ask questions. Just do as you're told. Now go on, both of you. We got business to talk over."

Mother and I walked in a daze through the cars to our compartment. The berths had been made up and I climbed into the upper with my clothes on; the train was due in New York in a few hours. Lying back on the cold hard pillow I tried to remember exactly what had happened, but I couldn't. I knew I had to report at the Ziegfeld Theatre, but for what show, I wondered. And who was Lew Brown?

"Mother?" I whispered. "Are you awake?"

"Of course I am," Mother said irritably. "Who could sleep on this noisy train! Other people, I notice, have drawing rooms and here we are cooped up in a compartment—"

"If Lew Brown is just a song writer how could he get me into the *Follies?*"

"Go to sleep," Mother said. "You heard what Waxey told us. Don't ask questions."

At eleven sharp the next morning Mother and I were at the Ziegfeld Theatre. The doorman directed us to a change room, where I put on my bathing suit, then with my coat over it, I went out onto the stage and joined a group of girls lined up at the footlights. There were only a few of them wearing bathing suits and I was glad I had put on my coat. Most of them wore dresses and suits. Diamonds glittered on their hands and arms and chests as they stood in the harsh glare of the work light that hung from the flies. They were unbelievably beautiful, and they knew it.

"Straighten out the line," the dance director said. His name was Bobby Connelly. I knew that because I had seen him on the train. I recognized his assistant, Sammy Lederman, too; they had both been with Lew Brown when he told me to report at the theatre. Their eyes went past me now as though they had never seen me before. "Hey, you, on the end," his assistant said to me, "straighten out that line." Then running back and forth in front of us he began writing down our names on a clip board. A red-haired girl down the line spoke her name, "Hope Dare," and the girl next to her said, "Boots Mallory"; the next girl giggled, "Oh, Sammy, you know all of us—" He must have given her a look because she stopped giggling. "Virginia Bruce," she said and he scratched away on the pad. "Jean Howard—Joan Burgess—Lorelle McCarver," then he was in front of me. "Name?" he asked.

I hesitated an instant. "Rose Louise," I said.

The moment I said it I was sorry. He knew who I was, and he'd think I was ashamed of my burlesque name. I wanted to take it back but I didn't. I *was* ashamed and the realization made it worse.

He stepped aside so the men in the audience could see us.

There were murmurs coming from the black void in front of me. I could see the outlines of men's faces and here and there a pair of feet resting against the velvet-covered orchestra rail. One of the shadows was Flo Ziegfeld. Perhaps at that very moment he was looking at me. I let my tweed coat fall open and I could feel a rivulet of perspiration roll down my arm. More than I had ever wanted anything in all my life, I wanted to be chosen for that Ziegfeld show.

One by one the girls were told to step forward or back. They moved slowly. Their necks were stretched taut, eyebrows arched and stomachs held in. Not one of them smiled. They looked as though they didn't care if they were chosen or not, but as their names were called I could feel them tense. Then I heard my name and I stepped forward. From the corner of my eye I looked down the line. There were nine of us. The others had been dismissed. "Same time tomorrow," the assistant said. "The Equity man will be here with your contracts. It'll be a long day so don't make any dates."

The girls drifted away and I waited a moment, then hurried to catch up with the dance director, who was walking toward the steps leading into the audience. "I beg your pardon," I said, "but does that mean I'm in the show? Am I in the *Follies?*"

"*Follies?* We aren't doing the *Follies.* This is a book show *Laid in Mexico.*"

"But I thought—I hoped it was a Ziegfeld show—"

He looked at me as though I were joking. "It *is* a Ziegfeld show. Don't you read the papers?"

He went down into the audience and I knew he was going to tell the men there what I had said. I ducked into the wings and waited in agonized embarrassment for them to laugh. Mother hurried across the stage to me. "We made it, dear," she cried. "I knew we'd do it. Hurry, dear, and get dressed. I have to talk to Ziggy about your contract."

A blonde girl, who hadn't been chosen, was the only one in the change room. She had taken off her bathing suit and was tucking her full breasts into a wispy black lace brassière. "Not one of the broads in that line had a shape like mine," she muttered angrily. I glanced at what was hanging over the top of her brassière and silently agreed with her. "Nobody gets in a show like this unless they know somebody," she said. "Not that I give a damn if I'm chosen or not. It's my boy friend's idea. He thinks having his girl in the *Follies* makes him look like class—"

"It isn't the *Follies*," I said. "It's a show named *Laid in Mexico*."

The blonde pulled her head through the neck of her black satin dress. "What? *Laid in Mexico*! For crissake, I might as well be working for Minsky."

"They're changing the name," Mother said calmly. "I was talking to the doorman. They're going to call it *Hot-Cha*! and they've already signed up Bert Lahr and Lupe Velez and Buddy Rogers— and Gypsy Rose Lee."

The blonde put on a silver-fox coat that came to her knees and slammed a red pouf of a hat on her bleached head. "Well they can have it," she said, snatching up her bag and gloves. "I'm more the Earl Carroll type anyway."

Waxey Gordon took Mother and me to La Hiff's Tavern after the show at the Republic that night. We sat in a booth. The four bodyguards were at a table nearby where they could keep their eyes on the doors. While the waiter took our orders I felt around in my purse for the roll of bills Mother had placed there. We had rehearsed exactly what I was to say and after the waiter left I began. "We can't ever repay you for helping me get in the Ziegfeld show," I said, "but we can pay you back for the dentist." I put the rolls of bills on the table in front of Waxey Gordon. "We can't pay it back all at once, but we can give you a little each week. There's twenty-five dollars on account."

Waxey Gordon picked up the roll of bills and unsnapped the elastic band. "I oughtta frame these," he said, counting the money. "It's the first time anybody ever paid me back anything."

Mother took one last look at the money before he put it in his pocket. "We don't owe a penny to a living soul," she said, not quite truthfully. But of all the bills we owed, Mother and I decided this one had to be paid first. It wasn't exactly gratitude; we wanted to be on the safe side. As Mother said, we didn't want to find ourselves floating down the East River with our feet in a cake of cement.

"At twenty-five a week," Mother was saying, "we figure it will take us twelve weeks to pay you back."

"How come?" Waxey Gordon asked.

"The dentist told us the bill would be four hundred," Mother said, very businesslike, "but considering all you've done for him I decided three hundred would be plenty."

On our way home Mother sat stiff and straight in the worn leather scoop seat of the secondhand Charnard Weckler we had traded in the old car for. It was a bright-yellow French car shaped like an old-fashioned bathtub. Under the snub-nosed hood were four toylike cylinders that made the noise of a Mack truck pulling up a steep hill. "It takes all kinds of people to make a world," Mother said, pitching her voice an octave above the motor. "Why, I couldn't believe my eyes when he took that money."

"But—we gave it to him." I said.

"We did nothing of the kind," Mother replied. "We *offered* it, but I certainly didn't expect him to be cheap enough to take it."

A soft snow was falling and the thin tires skidded on the upgrade of the Queensboro Bridge. "Shift into second," Mother commanded. With a grinding noise the gears fell into position and Mother sat back. "What a lucky girl you are," she said with a contented sigh. "Here you are, seventeen years old, with everything in the world a girl could ask for. . . . Just think of it! We have our own home, our teeth are straightened and we're in the Ziegfeld *Follies*—"

"*Laid in Mexico*," I said.

"Yes—" Mother replied uneasily. "I certainly hope Ziggy changes that title. It *does* sound Minskyish."

ACT THREE

3 1

THERE WAS A TRACE
of dead-white powder on Mother's face as she strode into my
Gramercy Park apartment carrying a wilted bunch of dahlias, a
net shopping bag filled with jars of home-made jelly, and Solly,
her favorite rooster, wrapped in a pink baby blanket. Bootsie and
Runty, the two poodles, scampered in behind her. Dropping everything but the rooster on the nearest table, she eyed me appraisingly.
"You look awful, dear. Has anything happened?"

"Mother, you saw me yesterday. What can happen overnight?"

Raising an eyebrow for an answer, Mother began unwrapping
the rooster. "Solly's been limping again," she said. "I'm taking him
to the veterinary."

"Don't put him down on the Aubusson rug!" The moment the
words were out of my mouth I regretted them. Mother's mouth
tensed as she held the rooster, his feet barely touching the rug. "I
guess he's not good enough for such a grand apartment," she
said. "Neither of us are. All we're good for is to work like horses on
that farm of yours. Day in and day out—"

"I didn't mean that at all, Mother." I tried to keep the impatience
from my voice, but it was after ten. My hair wasn't done, I wasn't
made up and the photographers were due at eleven. "You know
very well it isn't *my* farm. It's our farm. You're the one who wanted
it. You're the one who bought it. I'm just the one who paid for it."

"That's beside the point," Mother replied. "Could one of the staff make me a cup of coffee? I was so upset about Solly I didn't take time for breakfast."

"No one is in yet," I said. "I'll make it."

"Oh, I'll make it myself," Mother replied. Carrying Solly, she headed for the kitchen, leaving faint mud prints on the rug. "Four servants on the payroll and no one to make a cup of coffee. We were better off when we were eating at the Dew Drop Inn." The kitchen door swung closed on the hem of her mink coat and she pulled it free with an angry gesture.

I unpacked the jars of jelly and put the wilted dahlias in a vase. When Mother left I would throw them out. Even though I had planted them myself I hated them. The label on the clumps had promised they would be pale yellow, but instead they were a violent orange with maroon flecks. It had been the same with everything I planted around the country house. The hollyhocks were rusty and hungry-looking, the sunflowers came up like rangy trees. The peonies didn't come up at all. Mother had told me one either had a green thumb or one hadn't. Then, trying to soften her words, she had added, "After all, dear, you can't have everything."

She had told me the same thing about the garden in Rego Park but the bank foreclosed the mortgage before I had a chance to find out if I had a green thumb or not. Mother blamed me for losing the house. We lost it, she said, because of my stubbornness. Had I left Ziegfeld's *Hot-Cha!* when I knew how small the salary was, we wouldn't have gone so deeply in debt. She thought we might have saved the house had I gone back to Minsky's immediately after the Ziegfeld show closed, but instead, according to Mother, I had wasted weeks making the rounds trying to get into another Broadway show. She might have been right, because when I finally did go back to burlesque our nest egg was gone. The money bag was flat and the Minskys knew it. Instead of the $150 I had been earning when I left I went back for $100. Billy Minsky was dead and his brothers were running the theatre. Business, they told us, was very bad. Too many of our old customers were on street corners, selling apples. My salary, after a few weeks, dropped to $75, then to $50, plus $25 in I.O.U.'s, which were to be paid back when business picked up. The bank, holding our mortgage, wasn't interested in accepting Minskys' I.O.U.'s. They served us with a dispossess notice and three months later we were served again. This time with eviction papers.

As a last resort Mother had thought of asking Waxey Gordon for a loan. Considering how we had paid back the dentist money, at least part of it, she was sure he would trust us, but we didn't know where to find him. Later we learned he was in Lewisburg prison. It had been on the front pages of all the papers, but neither Mother nor I read the front pages. We read our news in *Variety* or *Billboard* or the columns. It was a shock to Mother to learn Waxey was serving eleven years for evading his income tax. She couldn't believe it. "They can't put you in jail for *that!*" she said. "If they could we'd be serving time ourselves."

When we were finally evicted, Mother and I were almost reconciled to losing the house. The lavender tiles were falling off the bathroom walls. The roof leaked. The Tilene in the kitchen had turned yellow and everywhere we looked there was something that needed repair. It didn't take us long to pack. In the two years we had lived in the house we had never really unpacked. Our wardrobe trunks were still opened against the walls in our bedrooms. The bureau drawers and clothes closets were almost empty. Habits of a lifetime aren't easily broken.

The furniture was no problem, either. We owed so many payments that the furniture company took care of moving it for us— right back to their warehouse. The few pieces we had salvaged were sent to the large, gloomy apartment Mother had rented on upper Broadway, and leased under a different name.

We left Rego Park late at night to avoid any unpleasantness. Mother tied the keys of the house to the front-door knob and we tiptoed away down the cement walk. As she said, we weren't trying to get away with anything. The bills would be paid eventually. By the light of the taxi we could see the yellowed lawn with the bare patches of dirt showing through. The two conical cedar trees at either side of the door were brown and scraggly, like the Christmas trees my sister and I used to troupe when we were on the Orpheum Circuit.

The cow head, tent, dancing dolls and gilded guns were already loaded on the taxi along with our suitcases and the monkey's case and the dogs' bags. The trunks had gone on ahead with the odds and ends of furniture. Mother took one last look at the house before she got into the taxi. "We've learned our lesson," she sighed. "Civilian life just isn't for us."

That year I went into George White's *Melody*. I had six lines in the show but managed to pad my part by saying "Ouch" when my bustle caught in the door on my exit. We opened in New York during the bank moratorium, and my salary, which had been one hundred a week, dropped to fifty. A few weeks after the banks closed, the show closed, and I went back to Minsky's again. Then Billy Rose opened a night club called the Casino de Paree and I went to work for him for sixty-five a week. I had a few lines in that show, too. I introduced three of the vaudeville acts: Eleanor Powell, Jimmy Durante and the dance team Gomez and Winona. There was no chance of padding my part with Billy Rose. He wanted a straightforward announcement and a subdued exit. "Like a white zombie," he said. "No sly winks or dropping of the shoulder strap." To make certain his orders were carried out, he would be backstage every show. He was married to Fanny Brice in those days, and one night when she was in the audience he came back just before I went on to announce the entrance of Gomez and Winona, the dance team. "Do a good show," he said with unusual cheerfulness. "Fanny Brice, one of the biggest stars in the business, is watching you." My knees went wobbly, and my mouth got dry. Would she remember me? I wondered. Would she recognize me?

She was sitting at one of the ringside tables, a sable scarf on her shoulders and diamonds on her arms. I tried not to look at her as I smiled my brightest smile, then, clearing my voice, I said, "And now may we present Wimez and Ginona!"

Billy Rose was waiting for me in the wings. "Get your money," he said. "You're through."

Now I was back in burlesque. For thirty-nine straight weeks I had played the Irving Place Theatre, off Fourteenth Street. Our bills were paid, we had a country house and a small annuity and I had my own apartment and Eddy.

An enlarged snapshot of him taken on his tennis court smiled back at me from a silver frame. I had never seen him on the tennis court but I could imagine how he would play: not gracefully, but with great flourishes and wasted gestures. I could imagine his long legs, muscles taut, as he ran to strike out at the ball and his little-boy disappointment should he miss. Back of the snapshot, in the same frame, were seven others; I changed them from day to day. One was of Eddy with three of his collection of antique cars, a Stutz Bearcat roadster, a Rolls Royce sports touring car, a Kissell, and Eddy, immaculate in his white sweater, standing in front of them, his tanned, almost too handsome face wearing a proud, pleased smile as though he himself had built them. There was another snapshot of him with his dogs, six Dobermans, one at the swimming pool, and another of him in front of his house that had nine bathrooms and looked like a summer hotel.

Opening a drawer in the table I hid the snapshots. The news-papermen might be inquisitive, and Eddy had a reason for not wanting publicity. The morning sun was pouring through the terrace doors. I opened them wide and stood there with my arms out-stretched and felt the warmth through my velvet dressing robe. How good it was, I thought, to be alive, to be in love and to be working.

My eyes traveled with pride over the living room. I had decorated it myself, with only the least bit of help from the antique dealers along Third Avenue. The blackamoors at the door didn't exactly match the period of the Chippendale sofa, and the Victorian chairs, upholstered in salmon-pink velour, might have clashed with the deep-red satin draperies held back from the windows with gold cherubs in flight, but as Elmo, from the Flea Market, remarked, "It's amusing, and its *you!*"

Mother came in from the kitchen, carrying a tray of coffee and cups and saucers. "I gave Solly a bowl of water," she said cheerfully. "It would have done your heart good to see him lap it up."

The rooster, following her, pecked at the flowers woven into the rug. He was a pure-bred Moroccan with large clumps of feathers on his feet. I had paid forty dollars for him because he was what Mother called the nucleus of her chicken farm. With Solly and ten hens she had planned on going into the egg business, but with his bad leg he hadn't been able to do much of that type work. The egg business had collapsed along with several other money-making schemes, including jelly that didn't jell, turkeys that didn't thrive and guinea pigs that didn't multiply. The barn was filled with slightly used brooders, feeding trays, watering pans and cases of brand-new jelly jars.

Now Mother was taking in paying guests. At three dollars a head per night six women slept in the converted hay loft, four others occupied my room, there were four more on the sun porch and three in what used to be the maid's room. There were no servants. Mother said they were more bother to her than they were worth and she'd rather have the money. She convinced her guests that part of the fun on a farm was pitching in and doing the work. Between them they had reroofed the barn, painted the chicken coop and widened the driveway. It was all good, wholesome outdoor activity, Mother said, and slenderizing besides.

"How are things at the farm?" I asked. Mother looked at me over her cup. "The usual complaints. I sometimes wonder if it's worth it. It's supposed to be a milk farm, Louise, but from the way those women guzzle you'd think it was a beer farm."

I went into the bedroom to put on my make-up and Mother followed me in. She smoothed out the pink satin bedspread before she sat down. "Louise, dear," she said, "do you remember that nice Mr. Gebhardt I told you about? The one who wanted to invest in my guinea pigs?"

"I'll never forget him," I said, remembering too well the scene he made in my dressing room the night he demanded his money back.

"Well, he called me yesterday and said he was serving us with a writ or something. He said I used the mails to—oh, what is the expression—?"

"Defraud?"

Mother's face lit up. "Why, yes," she said with a happy smile. "It's wonderful how you know all those things. I sometimes wish you'd had more schooling—who knows what you might have become?"

"What about Mr. Gebhardt?" I asked, rubbing the grease paint on my face and blending it in.

"Oh yes. Well, he said that when I advertised in the papers for a partner I let myself in for something or other and now he wants a hundred dollars."

"I already gave him a hundred. That's all he invested in the first place—"

"I know, dear," Mother said patiently, "but he says I mandamused something, and the extra hundred is for the inconvenience he suffered."

"I won't give it to him," I said flatly. "I'm sick and tired of being blackmailed by these partners of yours. He knew very well what he was investing in. Four guinea pigs—"

"They were very special guinea pigs," Mother said reprovingly. "And one of them was pregnant. Why, if they hadn't caught bronchitis we would have cleaned up." She sipped her coffee thoughtfully. "Mr Gebhardt can be very difficult," she said. "And he does have the law on his side."

I went over and moved the slipper chair and lifted up the loose end of the carpet. From the money I had hidden there I gave Mother two fifties. "Please, Mother, no more investments?"

Mother reached under her dress for the shabby old money belt. She felt around carefully for a flat pocket, then tucked the two bills into it. "Oh, yes," she said, "I almost forgot about the twenty-five dollars for the lawyer."

I gave her the extra money. "Get a receipt," I said.

"Of course I will," Mother snapped. "Do you think I'm crazy?" She smoothed her dress down over the money belt and picked up her cup of coffee. "How's Eddy?"

"Oh, he's fine."

"And how's his wife?"

"She's fine, too—I guess."

Mother sighed comfortably. She let her eyes wander around the room until they fell on the orchid plant. Seven pale blooms clung to a piece of bark. The sun filtered through the delicate petals, showing their tracery. Mother made a clucking noise with her tongue. "It must have cost him fifty dollars."

"Seventy-five," I said. "He told me so."

"Too bad he didn't give you the money instead," Mother said peevishly. "Not that he isn't generous, but things like this are such a waste."

"It gives him pleasure," I murmured.

"How like a man," Mother replied "Always thinking of himself."

I powdered over the grease paint, and began outlining my lips with a brush. When they were done I patted them with the make-up towel. "I'm having pictures taken," I said to Mother's inquisitive look. They're due almost any minute."

Mother shrugged. "Every time I pick up a paper or a magazine I see your pictures in it. I know it's good for business and all that, but I think people are getting tired of looking at the same old face."

There was a moment's silence while Mother thought over what she had said. "I didn't mean that exactly. What I mean is that there's such a thing as too much publicity. If you were in a Broadway show it would be different, but all this talk, talk, talk about you being in burlesque—why don't they ever mention how you headlined on the Orpheum Circuit?"

"June did that," I replied. "I didn't."

"But you were there, dear. She couldn't have done the act by herself. The proof is what has she done these last few years besides have a baby? There she is, working in that ridiculous barn of a theatre, way out in the country—"

"She's learning to act," I said evenly. "She's learning what she wanted to learn when she was a child."

"I don't like your tone," Mother said. "Both you and your sister get that edge to your voices every now and then and I don't like it. You had every chance in the world to learn when you were children. Why, the acts we worked on the bill with—"

"You don't learn how to act by osmosis."

"And that's enough of that kind of language, too," Mother said.

The photographer, along with a reporter, arrived before I had finished doing my hair. Mother let them in the apartment. The dogs yapped, and I could her her voice. "They won't bite—in fact, they have no teeth. This is the little mother and the other one is

her baby—down, Runty. Bootsie—shut up! If you just wait in the
hallway I'll lock them in the kitchen." There was a scuffling noise,
then Mother with the two men stood in the doorway of the bedroom.

"Louise, dear," she said, "the newspapermen are here. I'll get
them some coffee or a drink while you finish your make-up."

I twisted my hair into a chignon and pinned on a matching
switch, then I ran a comb through my bangs. I didn't have to dress
because the pictures were to be taken in the bathtub. With a quick
last look in the mirror I hurried out to the sitting room.

". . . General Neville gave Gypsy the mother dog when she was
a little girl headlining on the Orpheum Circuit—" Mother was
saying, and the reporter was making notes on a piece of yellow
paper. "She's a trained dog—"

"Would you gentlemen care to see the bathroom?" I asked. Leading the way, I threw open the door. It was done in black and gold.
The wall paper was a design of powder puffs on sticks with gold
bows between. The bathtub, sink and toilet were gilded. The
shower curtain was black lace. The towels were gold with a huge
G embroidered on them in black. "It has a Renaissance quality,
hasn't it?" I murmured.

The men didn't answer me. They were staring at the mink bath-
mat and matching toilet-seat cover. Mother pushed her way past
them. "Louise!" she gasped. "That's your old mink coat! How
could you do such a thing? Why, that's the first thing Eddy ever
gave you!"

One of the men cleared his throat and Mother turned to him
apologetically. "I guess I'm just a sentimentalist," she murmured.
"Souvenirs mean so much to me—"

I turned on the water tap and poured in a handful of soap flakes.
The men turned their heads as I slipped out my dressing robe and
into the bubbles. Mother snatched up the robe while the photographer focused his camera. "Lift up one leg like you're washing,"
he said. I lifted the leg through the bubbles and held it high as I
smiled in his direction. "Big eyes, dear," Mother said.

"Pretty snappy apartment," the reporter said. "Must have cost
plenty."

"My dear husband left us comfortably fixed," Mother murmured.
"So I see," he replied.

"He was a noted explorer. Alaska, you know. This nugget was
the last thing he ever gave me." She fingered the gold nugget hanging from a chain around her neck that she had bought in a pawnshop on Eighth Avenue. "I always wear it," she said softly.

"What about Broadway?" the reporter asked me. Have you any
ambition to do a big show?"

"We've been in three of them," Mother replied before I had a
chance to answer. "They were all musical comedies, though, and
Gypsy is more of an actress than the public realizes. Leonard Sill-
man has been after us for New Faces but it's another musical, and
that title doesn't exactly suit Gypsy. No—until the right play
comes along, we're going to stay right in burlesque, not just because
of the salary—we're getting a thousand a week you know—but
because of the training."

"A little more leg, please," the photographer said.

"Of course," Mother replied, swishing the bubbles away. "Not
too much smile, dear."

Holding my leg in the air, I smiled at the photographer. The
flash bulbs went off, and the reporter folded away his paper of
notes. "Thank you," he muttered. "I guess that's about all we
need."

The photographer packed up his bag and Mother saw them to
the door. Her voice carried over the sound of the dogs, who had
started barking again. "—did you happen to see the layout on
Gypsy in the Police Gazette last week? Four pages and the cover—"

In a moment she returned. "Well," she said, picking up the bath
sponge and a bar of soap. "As long as you're in there you might as
well bathe."

At two o'clock Mother had her driver drop me off at the theatre
for my matinee. She eyed the marquee distastefully as we pulled up.
"I just hope you'll soon be out of all this," she sighed. "Your poor
grandfather would turn over in his grave if he knew."

Kissing her on the cheek, I let myself out of the car. "Until next
Friday," I said.

Mother swallowed painfully. "If I live that long," she murmured.

32

THE UNSIGNED SHU-
bert contract lay on the coffe table, mixed up in a jumble of press
clippings, overfilled ash trays, highball glasses and three books Eddy
had brought me for my birthday: *The Waves,* a novel by Thomas
Mann, and a de luxe edition of Audubon's Book of Birds. His big
present sparkled on my wrist. The diamond in the center weighed
fifteen carats. I wore it along with three other bracelets he had
given me: one for Christmas, one for the anniversary of our first
meeting and one for Valentine's Day. The new bracelet was by
far the most beautiful. I wished I could say the same for the
Shubert contract. It had arrived in the mail that morning; a
blurred carbon copy of a contract for the Ziegfeld *Follies.*

The show had opened on Broadway a few months before and
closed suddenly when the star, Fanny Brice, was taken ill. Now it
was to reopen and the Shuberts, who had taken over the title when
Flo Ziegfeld died, wanted me to replace Josephine Baker. Bobby
Clark was to take Bob Hope's place. Cass Daley and Jane Pickens
would be added to the cast. Lee Shubert had told me I would also
do Eve Arden's scenes and a number with Bobby Clark.

On the surface, it sounded wonderful, but as Eddy had just
pointed out, there was no chance of a Broadway run. The Shuberts
were opening it in New York only so they could send it out on the
road and bill it as a complete New York cast. My salary, $250 a

week, was disappointing, too. Out of that I would have to pay agent's commission, costumes, hotels, sleepers and all my expenses. Eddy was right, it wasn't a good contract. But it was for the Ziegfeld *Follies* and I'd be a real principal, not a glorified showgirl with a few lines to speak. I put the contract aside. Eddy had told me to think it over and weigh carefully what going on the road would mean.

I sorted out the newspaper clippings with the big red circles marked around my name. I had brought them out to show Eddy—in case he hadn't already seen them. One was a long story about me that had appeared that month in *Town and Country*. Otis Chatfield Taylor had written it. He wrote, among other things, that I was the Gene Tunney of burlesque. Personally, I didn't get the connection, but I did like the part where he said Jean Cocteau, after watching my show, had burbled, "How vital!" and how invitations to my parties were cherished by gangsters, social registerites, artists and writers alike. And many, he had added, bring their wives.

There were several clippings about my attending the opening night of *Jumbo*. Some of them were just mentions, but Cholly Knickerbocker wrote: "Among those present were Mrs. Harrison Williams in carved rubies and sables, Mrs. Dolly O'Brian in diamonds and chinchilla, Lady Furness in pearls and silver fox and Gypsy Rose Lee in ermine (full length)."

O. O. McIntyre's column was longer and, I thought, more to the point. "Among the death watch at first nights recently has been the long-reigning Queen of Burlesque, Gypsy Rose Lee. She is among the celebrity curiosa that collects at smart soirees. An eyeful in a showy way, but not quite the over carmined type one might expect. She occupies an apartment, a perfect bijou, on the north side of Gramercy Park, a rendezvous where people strange to the leafy square drift in and out—a jiggled mosaic of the Broadway pattern. Gypsy is of an intelligence belying her calling. Quick on the trigger . . . as she continues her slink through the Park Avenue drawing rooms there are not many who do not angle for her, and in every instance, to those who have not seen her she proved a surprise package. Those who expected to find Miss Lee over rouged and thickly veined with Rabelaisian repartee, discovered instead, a

self possessed lady with a cough drop voice and a dress suit accent
who might have run up from Bryn Mawr for a prom. She scatters
effortless French phrases through her conversation and fits in
perfectly with the Dear Noel motif—"

Fortune magazine, in an article on burlesque and its effect on
real-estate values, gave me three pages and four pictures. *The New
Yorker,* inspired by *Fortune,* was not quite so enthusiastic. They
did say they "went for me—so to speak," but then they spoiled
everything by adding that the chorus girls at the Irving Place looked
as though they were wearing last year's Earl Carroll's costumes, and
the year before last's bosoms. Walter Winchell mentioned me twice
that week. Once he said, "Orchids to Gypsy Rose Lee's nudist
colony," and the second time, in commenting on the *Town and
Country* piece, he wrote that I read swell. "There's something
healthy," he added, "about females like that."

The picture taken of me in the bathtub the week before hadn't
turned out too well. I looked as though I had a double chin, and
my leg sticking up out of the soap suds appeared fat. The bump on
my big toe, from wearing short dancing shoes when I was a child,
showed, too. But the picture was on the front page and the caption
was nice. It read, "Gypsy Rose Cleans Up for Burlesque."

The clippings, ten of each, made a neat pile. I put them in a suit
box and shoved it under the sofa, then I emptied the ash trays.
The phone rang, but I didn't answer it. I knew it was Whitey, the
stage manager, calling to tell me I was late again for the matinee.
The Tiffany clock Eddy had given me said two forty-five—no time
for a full make-up. I grabbed up my Russian broadtail coat, and
gave a quick pat to the white elephant Flo Ziegfeld had given me
before *Hot-Cha!* closed; then, making sure my key was in my purse,
I flew out of the apartment and rang for the elevator. The operator
was all smiles, so was the doorman, and I knew Eddy had over-
tipped them again. I turned to the right when I left the building
and ran the two blocks to the theatre. In the middle of the first block
the street began taking on the character of the theatre. Gone were
the uniformed doormen standing under the canopies with the
boxed yews flanking them. The sedate private houses disappeared
along with the soft silence. The clean odor of earth and trees was

lost in a smell of popcorn and rancid butter. I turned away my head as I passed the stand so I couldn't see the candied red apples with their sticks in the air. A jewelry store, the window filled with trays of tie pins and old-fashioned watch fobs, was next, then a lunch-room with a griddle piled high with hot dogs behind the steamed-up window, and finally the stage door.

Georgia Sothern, her hair shining like a new penny, sat next to me in the dressing room. She took her feet down from the make-up shelf to let me pass. "You better hurry," she said. "Whitey's having a fit."

"To hell with him," I said, tearing out of my clothes. "I'm bored with his tantrums. Besides I'm thinking of giving in my notice. I might take that job in the *Follies*."

Georgia picked up a powder puff and patted it under her arms, then powdered carefully around her rhinestone brassière. "What did Eddy say when you told him about it?"

"He—he was very happy for me," I replied.

"And your mother, what did she say?"

"I didn't tell her yet. I wanted to make up my mind first."

Georgia threw the puff on the littered make-up shelf. "I love you, Gyp," she said. "You're one of the best friends I have, but so help me, sometimes I think you're nuts. If I had a guy like Eddy I'd hang on like a leech—young, handsome, generous—he's got everything. This damned Shubert show's going on the road and you know it. The moment you leave town some smart bimbo is going to latch onto him and that's the end of you. Then what have you got? A contract for a lousy two hundred and fifty a week with a road show."

"It's more than that," I said, pulling on my white Cellophane-fringe dress. "It's a chance to get out of all this—"

"Forget about Eddy for a minute," Georgia said. "Look at every-thing else you'll be giving up. What about your apartment? You've got a lease on it, haven't you? And the country place, who'll take care of that?"

"Mother will be there—"

"*Your* mother?" Georgia hooted. "You think *your* mother will stay buried out in that country place while you're on the road with a show? Like hell she will. Dogs, monkey, asthma and all, she'll be right there beside you."

"She wouldn't leave the farm for anything," I murmured. "Not with those paying guests and the chickens and everything."

Whitey threw my ermine coat in the room. "You can get this out of the office safe yourself tomorrow," he said. "I'm fed up being your personal maid. And I'm sick and tired of you dragging your behind in here when you feel damned good and ready to. Your contract says you gotta be in at half hour like everyone else—"

"Modulate your voice, please," I said. "It reverberates, and you can stop worrying about me. I may not be here much longer."

He helped me into the ermine coat, then followed me down the stairs. "Taking that job in the *Follies,* huh? Well, it's your own business, but if you ask me—"

"I know, I know," I said over my shoulder. "I've been through it all with Georgia."

The orchestra was playing my introduction, and Whitey ran to the microphone to make my announcement. I let them play another eight bars as I walked unhurriedly to the center of the stage. Rags Ragland was waiting there for me. "Give 'em the old one-two, Punkin," he said, holding open the curtain. "After your number I want to talk to you. We'll grab a quick beer at the Dutchman's." I nodded to him as I went through the folds.

While I was doing my number I could see him watching me from the wings. He had just finished doing the "Crazy House" scene. The long nightgown he wore was still wet down the front where the talking woman had squirted him with seltzer water. He stood with his knees bent a bit, both hands on his hips, a happy toothless grin on his face. Rags wasn't exactly toothless; on either side of his mouth he had two long teeth and a full set of lowers. He also had a very nice upper plate, but he rarely wore it. Most of the time it was wrapped in newspaper and tucked safely away in a cash register in one of the bars along Third Avenue. The false teeth had cost a lot of money and Rags wasn't taking any chances of losing them after he'd had a few beers too many.

Herman, the piano player, smiled up at me as he sequed into my first strip trailer. I unwrapped my ermine coat and let it slide

off my shoulders; then, stepping up to the footlights, I dropped it
into the orchestra pit. The tuba player stood close enough so that
I could drop it down his horn. I waited for the laugh, then with
my back to the audience I let one shoulder strap fall, then the other.
Holding the center fold of the curtain I turned slowly and flashed
the pink satin bows glued to my breasts. Pulling the curtain around
me I stood there in the darkness for a moment or two, my bracelets
glittering in full view of the audience while Mitch Todd, the
tenor, sang the opening chorus of the first-act finale: "Miss Lingerie
—you're a beauty, beyond compare—" The audience was still applauding, (the bracelets and a rustle of the curtains had helped) as
Rags and I walked up to my dressing room. "Throw a coat on over
your kimono," he said. "We don't have much time."

The Dutchman's, one of Rags's favorite bars, was close to the
theatre. The owner didn't object to us wearing backstage kimonos
in the place and he was very nice about allowing us to sign our bar
checks. There were booths in back and it was cool and quiet. Rags
walked a few feet ahead of me down the street as usual. His huge,
floppy comedy shoes with the elastic at the sides made a slapping
noise on the sidewalk as he strode purposefully toward the swinging
doors and the welcoming sign of the Dutchman's.

I took big steps, trying to keep up with him. "It isn't polite to
walk so far ahead."

Rags threw open the swinging doors "Don't gimme any of that
Lady Esther stuff," he said, then to the bartender, "Two beers. And
draw one for yourself." Sliding his long length into one of the
seats in the nearest booth, he placed his elbows on the table and
waited for me to settle myself. "Now," he said, "what's this stuff
you've been telling Georgia? About you giving in your notice?"

"I told you about them offering me the *Follies*—"

"But you didn't tell me you were going to chuck everything and
take it. What are ya? Nuts or something? In burlesque you're a big
star, your name in lights, audiences coming to see you in limousines
—look at the publicity you've been getting. Front pages, columns,
magazines. You think you'll get all that in the Ziegfeld *Follies?* Like
hell you will. You'll be a face in the crowd, that's what you'll be.
You'll get plowed under. New York's a funny place, Gyp. Right

now you got it in your pocket but you go away for a year or more
and they'll forget you ever lived. I seen it happen before. Look at
Peaches Browning, for instance—one minute she's all over the
papers and the next day? Gone!"

"But she wasn't a real star—"

"She had her name up in lights in burlesque!" Rags said. "Same
as you have."

The Dutchman brought over two beers and placed them in front
of us, then he squeezed in beside Rags. "I got two barrels a beer for
the party tomorrow night," he said. "Think that'll be enough?"

"Plenty," Rags replied. "Lots of us'll buy the hard stuff anyway.
Why fill 'em up for free? Beefsteak and beer on the house is
enough." Rags looked down at his beer, then smiled up at the red-
faced bartender. "It's pretty swell of you to toss me this testimonial.
. . . I've never had a beefsteak in my honor before."

"Ten years in burlesque is something to celebrate," the Dutchman said expansively.

With the money Rags spent in the bar he had a beefsteak supper
coming to him in dividends, but I didn't say anything. He was too
proud and happy for me to say something that might spoil it. He
gulped down his beer in two swallows and pushed out of the booth
after the bartender. "Put the beers on my tab," he said, sauntering
past the bar and out the swinging doors. I snatched up my coat and
hurried after him.

Whitey was waiting at the end of the stage alley. "You're damn
near on," he screamed. "Come on, run! Gawddamnit awmighty,
I'm so fed up chasing you through alleys I could—come on!"

I ran, just to make him happy, but my heart wasn't in it. If I
were in the Ziegfeld *Follies* the call boy would tap on my door and
whisper, "Places, please, Miss Lee—if you're ready." I would sing
out a gracious "Thank you" and walk like a lady to the wings. The
stage manager would bow to me. . . .

"Pick up your big feet and run!" Whitey yelled. "I'm fed up
with you broads missing cues—"

"Don't you call me a broad!" I called back at him. "I'm the star
of this show and don't you forget it!"

I ran up the stairs and snatched the pale-green costume off the

hook. I was so angry I could hardly pin the flittered leaves to my
leotard. Then, when I was dressed, I grabbed up the apple I used
in my number and sailed down the stairs to the stage, holding up
the green net, so it wouldn't drag. "And now," Whitey said into
the backstage microphone, "We take great pride in presenting the
star of our show, the one and only Miss Gypsy Rose Lee." I
smiled at the unseen audience and went into my song.

> I'm a lonesome little Eve
> Looking for an Adam.
> Gee I wish I had him,
> Cuddling me, 'neath the shade of a tree,
> And in our garden we would be so happy.
> I'm a lonesome little Eve.
> All I do is sit and grieve.
> Like Eve I carry round this apple every night
> Looking for an Adam with an appetite.
> And if I could find one who would take a bite
> We'd be just like Adam and Eve. . . .

There was no runway at the Irving Place Theatre. The fire
department had made us take it out, but there was a circular stairway leading down into the audience from the apron of the stage.
With the apple in my hand I went slowly down the steps, singing
to a baldheaded man in the second row:

> Would you for a big red apple?
> Would you for my piece of mind?
> Would you for a big red apple,
> Give me what I'm trying to find—

One after the other I coaxed the men in the audience to eat the
apple, then when there was nothing left but the core, I ran up the
steps toward the wings. Just before exiting I tossed the core to a
man who was leaning over the railing in the lower box. The spotlight shifted to him as he lunged. It was always good for a laugh,
but that day the customer leaned over too far and fell, right into the
orchestra pit. There was a stunned silence, then a burst of applause
as he got to his feet and waved the core triumphantly in the air.
The drummer and I helped boost him back into the box, and while
I was about it I made a mental note to keep that bit of business in
my number. It would be difficult finding someone who would fall

out of the box twice a day, but it was worth the trouble. For the night shows anyway. Then, as I was running off stage with the sound of applause and laughter in my ears, I suddenly thought of the Ziegfeld *Follies* and how different it would be. The Shuberts wouldn't allow the customers to hang over the railings, or fall into the orchestra pit. They wouldn't allow me to go into the audience with a powder puff or an apple. They might not even allow me to do my specialty. The orchestra went into a chorus of "Lullaby of the Leaves," my strip music, but I stood frozen in the wings, frightened at the thought of leaving everything I was so sure of. Rags and Georgia were right. Eddy was right. I'd be a fool to leave all this.

Herman looked up from the pit, a worried frown on his face, then he broke into a smile when I paraded on, holding up the full skirt of the green costume, and swirling it about me. Stepping out of it, I posed for an instant in the leaf-bedecked leotard, then slowly began unpinning the leaves, one by one, and throwing them into the audience. I had planned on renting a wind machine for this part of the number, but they wanted fifty dollars' rental for the thing. Besides it wouldn't blow the leaves off slowly enough, so I went back to unpinning them. In that way I had complete control of the three vital ones.

Whitey was in the wings at the end of my number, beaming at me. "Great bit of business having that guy fall out of the box," he said. "Only you should of left him lay there. We could have charged him sixty-five cents extra."

I walked past him without a word. He wasn't going to get back in my good graces that easily.

"There's a note I left ya on the make-up shelf," he said. "It's from the Taylors, those society friends of yours."

I wished again he wouldn't use that expression. Society sounded so burlesquey. People, I had learned, were either in the social register or they weren't. It just happened that the Taylors were. I knew that because I had looked them up. During the past few months I had been looking up all sorts of people in the book. Those who had invited me to dinner parties and luncheons and who had come to see me at the theatre. It was surprising who was in the book. Eddy, for instance, with all his money wasn't, but that nice couple who looked so shabby and took me swimming at the River Club were.

The Taylors' note was to tell me they were catching the show the following night and were bringing the Earl of Gosford. They would be in the lower-right box. Would I please "play up" to him in my audience number? I tucked the note in the frame around my mirror. An Earl, I mused. It sounded like some kind of royalty. I wondered how I could look that up.

"More of the snob mob dropping in, huh?" Bubbles, wrapped in a skimpy kimono with a towel over her shoulder, was reading the note. "I don't like audiences looking at me with field glasses," she added, "like I was a racehorse or something."

I didn't bother answering her. Bubbles and I didn't get along too well since the time I made the bosses cut her audience number, an obvious steal from mine. She dropped her kimono and began splashing cold water on her breasts. Bubbles spent a lot of time on her breasts. When she wasn't rubbing them with cocoa butter to make them larger she was patting them with ice or cold water to make them firmer. As she often said, they were her meal ticket and if she didn't take care of them who would.

"I guess that means you won't be going to the beefsteak supper," she said. For a moment I had forgotten all about the party. If the Taylors asked me to join them, and I was sure they would, I'd have to refuse. I wondered if it was proper to say, "No, your highness" to an earl, or "No, your earlship."

"We'll miss you," Bubbles said sarcastically. "There won't be a soul there to lend tone to the joint." She leaned over the sink and I was tempted to let her have it, but just then Whitey stuck his head in the door. "Get your note?" he asked.

"Yes, I did," I replied coldly, snatching up a make-up towel to cover myself. "And I wish you'd learn to knock."

"Anything you got, kid," he said cheerfully, "I seen better."

Bubbles snickered. "He can say that again."

If I'd had the Ziegfeld contract in my hand at that moment I would have signed it regardless of what I was giving up. "Consider the source," I said to myself, controlling my anger. "*Sois chic. Sois gentille—*"

"Her name is Rose Lee—but she's askin' all her friends to call her Gypsy!"

Denys Wortman

Reproduced permission *New York World Telegram*

A Trainman's Last Strip

News Item:—"Mob of 100 women, sympathizers with striking Louisiana & Arkansas Railway Workers, ambush train and strip clothes off of fireman."

New York Journal-American

"Ferguson! Look!! Gypsy Rose Lee!!"

— AND NOW WHO WOULD YOU LIKE ME TO IMITATE, FOLKS?

GYPSY ROSE LEE !!

ARTHUR BORAN

CHELMOW

Cartoon by Gard. The New York Herald Tribune

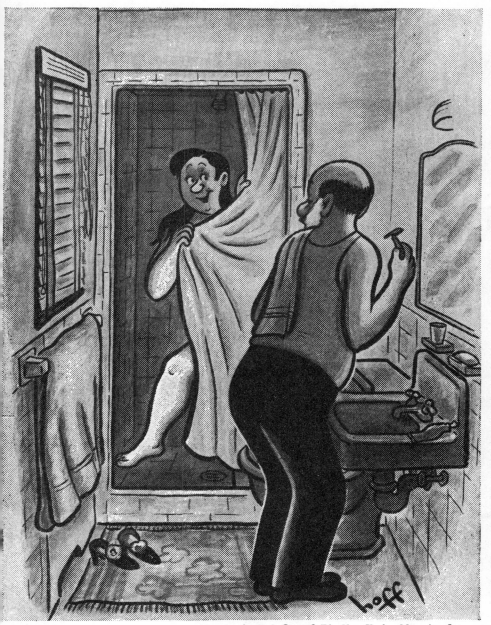

Drawing by Hoff. © *1948 The New Yorker Magazine, Inc.*

"Hey, Sam—Gypsy Rose Lee!"

Backstage Chivalry at "Ziegfeld Follies"

Cartoon by Ken Chamberlain. The New York Herald Tribune

Stage hands turn their heads away when Gypsy Rose Lee finishes her strip-tease act and backs into the robe held by her maid.

33

THERE WAS QUITE A crowd gathered around the backstage peephole before the show the following night. News had gotten about that an earl was in the theatre and everyone wanted to get a look at him. I waited my turn, then put my eye to the hole cut in the front curtain. There were six people in the lower-right box. I recognized the Taylors, but the others all looked alike: the men in tuxedos and the women in lace evening gowns. The man nearest the rail I guessed was the Earl; the Taylors would have put him there so I could reach him in my number.

"We're sure getting la-de-da around here," one of the chorus girls murmured.

"Yeah," another one said. "This would be a great night for the cops to raid the joint."

I waited in my dressing room when the last finale was over. I had the feeling I had given a good show; it's an inside feeling but it left me with a glow that made my cheeks red and my eyes clear and bright. I could hear Whitey's voice and I knew he was bringing my guests upstairs. I threw a make-up towel over the littered shelf and hid a few untidy bits of net and rhinestones. "They're redecorating the green room," Whitey was saying in a lifted-pinky voice. "Sorry your lordship has to hike up these crummy stairs . . ."

"Not at all," a very British voice answered. "We don't have anythink like this in London, y'know, and I must say I've enjoyed every moment of it."

Whitey stood aside as the six people crowded into the dressing room. I noticed that he had put on a clean shirt, his hair was slicked down with Vaseline. The Taylors embraced me, then introduced their friends. The Earl of Gosford came forward and held my hand. "The most delightful evening I can remember," he murmured. His black tuxedo glittered with green flitter where I had brushed against him during my audience number. His trousers, where I had sat on his lap, were flecked with the stuff. "Your suit!" I gulped. "It's covered with that damned flitter!"

The Earl looked down at the glittering tuxedo. "So it is," he replied, flicking away at the specks that clung to the wool.

"It won't come off that way," I said hastily. "It has a glue base. Please, send it to me tomorrow and I'll have Winzer, my theatrical cleansers, get it cleaned up for you. . . ."

"My dear," the Earl replied," I wouldn't think of it. I shall leave it just as it is forever, to be worn only on special occasions."

Bubbles, from her side of the partition, made a snorting noise. The Taylors, used to these distractions, covered it up by asking me to join them for supper. "We'll go to the Oak Room, or some other quiet place and have a little evening."

"I'm so sorry," I said. "I'd really adore it, but I must say no. I have to be up so early tomorrow—I have an ethnological dance lesson at nine—my French lesson at eleven, and a fitting at one. Please forgive me?"

When the door closed behind my guests I was exhausted. It was like giving a performance, I thought, only harder. I was pleased with myself though. Especially about the ethnological dance lesson. I wasn't sure what it meant, but it sounded good. Glancing through the dresses I kept on a nail on my side of the room I wondered which was the most proper for a beefsteak testimonial supper. Deciding on a red-and-black-flowered satin (picked up on sale at Bergdorf's), I pulled it on over my head and slipped into a pair of red satin shoes. As an afterthought I threw my ermine coat over my shoulders. Rags was waiting for me at the foot of the stairs. He wore his navy-blue suit for the occasion, a clean white shirt and his comedy shoes.

"They might want me to make a few funnies," he said, catching my disapproving look at the shoes. "I don't feel right without the Juliets."

The party was in full swing when we arrived at the Dutchman's. The whole cast from our show was there, along with most of the people from the Republic and the Eltinge and others who were laying off. A few of the comics were wearing their trademarks, like Rags's shoes: an oversize collar, a shirt dickey and cuffs with no shirt, a putty nose. Harry Clexx wore a tie that was so long it dragged on the floor, Mandy Kaye's hair stood out around his head like a coonskin cap, Joey Faye wore a sport shirt open at the neck with a four-inch square of fur glued to his chest. I was the only woman, I noticed, wearing an evening gown.

A large table covered with a red-and-white-checkered tablecloth held loaves of sliced bread and platters of rare, juicy beefsteak cut in thick slices. Two barrels of beer with glass mugs stacked up beside them were cradled on stands on the bar. Waiters carrying trays loaded with beer and drinks weaved in and out through the crowd. The sawdust on the floor was wet already with spilled drinks and the air was heavy with smoke.

Rags and I stood on the top step of the three leading into the room. "As your mother would say," Rags whispered, "I can see the handpainting on the wall; it'll be a rough night tonight!"

He passed my ermine coat over to the bartender, then, taking his teeth from his pocket, gave him those, too. "Put this stuff in the safe for us, will ya?" He asked. "When the fur starts flying we don't want to be encumbered with no encumbrances."

Walking through the crowd, Rags accepted the congratulations of those who were still sober enough to remember what the party was all about. Once or twice he stopped to say, "You know my friend, Gyp?" then before I'd have time to catch the name he'd move on again. A blonde squeezed up to him and wriggled around for a moment. "You remember me, don't cha?" she asked, gazing up at him with a bleary eye.

"I remember the face," Rags said, "but I can't place the body."

The blonde giggled, "Fresh!" and six comics in a chorus shouted, "If it's fresh, I'll take some."

"Great party, isn't it?" Rags said to me. "I didn't know I had so many friends."

Moey Briskin, Rags's straight man, had just finished singing a dramatic version, complete with recitation, of "Brother, Can You Spare a Dime?" and Joe Freed was up on the platform doing his specialty with four soup spoons. It wasn't very musical, but it was loud. Georgia grabbed Rags's arm. "Come on, you have to do something," she said. "Everybody's doing a number or something—"

Rags finished his drink, then let Georgia drag him over to the platform. "I want to thank you all for showing up for my party," he said. "And to show my appreciation, I will render my own version of the 'Dirty Bartender,' which I copped from Red Marshall, who copped it from Frank Silk, who copped it from Harry Clexx, who copped it from me."

With a few hurriedly collected props Rags did the scene. The noise in the room silenced, even the smoke seemed to clear away. The audience, who appreciated pure comedy and timing, knew they were watching one of the best comedians in the business. There wasn't much applause when Rags finished. The applause was in the hearts of the audience. Rags knew it. He took his bows humbly, but I knew how proud he was inside. "You could be a big star if you really worked at it," I said to him.

Rags snatched a drink off a tray that was passing. "Not me, Punkin," he said. "Why should I knock myself out doing six shows a day at the Roxy?"

"The Roxy? Who said anything about the Roxy? I'm talking about Broadway, Rags. The Ziegfeld *Follies*—Hollywood, even."

"Not for me," he said, downing his drink in one gulp. "I'll stick to burlesque. I know where I am in this racket."

"You're afraid," I said. "You're afraid to get out of it."

"Damned right I am," Rags replied. Stinky Fields yelled at him from the far side of the room. "I got us a table—come on." And Rags pushed his way through the crowd. I picked up the train of my dress and tried to follow him. Bubbles, standing in my way, smiled at me. "Look who's here," she said. "All dressed up like she's pouring tea at Lady Goo Flops. What are ya doin'—slumming?"

Rags looked back over his shoulder, "Come on, Gyp. She's just clowning."

"Don't bother with the apologies," I replied, looking straight at Bubbles. "She's obviously drunk."

"Well, get her," Bubbles sneered. "Soddy I didn't bring my lorgnette—not that I need it to see through a phony like you."

I tried to push past her. "Don't be vulgar," I said.

"Vulgar, my behind!" Bubbles yelled. "I'm fed up to here with you. You think you're such great potatoes. Do you know what you really are? You're the laughingstock of burlesque. That's what you are. You and your half-assed society friends. Friends! You should hear 'em laughing at you! Sure they invite you to their parties—for the laughs you hand 'em. You and your French words and your big head. You know what I think? I think you stink."

I gave her a push. "To whom do you think you're speaking?"

"To youm, that's whom, and look out who you're pushing or you'll get hurt."

Rags elbowed through the crowd and held my arm, and suddenly Georgia was there between Bubbles and me. "Come on, now," they were both saying. "This is a party—let's all have a drink and forget it."

"She pushed me," Bubbles bawled. "No phony is pushing me around!"

"Don't you call me a phony," I said, shaking off Rags's hand. "You cheap two-bit hootch dancer!"

"Me? A hootch dancer?" Bubbles screeched. "Let go of me—I'll show her who's a hootch dancer." She snatched up a mug of beer from the table and let me have it right in the face, mug and all, and the fight was on. I gave her a slap on the neck, and when she leaned over for another mug of beer I brought up my foot and gave her a swift kick on the behind. Then with all the screaming and yelling and pushing and shoving I couldn't tell if I was kicking her or somebody else. All I could see was a mess of arms and faces and glasses and ice cubes flying around. Once, for a moment, I was on the floor with sawdust getting up my nose, then I was on my feet with my fists flying at anything that came near me. Voices were yelling, "Break it up—cut it out now"; then someone else would say, "Kick her again," and over all of it I heard the noise of a whistle and Georgia was shaking me very hard. "It's the cops," she was saying. "Sit down and be quiet."

Bubbles, holding her hand to her mouth, was whimpering. "My tooth—that bitch loosened my tooth—"

Then suddenly everything was still. The upturned chairs were placed at the tables right side up, and a silence fell on the room. Rags straightened his tie and led me, my dress torn and hanging down over my shoulders, to a table. Someone slapped my chignon on the checkered cloth. "Your hair, I believe?"

The bartender who had been in the middle of the fight was back of the bar now, nonchalantly polishing a glass. Bubbles' dress was torn, too, and she had one shoe off, gazing at it in her hand with the heel hanging by a bent tack. A long red welt ran down her shoulder to the top of her soiled pink brassière. She looked up balefully, out of breath and panting, at the two policemen who walked into the barroom, their clubs swinging by their sides.

"What's going on?" one of them asked the Dutchman.

"Where? Here?" the Dutchman said. "Nothing going on in here that's unusual."

The policemen glanced around the room. A few broken glasses had been kicked under the tables, but aside from that things looked pretty much as they always did. Then one of the policemen looked at me, and at Bubbles. "What happened to them?" he asked.

Rags smiled at him. "Just a couple of strip teasers rehearsing a new number.

The policemen took another look, then they turned around and headed for the door. "No more noise," one of them said. "We got a complaint about the racket—keep it down, or I'll run you all in for disturbing the peace."

"Peace on you, too," one of the comics muttered. There was a babble of voices when the policemen left. "They're public servants, aren't they?" someone said. "I shoulda asked 'em to get me a drink." All the old policeman jokes were dragged out and dusted off, a few of them too dirty to use in burlesque, and all of them too old to be disinterred. Rags handed me his handkerchief. "Wipe the sawdust off your face," he said. My jaw hurt when I touched it. My ear hurt, too, and I had a broken fingernail. Pushing away from the table I started for the bar where my coat was.

"Don't be a bum sport," Rags said, following me. "So what? Bubbles had a few too many, that's all. You were pretty quick with the fists yourself. Let's have a coupla brown boys and forget it."

"That's right. Stick up for her. Go on—it's your party. You're the one who's celebrating ten years of all this. Go on, let them tell you what a funny guy you are, make faces for them. Maybe ten from now they'll throw you another beefsteak party, but I won't be here to enjoy it because I'm getting out. Right now!"

I grabbed my ermine coat from the bartender and ran up the three steps to the door and slammed it behind me. Outside through the window with the half curtain on it I could see Rags shaking his head back and forth as though he felt sorry for me. A blonde struggled over to the platform and leaned on the piano. Her voice was like a hoarse whisper, "I wanna be loved with inspiration—"

I pulled my coat around me and ran down the street toward a parked taxicab. Why should he be sorry for me? I thought. Why should anyone be sorry for me? I had a house in the country, diamond bracelets, an annuity—and I was going in the Ziegfeld *Follies*.

"Where to, lady?" the cab driver asked.

"Gramercy Park," I said, then I began to cry. My mascara was running but I couldn't stop. Big wet tears fell on my face and burned my cheeks and lips.

"You all right?" the cab driver asked. "You ain't sick or anything?"

"No, I'm all right," I sobbed. "I—I just said good-by to some friends."

34

THE *FOLLIES* RAN
longer than Eddy thought it would. We opened at the Winter
Garden in September and twelve weeks later were still playing to
packed houses. The critics agreed that we were a hit, but the
follow-up reviews were even better for me. I had been featured in
thirty-seven magazine articles, including a picture in the first issue
of a new magazine called *Life*. Walter Winchell had mentioned
me forty-one times, Louis Sobel eighteen. Ninety-seven press
photos of me had appeared in the New York papers, and seventeen
cartoons. I had been elected Queen of Columbia College by the
senior students; had starred in the Beaux Arts Ball, where I appeared in a few gold spangles, as the eclipse of the sun; and had
been held up and robbed of almost all my jewelry. As Mother said,
everything nice that could happen to a girl on her way up had
happened to me.

Not all of my publicity had been complimentary. In fact some
of it was most unflattering, but there was a lot of it and, to me, that
was what counted. Ed Sullivan, giving me two-thirds of his column
wrote: "Next to Wallis Simpson . . . Gypsy Rose Lee emerged this
season as the most successful space grabber of all . . . the tall, well
upholstered Miss Lee, was graduated from Burlesque to the Follies
. . . the point of origin is not to be held against her because Jim
Barton, Jay C. Flippen, Willie Howard, Bert Lahr and Fannie

The Steiners

Now my
costumes
were made
in Paris.

Bruno

Minsky's, 1931.

The Steiners

The Steiners

Charles James
dressed me.

Bruno

World's Fair, 1940.

🐚 In the Ziegfeld *Follies*
Winchell said I showed
a lot of talent…

Valente

Bobby Clark's *femme fatale...*

Jerome Robinson

In the Major Bones scene (with Stan Kavanagh, Cass Daley, Ben Yost and Fanny Brice) I was a dowager in a gray wig, and played the kazoo with two cymbals strapped to my legs.

Mr. John made our hats.

Michael Todd's
Star and Garter.

Vandamm

A lot of star,
less garter.

 On the road…

The Steiners

…and at home.

A family portrait:
June and I with our children, Erik and April.

Brice came out of the Burlesque incubator. It is beside the point that Miss Lee lacks the talent of this distinguished group of alumni . . . it is beside the point that Mother Nature did not bequeath her a streamlined chassis to compare with the smoothly contoured torsos of the Follies chorines who parade behind her. Lacking all these things, she compensates for their lack with a divine talent for keeping her name in print, and at the box office that passes for talent. How does Miss Lee operate? I am not privileged to take you behind the scenes with this distinguished strip-tease artist but I can reveal her technique for prodding paragraphs. Not long ago, a Broadway columnist, a contemporary, attended the Follies and sat in row "A" . . . to the other performers he was just another customer, in on the cuff . . . but Gypsy Rose Lee was more alert . . . she sent a note out to him, a shy little missive in which she related that the presence of the great big mans was so thrilling that she couldn't give a performance of artistic integrity. The great big mans was thrilled, too. . . . Since then she has been mentioned daily in his columns two and three times."

The *Daily Worker* panned me and burlesque as well. Strip tease, they wrote in an editorial, is a capitalistic cancer, a product of the profit system. Girls who turn away from street walking, they added, took up strip teasing.

Good or bad, everything went into my scrapbooks. I had five now, and was working on the sixth. I didn't get all the publicity on my own. Joe Flynn, the press agent for the *Follies*, was a past master at getting space. It was Joe who, a few seasons before, had a girl, wearing nothing but a long blond wig, ride a white horse down Broadway. We were both sorry he had already used the stunt. It would have been perfect for me.

Minskys' press agent, Mike Goldryer, helped a lot too. He broke the front pages of every paper in the country with his story about the foreign invasion of strip teasers, and how they were taking jobs from the more deserving American girls. "Strip teasing," he had Minsky say, "is pure American art. It is an infant industry, and we must protect our rights."

Representative Sam Dickstein, a Democrat, from New York, brought the issue before the House, and that night the newspaper headlines read: "Congress Learns of Gypsy's Art" and "Congressional Hearing Halted for Reverie at Mention of Gypsy Rose Lee." The stories were accompanied by pictures of me snapping my garter. Heywood Broun, in his column on the subject, wrote: "Gypsy stands in no need of protection. In free and fair competition she can meet all competitors from all alien lands and hold her own. . . ."

Other strip teasers, spurred on by their press agents, helped fill my scrapbooks. June St. Clair, for instance, complained to the Associated Press that I was a fraud. "Gypsy's work isn't art," she was quoted as saying. "She's fooling the public. Why, she doesn't even strip!"

Margie Hart managed to be heard. "Unlike Gypsy Rose Lee," she wrote Ed Sullivan (who evidently appreciated a shy missive himself, when it was sent to him), "I do not read Tennyson, and Einstein's theory of relativity leaves me cold. . . . I owe whatever success I enjoy to reading the *Police Gazette* and Broadway columns, but I find pictures easier to understand. . . ."

"She would," I replied in print, via the United Press.

Mike Goldryer hit the front pages again with a scheme to have the Minskys present me with a degree, "Doctor of Strip Teasing." Six professors from New York University were cajoled into taking part in the ceremony, which was to be held after the show one night at the Oriental, Minskys' new theatre. Ten strip teasers, wearing transparent gowns and caps, were to be awarded lesser degrees. Bernard Sobel, author of *Burleycue,* and keeper of the burlesque archives, was master of ceremonies. After ten minutes of speeches, the proceedings were interrupted by a raucous voice from the balcony, demanding that they bring on the dames. The six professors squirmed uneasily on their chairs, and Reginald Marsh, the artist, went up to the lectern. "The strip tease," he said, "is classical, it is eternal, it is—"

"Get the hell off!" another voice from the balcony yelled. Mr. Marsh obliged, and, as the pop bottles began rolling down the aisles, the graduating class tripped on stage, but I refused to budge.

"It was to be a dignified ceremony," I insisted, holding my ground in the wings. "This is a clambake and I'll have no part of it." Wrapping myself in my mink, I stalked out through the stage door.

The next day I was embarrassed to learn that Gertrude Lawrence, with a true show-must-go-on attitude had accepted my degree *in absentia*. She gave it to me reluctantly, a few days later. "I should like to have taken it back to England," she said. "They would have thought me such a success."

All these stories helped, but the jewel robbery was what I called the *coup de grâce*. The police never did catch the hold-up men, and for months, when anyone else was robbed, mine was the name that grabbed the headlines. The value of my jewelry grew with each new robbery, and I became so used to the upped value that when my insurance check arrived from Lloyd's of London I felt as though I'd been cheated. The insurance money went to pay the mortgage on the country house. As Mother said, I no longer needed diamonds. The jewelry had served its purpose. Besides, I had begun to notice that glitter didn't necessarily mean chic.

When my publicity quieted down I made a few well-timed entrances into the Stork Club, or was seen dancing in a Charles James gown at the Mayfair or lunching in a Schiaparelli at the Colony.

Joe Flynn saw to it that Adele Moon, my maid, was offered a job, which she promptly refused, at sixty dollars a week to do a strip tease in a Harlem theatre. (After fifteen years with Fanny Brice, Adele was wise to publicity stunts.) Julie Bryan, my understudy in the *Follies* (less experienced than the maid), went to work as featured strip teaser for the Minskys. I made a screen test for Darryl Zanuck and took up ballet for one day while the photographers took pictures to prove it.

The city, during all this, had broken out in a rash of Gypsy Rose Lees. Uptown there was a sepia Gypsy Rose Lee. Downtown there was burlesque's Gypsy Rose Lee, billed as younger and prettier. The Young Communist League advertised one of their entertainers as "Our Very Own Gypsy Rose Lee." A female impersonator, wearing a brassière filled with birdseed to give it a lifelike movement, billed himself as the Brazilian Gypsy Rose Lee. Hubert's Museum, on Forty-second Street, featured a "Gypsy Rose Flea."

The old Mae West jokes were dragged out and dusted off and

attributed to me. There were rumors about that I was illegitimate, a dope fiend, a Lesbian. It was all very gratifying and I did my best to keep the ball rolling.

One night, during the show, Fanny Brice asked me if I wanted to buy her Minerva town car. "I'm tired of paying storage on it," she said. "It cost me fourteen thousand new, but I'll sell it cheap. I feel like a damned fool riding around in it, but it would be a swell publicity gimmick for you."

She gave me the address of the garage where it was stored, and the next Friday, when Mother was in town, we went up to look at it. Mother and I had never heard of a Minerva, but it was the most beautiful car we had ever seen. It was a landau, with the chauffeur's seat out in the open. The paint was gleaming and perfect, without a scratch on it anywhere. The tires were almost new. There was less than six thousand miles on the speedometer.

"We have to have it," Mother breathed. "I just can see the neighbors' faces when we drive up."

The mechanic watched us as we felt the gray upholstery, and ran our fingers over the polished body. "Will it go?" I asked him.

He thought it over for a while. "Depends," he finally said, "on where you're going. I won't say it'll go far. If you're lucky you'll get about five miles to a gallon a gas. It takes two hands to shift gears and damned near a whole city block to park it in."

Mother gave him a big smile. "You can't discourage us," she said. "We know you like having that storage money coming in every month."

That night I asked Fanny how much money she wanted for the car. I reminded her how difficult it was to drive, how much gas it used and how, after all, it was a used car. Fanny bit her lower lip as she thought it over. "Connie Bennet offered me ten thousand for it," she said. "Of course, that was a long time ago, but I haven't had it out of the garage since." I could feel the car slipping through my fingers. Even half of what Connie Bennett offered was more than I could afford.

"Tell you what," Fanny said. "You give me fifty bucks for the car and I'll throw in the fur lap robe."

We made the deal then and there. The registration was made

over in my name and now I had an annuity, a country house, a mink coat and a town car.

Angelo, a cab driver I knew, came to work for me as chauffeur. He took off a few minutes each night to drive me to the theatre. Then, parking the Minerva, he'd go back to hacking until the show was over, when he'd pick me up. He drove me to the theatre on matinee days, too.

I loved playing matinees with the *Follies*. It was nice to look out front and see so many women. Their brightly colored hats and dainty veils and perfume made the audience like a spring bouquet. The sounds they made, chattering and giggling, were so different from the audience sounds I was used to. They squealed with delight before I took off a thing.

After the show they would wait at the stage door with their programs to be autographed. I dressed carefully for these apperances; women are so critical. I made sure my nail polish wasn't chipped, that my seams were straight. The Minerva, with Angelo at the wheel, would be waiting at the curb. Letting my furs drag a bit on the sidewalk I would smile at the ladies, and pretend to be surprised when they asked for my autograph. My ears picked up every comment.

One Wednesday, I remember, there were the usual remarks. "She's rather sweet, in a stagy sort of way—"

"I thought she was much taller."

"Is that mink? Or sable?"

"She must be at least forty—"

I saw a familiar face in the crowd. First I saw the red fox coat and muff to match, then the dress: black satin with a green chiffon scarf. Green shoes, hat and gloves made up the ensemble. None of the greens matched very well, but the face under the hat was radiant. It was Nudina, the snake dancer from the Republic Theatre.

"I just caught the show!" she said, throwing her arms around me. "I'm working at Minskys' but I told 'em I was sick. I just had to catch your show before ya went on the road. It was so wonderful, Gyp, I just can't tell ya. I sat there and cried like a baby every time you came on."

The matinee ladies were all ears. I eased Nudina toward the car and helped her in. "Let's have dinner and talk," I suggested. "Sardi's," I said to Angelo, and, squeezing Nudina's hand, I waved gaily with the other to the bobbing heads and pink, veiled faces at the stage door.

"My gawd!" Nudina said, taking in the car. "Is this *yours?*"

"A gift," I replied. "From a friend."

Vincent Sardi met us at the door. "The usual table?" he asked, and as I smiled and nodded at him I could feel the eyes of the other diners resting on me. Their whispers passed from table to table. I hoped Nudina was aware of the stir my entrance made. I glanced at her from the corner of my eye, but she was too busy admiring the room. I waved at Leonard Lyons. "Lennie, darling. I have a very funny story for you—"

Leonard smiled back at me, and I knew he'd stop by later. I knew, too, that I'd have to think up a funny story in a hurry. Leonard wasn't interested in gossip; the story would have to have a point to it. I decided to tell him the one about Mother and the turkey raffle.

"This way, Miss Lee," the headwaiter said. Nudina, gazing at the walls covered with caricatures of celebrities, tripped along behind me. "Where's *your* picture?" she asked me. I didn't answer her. The fact my caricature wasn't on the wall was rather a sore spot. "Don't look now," I said, changing the subject, "but there's Katharine Cornell."

"Katharine who?" Nudina said loudly.

Then when we were seated, and the napkins were spread on our laps and the menus were in our hands, Nudina looked over at me and smiled. "It's like old times, isn't it?" she asked. "Like when we used to get loaded between shows at the Dutchman's."

The waiter cleared his throat, and Nudina glanced down at her menu. "What's cannelloni? I'll have it. And potato salad and pumpkin pie and coffee."

"And for you, Miss Lee?" The waiter asked. "The usual?"

I gave him a rueful look. "One egg, soft boiled, and a glass of milk."

"A small pat of butter?" he suggested.

"No—later I'll have the mousse."

"Mousse?" Nudina exclaimed. "I heard you had an ulcer. How come the doctor lets ya have meat?"

The waiter was too well trained to laugh.

Nudina pulled off her green gloves and settled back in the booth. "Gyp, you'll never know what a kick I got outa watching you in that show. There you are, doing the same old number you done in burlesque and those dames in the audience from the Astoria Garden Club just eating it up—"

"The number's a little different—"

"Yeah. The pants are bigger." Nudina smiled with satisfaction. "Here we are," she said. "You starring in a Broadway show and me breaking the house record at Minskys'."

"Funny, isn't it?" I said, after a thoughtful pause.

"Yep," Nudina agred. "Both of us on top of the heap."

"Do you ever see Georgia?" I asked. "Or Tessie—or Rags?"

Nudina laughed. "My Gawd, you'd think you been in Siberia or someplace. It's only been a few months since you were working with all of 'em. Georgia's at the Old Howard in Boston this week and Tessie? Gee, I dunno—last I heard she was working on a carnival."

"And Rags—what about him?"

"You mean you didn't hear about him?" Nudina let her voice go up on the last word and every head within six tables around us turned and stared. "You're probably so busy reading your own publicity you don't take time to read other people's. Rags is going inta *Panama Hattie*, with Ethel Merman."

"Oh—I'm glad for him. Is—has he married or anything?"

"Of course not," Nudina said. "You know Rags."

Our food arrived and for a while we were too busy to talk. Besides, we'd run out of topics. The aroma of Nudina's cannelloni mixed up with her Shalimar was almost more than I could stand. For eight weeks I'd been on an ulcer diet: milk and eggs with an occasional dish of rice pudding or mousse. The doctor had told me my ulcer came from worry and anxiety, but I couldn't believe that. Not even when I saw the x-rays. I had told Fanny about it at the theatre the same night. "What have I got to be anxious or worried about?"

"It's having your name in lights that's done it," Fanny had said, more convincingly than the doctor. "You've got a billing ulcer, kid. Getting to be a star is easy, nobody gets ulcers on the way up. It's staying there that's hard."

"A penny for your thoughts," Nudina said. I tried to think of something we had in common. "Still working with your snake?" I asked.

"It died," she replied with an angry toss of her head. "I paid seventy-five bucks for him, too. Me, that's never paid more than ten bucks for a snake in my life, to let that guy talk me into a seventy-five-buck python. He was so heavy, Gyp, I could hardly work with him."

"I'm sorry you lost him," I said.

Nudina shrugged. "I never cared much for him personally; it was the seventy-five bucks that got me sore. Sam is the only snake I ever really loved. You remember Sam, don't ya? The boa constrictor? What a snake that was. Remember that sweet wet nose of his? I always thought if anything happened to that snake I just wouldn't want to go on—I mean it. I loved that damned snake."

"How—how is he?" I asked.

Nudina dropped her fork. "My Gawd, Gyp," she whispered. "Didn't ya know? Sam passed on five months ago."

"I'm sorry," I murmured. "I hadn't heard."

"That's okay," Nudina said. "I'm sort of over it now. I was almost reconciled to losing him anyway. He was getting on in years, ya know. You can always tell when they're nearing the end. Their eyes get glazed-like."

I didn't want to know the details, but I thought it was my duty to ask. "Or maybe you'd rather not talk about it" I added hopefully.

"It does me good to get it off my chest," Nudina said. "So help me, it'll haunt me as long as I live. It was the night I bought Joe, he's that seventy-five-dollar python I was telling you about. I was making this jump to Chicago and I had to fly. They won't take snakes on a plane unless you have 'em crated, ya know. They got some half-assed law; anyway, there I am. Two snakes that don't know each other and me with only one crate. I was stuck. Believe me, but good. So what can I do? I put Joe, this new guy, in the crate, then I roll Sam, bless his memory, around my waist and put my coat on over both of us. He curled up like a baby. In a minute flat he was sound asleep. You know, Gyp, how I hate to fly? Well, I take two sleeping pills and I don't know a thing until we're circling over Chicago. When we land I unfasten the seat belt, being careful to not wake up Sam. He'd been such a baby doll, not a peep out of him. I get off the plane and open my coat and what do you think?"

I was afraid to think.

"Dead!" Nudina said. "He was stiff, he was so dead!"

There was a long pause while Nudina collected herself. She dabbed at her eyes with a tattered Kleenex, then shoved it back in her purse. "It took four guys to unwind him," she said. "Rigor mortis, ya know."

Leonard Lyons was working his way to our table. Asking the waiter for our check, I signed it hurriedly. The story of Mother's turkey raffle could never top Nudina's tale about Sam. Not that I wanted to cheat Leonard out of a story, but there is just so much space in a column.

Outside Sardi's Nudina and I kissed each other good-by. "It's been swell talking over old times," she said.

"We have to get together again," I agreed. "Real soon."

I waited until she was down the block, then I went back into the restaurant, looking for Leonard Lyons.

35

CLOSING NIGHT OF
the *Follies* Mother called me on my dressing-room phone. She forgot
to reverse the charges so I knew it was important. She was angry,
too, I knew that from the tremolo in her voice. "I just want you to
know," she said, "that I'm suing the New York *Daily News!*"

"Suing?" I gulped. "The *News?*"

"For that awful story they printed about us. I don't ask much of
you and your sister, and I certainly know better than to expect gratitude for the years I scrubbed and slaved to make stars of you both,
but I am entitled to a few crumbs of appreciation. I opened that
paper and there it was, staring at me in black letters splashed all
across the page, a full page! 'Gypsy's Secret Sister'—all about how
she's had to put up with being known as your sister and how
it's almost ruined any chance she might have had for success. Not
a word about how I took care of her baby all summer or about you
giving her your old ermine coat after you'd promised it to me.
Nothing but one lie after—wait, wait a minute. My jelly is boiling
over—"

"I didn't give her the coat, Mother, I traded it for my sewing
machine and she paid—" I realized then I was talking to a dead
phone. In a moment Mother was back. "You have to keep an eagle
eye on jelly," she said cheerfully. "That's why I had the phone put
in the kitchen. Do you know, Louise, I think we'll get almost two

hundred pints from the gooseberries this year. Now, where was I?—
Oh, yes, that story. Lies, Louise, nothing but lies. They're starting
a feud in our little family—"

"Please, Mother. Overture is in five minutes and I'm not dressed
yet. I saw the paper and—"

"You saw it?" Mother gasped. "Then why didn't you stop me?"

"It's good publicity," I said. "Besides, it's true."

"What has that got to do with it?" Mother asked tearfully. "It's
all right for you girls to have a publicity feud, but not at my expense.
It makes me look like an unnatural mother."

"But, you aren't mentioned in the story."

"That's just it," Mother cried. "If anyone deserves to be in a feud
with you two girls it's your mother!"

While Mother went on complaining I glanced down at the paper
lying open on my make-up shelf. There, under a big picture of
June holding a cigarette, although she didn't smoke, was a cartoon
of me, all legs and glitter. "The world knows," I read, "of Gypsy,
star of the Follies, darling of the literati, lily maid of the Minskys,
but who knows of her younger sister, June, whose talents were the
mainstay of the family for years. . . . Her show, Forbidden Melody,
may not be a hit, but June Havoc, secret sister of Gypsy Rose Lee,
most certainly is. Broadway is still ringing with the applause. . . ."

" . . . I could have given them the true story," Mother was saying
when the operator interrupted, "Beg pardon, but your three minutes
are up." Mother argued with her for an instant, then there was a
clicking noise and the phone went dead. I placed the receiver back
on the buttons and reached for my opening costume. While Adele
was hooking me up I tore out the pages from the newspaper. One
would be sent to Big Lady, back in Seattle, one to our real father
in Los Angeles, and one would be pasted in my scrapbook. This,
I knew, was the beginning for June. A new beginning.

After the show that night I closed my make-up box and said
good-by to my dressing room. I had been packing, little by little,
since the notice went up on the call board. Now there was almost
nothing left. The telegrams and pictures and notes had been taken
down from the wall around the mirror. The vases and flower baskets
had been given to the prop man. Adele had packed my chair covers

and wardrobe sheets. My costumes, as I finished with them, had been put in the big crates marked THEATRE and RUSH. I took one last look around, then, remembering that Beatrice Lillie's show was coming in the following day, I wrote "Good Luck" on the mirror with my lipstick.

The *Follies* let out earlier than *Forbidden Melody*. I was at the Chinese restaurant before June. Sitting at our regular table, I ordered for both of us. Because this was our last night lunch together for a long time I ordered a fancy one: Lobster Cantonese, egg roll and roast pork. "And plenty of tea," the waiter, who knew us, added.

When June first came to New York we had met almost like strangers. Since then, once a week, and sometimes oftener, we would sit at the House of Chan with a pot of tea, after our shows at night, until the waiters began piling the chairs on the tables. There was so much, it seemed, to talk about: her marriage, divorce, and April, the baby. My Eddy, his wife and, of course, Mother. And our ambitions, our fears and our futures. June had definite ideas about where she was going. I wasn't so certain.

"I'm going to be a real actress," she told me again that night while our egg rolls were getting cold. "I don't care how long it takes me or how hungry I get. Someday I'm going to play Anna Christie and Sadie Thompson and Hedda Gabler. . . ." Stray wisps of blond hair peeked out from under her beret. Her polo coat, cheap and a bit shabby, was thrown over the back of the chair. "My show's closing," she said. "I know I should be sorry, but I'm not. I'm almost glad. I'm going back to summer stock, Weese. I don't care what parts they give me or what they pay me. I'll move scenery, I'll clean out the dressing rooms, I'll do anything if they just let me act—there's so much I have to learn. So much I have to unlearn."

I remembered that day at Roxy's Theatre when she had used the same words. Her hands had been doubled into fists then, too, and there was the same fierce anger in her eyes. In a flash, the anger was gone. "I've talked enough about me," she said. "It's your turn now." Lifting the silvery top off the bowl she breathed in the garlicky aroma of the lobster. "You ought to take lessons yourself," she said.

I almost choked on my egg roll. "Lessons? For what?"

June served me a lobster claw, and fished out one for herself. She avoided my eyes when she spoke. "You can't go on doing this same act all your life, Gyppy. You can get away with it now while you're young and beautiful but you have to grow and develop. You have to have an aim, something real to shoot for." We ate silently for a few minutes. June had never approved of the act. From the beginning, way back at the Rialto Theatre, she'd been ashamed for me. Being in the *Follies,* with my name out front in lights hadn't changed her attitude a bit, but she'd never been quite so blunt about it.

"Maybe," June said, "you could do something with your voice."

"Or take up the saxophone?" I suggested. "Or an accordion?"

June shrugged. "The trouble with you is you've let a few childhood failures destroy your self-confidence. Since I've had one of my own I've learned a lot about children. They need approval from those they love, applause for their successes—"

"What successes?" I asked. "I'm a Hard-boiled Rose? That's the only success I can remember. From Hard-boiled Rose to Gypsy Rose—the story of my life."

"Maybe that's what you could do," June said. "Why don't you aim at that? Writing a story, I mean. Or a book, or a play. I'll bet you could do it, Weese."

The waiter hovered over us, check in hand. I made a move for my purse and June stopped me. "I want to pay it," she said. "I want this to be my night, right down the line. I'll put it in my diary as the night I found a direction in life for my big, fat sister."

I scooped up what was left of the Lobster Cantonese and divided it into the two containers the waiter had brought us. June divided what was left of the roast pork and put that on top. "But if you don't write the story," she said, "you owe me four dollars and sixty cents."

She put on her polo coat and I put on my mink. Then, picking up our containers, we walked, arm in arm, out of the restaurant. We said good-by on the street corner. "And you won't forget to water my philodendron?" I asked.

"And I'll keep Fridays open for Mother and have your phone disconnected and—Weese?"

"What?"

"I'm glad we finally got to know each other. I'm not sure I liked you when were were kids, but I like you now."

"I like you, too," I said. "I'd like you even if you weren't my sister."

The next day Mother and Eddy went with me to the station. Neither of them got out of the cab. Mother wanted to get back to the farm—one of her turkeys was sick—and Eddy was afraid he might run into someone who knew him, or his wife.

Surrounded by my eighteen pieces of luggage, I waved to them as the taxi pulled away. "I'll be back!" I yelled but I don't think they heard me. The rest of the *Follies* company was gathering and the noise was terrible. Fanny, whose luggage topped mine by seven pieces, was getting out of a cab. Besides the usual number of suitcases, hatboxes and shoebags, she had an electric hair drier, a folding massage table, a paint box and an easel. I had a Victrola, my two-burner hot plate, the sewing machine, five dachshunds, a Mexican chihuahua named Chiquita and a bowl of goldfish I'd won at Coney Island. Ordinarily I wouldn't have trouped the goldfish, but we were going into Chicago for a run, and I had become attached to them.

Before we closed at the Winter Garden, Fanny and I had decided to room together on the road. We had wired ahead for a suite with a kitchenette and two bedrooms, one for Fanny and me, the other for Adele and Claire, our maids. I had wanted to stay at the Ambassador East, but Fanny held out for the Sherman House. It was walking distance from the theatre, she said, and we could save money on cab fares. The only hotel I really knew in Chicago was the Grant, so I didn't argue with her.

Fanny had a clause in her contract providing her with a drawing room. I had no such clause in mine, and when she invited me to share the accommodations I accepted gratefully. "You can have the upper," Fanny said, "for exactly what you'd pay the railroad. No tax."

It was going to be crowded in an upper with a chihuahua and five dachshunds, but not half so crowded as the corridor outside our room, or the platform at the end of the train. The overflow of our combined luggage was piled to the roof. I fished around in my purse for the money and tipped my redcap two dollars.

"Split that with my boy," Fanny said to him, closing the door. Then she turned to me. "Now look, Gyp. If we're rooming together you have to cut out that overtipping business. I play this same route year in and year out. I don't want any Johnny-come-lately spoiling these guys for me."

"But, Fanny—eighteen pieces—"

"That," Fanny said, "has nothing to do with it. Nobody expects big tips from show people."

I didn't remind her of the bicycle she'd bought for the newsboy at the theatre, or the layette for the doorman's granddaughter, or the hospital bills she paid for the wardrobe woman. Fanny didn't like being reminded of those things.

"We've got to be businesslike about this," Fanny said. It was decided that instead of us both fumbling for our purses, Fanny would tip on the way out of a stop. I would tip on the way in. "But remember," she said, "one buck is plenty."

A friend had given her a case of home-made tamales as a going-away gift, and before the train left the station we opened a jar and ate all eight tamales cold. Then Fanny took two bottles of beer from a bag. "That's a quarter you owe me," she said, handing me one.

Taking off our shoes we leaned back on the green velour seats. "I don't know why it is," Fanny mused, "but I feel more at home when I'm on a train than I do when I'm home. I guess it's vaudeville that did it to me."

"Me too," I said. We sipped our beer thoughtfully as the train puffed and hissed and started to move, and the realization of what was happening hit me. "This is the first time in all my life I've ever gone anywhere alone—without my mother, I mean."

Fanny loosened the belt of her dress and peered out the window at the darkness. It reminded me of the time we stood at the doorway of her dressing room in San Francisco when she told me she was cutting Mary Rose because the act needed a comedy number in that spot. She knew then, too, that I was on the verge of tears, and that I wanted to cry by myself. After a while she took another gulp of beer and waited for the belch that followed. "Nothing better," she said, "than a good gripeswasser after tamales."

It took three cabs to get us to the Sherman House when we hit Chicago. Four bellboys began unloading the luggage and Fanny waved off two of them. "We don't need the whole staff to help us with a few suitcases." The dismissed bellboys smiled broadly. "It's like old times having you back with us," one of them said.

Fanny nudged me. "See, kid?" she said. "They respect you more when they know you aren't a sucker."

The assistant manager showed us to our suite. It was one of the newly decorated ones, very *moderne*. Fanny eyed the furniture with distaste. "How I hate this constipated furniture," she said. "Give me one good antique and I'll decorate a room around it, but this agonized stuff makes me want to vomit."

"We have one of the older suites," the manager suggested.

"Cheaper?" Fanny asked.

"Well, not exactly—"

"Then we'll stay right here. Bring in the bag, boys." With a finger she indicated which bags were to go where. "That," she said, pointing to the Victrola, "goes in the sitting room. The easel goes here, the goldfish in the bedroom. Be careful of that one, boys, it's my paint box—"

Half an hour later the two sweating bellboys carried in the last four pieces. Fanny gave me the nod. "You tip in," she said. "I tip out." I gave the boy a dollar, then when Fanny wasn't looking I slipped a fifty-cent piece under it.

"I caught that!" Fanny said, right in front of the bellboy. "Tipping like a whore again, eh?"

Fanny didn't believe in being extravagant on the road. In some respects she was almost too generous, but in others she practiced economies that would have done credit to Mother. She didn't take off her make-up with Crisco but she made up for it by economizing on other things, room service for instance. Instead of ordering à la carte Fanny would order the less-expensive combination breakfast. The toast and coffee she would keep for herself. The orange juice and oatmeal went to Claire, the maid. Fanny was a cigarette hoarder, too. There wasn't time during the show for her to smoke a whole cigarette, so she would take a few puffs of one, then cut off the burned end with a scissors. Blowing the smoke out of the butt she would put it aside for the next costume change. "Spend your money where it shows," she often said to me. "Better yet, don't spend it at all. An actor's best friend is his money, kid. They can talk all they want about scrapbooks, it's the bankbooks that count."

The *Follies* was even more of a hit in Chicago than it had been in New York. The critics called the show lavish, beautiful, in the Ziegfeld tradition, glorified and a laugh riot. Fanny's notices were raves. So were Bobby Clark's. Mine, even though I had been spoiled with all my New York publicity, delighted me. Ashton Stevens wrote: "I think that General Robert E. Lee would be proud of the undebatable artistry of this Minsky member of the Lee clan. She is the only member of the cuticle sisterhood who can make nudity witty . . . she removes her garments as delicately and calmly as she would remove the leaves from an artichoke . . ."

Gail Borden said I was surprisingly capable; Carol Frink was surprised, too. Her eyebrows went up at the beginning of the show and stayed there until the finale. Lloyd Lewis wrote of my many appearances in the show and guessed that I might serve to give the *Follies* its largest box-office impulse.

I made eleven appearances in the *Follies,* not because of my ability but because the Shuberts didn't believe in paying for two performers when one of them could double in brass. Five of my appearances were with Bobby Clark. First as his secretary in the Federal Spending Administration scene, then as a nurse to his Doctor Fluegal, and as the *femme fatale* in "Yokal Boy Makes Good." I was the virgin in "The Petrified Elevator" and the gray-haired dowager in the Major Bones scene, a satire on Major Bowes' Amateur Hour. Wearing a gray wig, I played a kazoo and accompanied myself with two cymbals which were strapped to my knees under a pink lamé gown. I was also Fanny Brice's mother in the Baby Snooks scene.

Besides my strip tease, which was just before the finale of the first act (my old burlesque spot on the bill) I did a Gershwin number with the show girls, and in the second act with Bobby Clark I did one of the hit numbers in the show, "I Can't Get Started with You." Those appearances, along with both finales, kept me moving faster backstage than I had in the "Newsboy Songster" act. In fact, I moved so fast that one show I didn't have time to fasten the strap on my shoe for my duet with Bobby Clark.

Toward the end of this number Bobby and I did a burlesque kiss. He would bend me over in an embrace and I would slide down the side of his leg and thump my bottom on the stage. As the laugh grew Bobby and I added to the original bit until I was doing a female Leon Errol. It wasn't just a kiss now; it was an acrobatic act. At one point, when I was collapsed, Bobby would look out at the audience and say, "Is there a blacksmith in the house?" Then, kissing me again, he would pull a string that made his coattails roll up his back like a window shade. Opening his coat, he yelled, "I guess I gotta fight fire with fire!" Pinned to his underwear were two black lace bows identical to those I wore in my strip tease.

That matinee the ladies in the audience were almost hysterical. To keep up the laugh I took an even bigger thump on my bottom. When I slid down Bobby's leg I really put my heart into it. The laugh was so big I hardly realized my foot was doubled under me. It didn't hurt at all until I got off stage. I went on with the show, but after the finale my foot began to swell and the house doctor who examined it said I had torn five ligaments in my metatarsal.

"In her *what?*" Fanny said. "Her metawho?"

I was stretched out on three chairs in Fanny's dressing room. The stagehands and chorus girls crowded around at the door. Bobby Clark stood over me, his face a white mask of sympathy. I tried to tell him it was my own fault, that I hadn't fastened the strap on my shoe, but I couldn't. The doctor began putting his things back in the little black bag. He was a theatre doctor, so he knew how important it was to patch me up. He looked down at me and gave the bandage on my foot another pat. "You'll be as good as new in two, three weeks," he said. "I'll bring a pair of crutches over to the hotel tomorrow—"

"Crutches?" Fanny gasped. "She can't work with crutches!"

"She won't be working," the doctor said. "With a foot like that if she was a horse we'd shoot her."

There is nothing worse than to be sick on the road. It isn't too bad during the day, but when seven thirty comes along and you know the show is going on without you a sort of desperation sets in. That is what happened to me the following evening. The crutches had arrived earlier and, gritting my teeth, I tried to rehearse with them propped under my arms. My costumes, I knew, would look all bunched up and awful; besides I didn't know to use the crutches. I'd swing back and forth on them, then land on the bum foot. "I can't do it, Fanny," I cried. "I just can't go on."

"Of course you can't," Fanny said. "But don't worry about it. Any of the chorus girls can do your scenes. One of the showgirls can do your number—"

I was dressed in five minutes. Two bellboys carried me, crutches and all, to a taxicab, and on the way to the theatre I decided on how I'd get through the show. As the secretary in my first scene it would be easy; I could lean on the desk. As the nurse I could make it from chair to chair. My number with the girls wouldn't be difficult; I had eight of them to support me and my number with Bobby would be all right, too. As the *femme fatale* I could play the entire scene on a chaise lounge. It was my strip tease that worried me. One of the stagehands came up with a solution. I would do the number sitting down. They would carry me out and put me on a chair, then pull away the curtain. I could rise toward the end to roll down my stockings and whip off my skirt. At the blackout they would pick me up and carry me back to my dressing room. That is exactly how I did it. I covered the bandage with body paint so it wouldn't look so antiseptic, and, leaning against the chair, I finished the number, then waited to be carried off.

Four days later I was doing the show without any help at all. The doctor said it was one of the most amazing recoveries he'd ever seen. He looked at the X-rays, then at my foot, and shook his head as though he couldn't believe it. "I don't see how she does it," he said to Fanny. "Those ligaments are in ribbons."

Fanny smiled that special smile of hers. "You should have caught the show, Doc. She laid a bomb."

That was true. The audience that expected more from me was too startled at seeing the world's first sit-down strip tease to laugh or applaud. My number was the flop of the show. Four days of that was all I could take. Pain or no pain I managed to hobble through the number and to walk off without the aid of the stagehands. My foot still hurt, but no one in the theatre knew it. The doctor took back his crutches and the show went on as usual.

We had hoped for a run of six or eight weeks in Chicago but instead we ran for twelve. There was no jewel robbery to help my publicity, but Darryl Zanuck, after weeks of thinking it over, finally decided to put me under contract to his studio. The first I knew of it was an item I read in Louella Parson's column. Then all the papers picked up the story and for a while it was even better than the robbery. Most of the stories were speculative. "Just what," the papers asked, "will Gypsy do in Hollywood?" It was a question I asked myself from time to time, so I had no answer for them.

My contracts arrived from the Coast during a matinee. Fanny read the original and I read one of the carbon copies. It took seven pages to say I was to receive two thousand dollars a week for the first year, and, at the end of five, should all the options be exercised, I would be earning five thousand. Then I came to the starting date. I had to read that twice because I couldn't believe it. "It's for the fifteenth of June," I said. "I can't make it—we're booked in Detroit that week."

Fanny shrugged. "So? The Shuberts'll get someone to replace you."

I wasn't sure I liked the way she said it. She made it sound too easy.

"We'll miss you though," she added, and that made me feel a little better. "Anyway, June's a long way off. Don't crowd the calender."

I wondered why the Shuberts were letting me go. There was no way for me to know they had been paid twenty thousand dollars for my run-of-the-play contract.

36

They CAN HAVE their long New York runs," Fanny often said. "Give me the road any day. Trouping to me is like a vacation with pay."

In a way, I agreed with her. But Fanny didn't have to pose for pictures with the delegation of distillers at nine in the morning, or make speeches at eleven for the Daughters of the Green Circle, or put on a pair of boxing gloves for a picture with Man Mountain Dean. Joe Flynn would have liked it had Fanny been agreeable to these stunts, but it was easier for her to say, "Let Gyp do it. She's the one who's stage struck." When one after another of the pictures appeared in the papers and magazines, I began to wonder if Mother hadn't been right when she said people were getting tired of looking at the same old face. I was beginning to get tired of it myself.

On off days, when there was no matinee or publicity stunt, Fanny and I would go to picture galleries or museums or the horse parlors. Fanny could sit in a horse parlor for hours, watching the names of the horses as they were changed on the boards and listen to the touts and characters who all knew her, and usually followed her betting advice. "Play him for fifty to win and show," Fanny would say to me, pointing to a name on the board. But I never did. Sometimes I was sorry, most times I was glad. To Fanny a good day was a day when she lost under five hundred.

Then during our second week in Chicago the calm was broken.

Fanny was sued for fifty thousand dollars by the lawyers of a
writer's estate, who claimed their deceased client had originated
Baby Snooks, one of Fanny's characterizations. Fanny never kept a
scrapbook or any records. Her memory about certain things wasn't
good, either. She was half convinced the lawyers were right. The
papers were spread out on her make-up table and while she was cold
creaming her face she read through them, trying to sort out the
wheretofores and thereofs. "Why the hell," she said, "can't lawyers
learn actor talk!"

"Is this the same writer who wrote the baby song you did on the
Orpheum Circuit?" I asked. "In 1925?"

"In 1925 this guy wasn't weaned yet," Fanny said. She loosened
the black, waxy cosmetic from her eyelashes and placed it carefully
in the soot-covered pan to be melted and used again. She was thinking very hard. "Let's see. . . . It was Blanche Merrill who wrote that
song! I remember it vaguely. It—how the hell do *you* know?"

Then I told her, for the first time, about working on the bill with
her, and how Mother insisted June and I catch her performances.
I told her about Mary Rose, too, and was glad she had forgotten.
She had forgotten the baby song also, but I hadn't. I sang it for
her, then and there, complete with gestures;

> Poor Little Moving Picture Baby,
> Poor little star that doesn't shine.
> I can't even get a job in a scene where there's a mob.
> I guess that they don't want a face like mine. . . .
> I'll take Baby Peggy's place, I'm told,
> When Baby Peggy gets too old,
> Poor Little Moving Picture Baby.

Fanny watched me with her mouth wide open. She had great
respect for a good memory. Then suddenly she came to life. "Get
somebody to take this all down in shorthand!" she screamed. "Go
get me a stenographer—we've won the case! I'll show those lawyers!
Trying to tell me he originated Baby Snooks!"

Fanny had started a painting of me before we left New York
and when we went on tour the unfinished picture went along. It
was Fanny's version of a Degas painting: the one where the model
is sitting with one leg up, drying herself with a towel. It wasn't an

easy pose to hold, and the kitchenette table I sat on left a lot to be desired. It was a gate-leg table and every time I took a deep breath it pinched me.

"Sit still!" Fanny would say. "How can I paint when you're squirming around like a whirling dervish?"

"If you had to sit here with your bottom getting pinched you'd squirm, too!" I replied.

"Look, kid," Fanny said, wiping the paint brush on her chest, "I'm the artist, you're the model, so shut up and sit still."

Fanny always cleaned her brushes on her chest. Her pajama tops had become so caked with paint she couldn't wear them, so now, she painted in just the bottoms. After a long session Fanny's chest was usually covered with streaks of burnt sienna, yellow ochre or cadmium blue. The chambermaid came in one day when Fanny had been working on the crimson background. She took one look at me with my upraised hands and one look at Fanny's chest and went screaming into the hall, "Help! Murder! The lady in 809 is killing the other one!"

Fanny painted water colors, too. They were mostly still lifes: a jug of paint brushes, a teapot and cup or one rose in a vase. Sometimes, after the show at night, Fanny would paint three or four. When they were finished she would soak them in the bathtub until they took on a diffused look. Other times she would rub them down with a dirty make-up towel to give them an oil effect.

She once rubbed a water color with what was left of a lox sandwich, and if smoked salmon hadn't been so expensive she would have used it more often. "Look at this texture, Gyp," she said, holding up the picture. "It's got a real Monet quality, hasn't it?" I didn't know enough about Monet to say one way or the other, but I had to admit it was interesting. Like an Easter egg that had gone wrong.

Mother wrote once a week. Her letters were brief and written with pencil on both sides of the paper, but the envelopes bulged with newspaper clippings and notes hurriedly scribbled on pieces of wrapping paper or grocery bags. Some of the newspaper clippings had nothing to do with Mother or me—a recipe for lemon whip tapioca, for instance, or a Winchell column without a mention of my name—but others were more newsy. The Minskys, I learned through one of the clippings, were in trouble. They had been forced to take the name burlesque off their marquee. The Minsky *Follies* replaced it. *Variety*, in a full-page story, said burlesque, under that name or any other name, was dead. "What Adah Isaacs Menken started Gypsy Rose Lee—and the Minskys—finished. And how!" On the margin, Mother had written, "Serves them right!" and "Thank God we're out of it, dear."

A two-inch ad was underlined by Mother with a red crayon. The ad read: "Artiste Wanted to Replace Gypsy Rose Lee in Ziegfeld Follies. Experience not necessary. Apply stage door Winter Garden Theatre 2:30 Friday."

The red crayon was Mother's only comment.

Since the robbery my insurance had been canceled. I didn't have much jewelry left, but Mother worried about what I did have. She worried about me being kidnaped, too. Most of the scribbled notes were warnings: "Be careful on the streets at night," and "Don't talk to strangers!" In one note she offered to send me the old money bag. "There's room in it for Fanny's jewelry, too," she added.

Fanny had tried to get insurance on her jewelry before we left New York. Besides her diamonds she had $450,000 worth of pearls. Fanny loved pearls. She knew real ones, too. She could walk into a restaurant and spot a string of pearls twenty-five feet away. "Japs," she'd say and most times she was right.

The insurance rate on her jewelry ran into the thousands and Fanny decided against it. I asked her why, since she didn't want to pay such a high premium, she hadn't put her jewelry in a vault while we were on tour. Fanny looked at me as though I were soft in the head. "Don't you know *anything* about pearls?" she said. "You gotta wear pearls, kid, or they'll die."

The jewelry was with us, every last bead of it, and each night when we left for the theatre we'd hide it someplace in the hotel suite. Fanny was a great believer in the purloined-letter trick. One of her favorite hiding places was under the pillow. "That's the first place they'd expect us to hide it," she would say. "Then they'd think nobody would be dope enough to hide it there so they won't look."

Other times she'd hide it in the oven, or under the bed or on a shelf in the closet. Fanny didn't trust hotel safes. It wasn't exactly the safe she distrusted. It was the clerks who had the keys to it. The first thing we'd do when we got home from the theatre was to look for the jewelry. Sometimes we'd forget where we hid it. The longer we had to look, the better Fanny would feel. "How can crooks find it," she'd say, "when we can't find it ourselves?"

After we'd had our night lunch, and our faces were covered with cold cream and our hair rolled up in curlers, Fanny would open the jewel box and begin to divide the pearls. A ring for me, a ring for her, a necklace for me, a necklace for her, a strand for me, a strand for her. Then, with $450,000 worth of pearls on our fingers, ears and necks, we'd turn off the lights and go to bed. "No damned pearl of mine is going to die on me," Fanny would say, as she rolled over and buried her face in the pillow.

The first I knew of Fanny's pharmaceutical trunk was when I complained of a headache one night at the theatre. Fanny brought me into her dressing room and opened the big H and M. There were four shelves in the trunk and every shelf was filled with bottles and boxes of pills and prescriptions and salves and ointments. Fanny told me she had a cure for anything and I believed her. "I've got cures for sicknesses," she said, "that haven't been invented yet."

She had pills to put you to sleep and pills to wake you up. Pills for expectant mothers and pills for those who didn't want to be. Headache pills, cold pills, laxatives, aspirin, codeine and stomach pills. Some of the bottles and boxes had dates on them going back five years or more. Pills had completely collapsed in other bottles and were now dispensed by Fanny as "powders." Pink pills had turned yellow. Others were stuck together in such a mess they wouldn't come out of the bottle. The boxes and bottles with question marks on them were those Fanny had forgotten the contents of, but that didn't stop her from handing them out.

Besides dispensing pills, Fanny also diagnosed illnesses. A few questions, a quick look at the tongue and the invariable query about the bowels and Fanny was ready to give her verdict. "You've got colitis, kid, and I've got just the stuff to cure it somewhere in my trunk."

Most times she was right. If Fanny said it was colitis, chances are it was colitis.

Fanny might have had a cure for body parasites in the trunk but I didn't have the nerve to ask her, although three days after we opened in St. Louis I knew I had them. I'd had them before and knew the best and quickest way to get rid of them was with blue ointment. Mother had always bought it for us though, and that day when I went into the drugstore in St. Louis I lost my courage. I looked at the druggist and gulped. No words would come. Suddenly, I remembered Chiquita. Holding up the chihuahua so the druggist could get a good look at her I said, "My little pet has lice. She's had them before and because her skin's so sensitive I can't use ordinary flea powder. I used something—oh, what was the name of that— could it have been—blue ointment?"

The druggist reached behind him and took a tube from the shelf. As he was wrapping it he said, "You'd better buy a bottle of Lysol, too, for that toilet backstage. Everyone in the show has been in with the same trouble."

Fanny never accepted dinner engagements when she was on the road. She liked to eat early and rest before the show. It was a nice habit, I decided, to get into. Most times we'd order dinner in our rooms. Then, while it was being prepared, I'd put on my body paint and glue on my brassière and pants, and by the time dinner was over the glue would be dry. But the dinner party we were invited to in St. Louis was one we accepted. The Stage Coach Ball in St. Louis was, we were told, one of the social events of the year. The men all wore pink hunting coats, the ladies, their loveliest gowns. Many of them went to the ball in a tallyho. Dinner parties were given before the ball by every important hostess in the city. Usually when we were invited to such an affair Fanny would say, "You go, kid, and tell me about it tomorrow." This was different. It was the pink hunting coats that intrigued her. "I have to get a load of those guys in the rented Guttenbergs," she said.

We started dressing early. Cocktails were being served at six and at a quarter of Fanny was still trying to decide which teeth to wear. She had three upper plates. One set was for the theatre;

Fanny called those her funny-face teeth. Another set was for eating; those she called her choppers. Her favorite set she called her Gentile teeth because the dentist who made them was Irish.

Sitting in front of the mirror, she tried one set after another. "I can't eat with the funny-face job, I can't make faces with the choppers and all I can do with the Gentile set is look pretty."

"Come on, Fanny," I said. "We'll be late."

"Look, Gyp, I happen to have a problem," Fanny replied evenly. "For you it's simple. All you have to do is glue on the pants and you're ready for anything."

She finally settled for the Gentile teeth and carefully placed the others in her petit-point evening bag. We made a delayed entrance at the party. As we stood in the doorway a hush fell. I'm sure neither Fanny nor I was what they expected. There wasn't a rhinestone to be seen on me and my white kid gloves came to above my elbows. Fanny, in her simple Mainbocher gown with two ropes of pearls, looked almost regal. She was by far the most chic woman in the room, and all the women knew it.

At dinner Fanny discreetly switched from her Gentile teeth to the choppers. After dinner she changed to the funny-face teeth and convulsed the party with a joke. Then, just before saying good night to the hostess, she switched back to the Gentile teeth for a pretty exit. On our way to the theatre Fanny stretched out, exhausted, in the limousine. "And you ask me," she said, "why I don't like to go to parties."

From St. Louis we played Pittsburgh, Cleveland and Kansas City, then two weeks of one nighters when we lived on the train and went for days, it seemed, without a bath. My goldfish died, one after the other, in Des Moines and I buried them in the alley outside the stage entrance. Fanny came to the funeral. "I never liked goldfish," she said, while I was digging the little hole in the ground, "but I'm sure as hell going to miss those two."

Indianapolis was a four-day stand. For the first time in over two weeks Fanny and I were to have our hotel trunks and the luxuries we had almost forgotten about, such as the hot plate, the Victrola and the hair drier. On the train we planned on the things we'd do when we hit town. First of all, there was the laundry to catch up on, the dogs would be bathed, we'd manicure our nails, wash our hair and rest.

Fanny had the rest, I didn't. The moment we got off the train the newspapermen grabbed me and for four days they didn't let go. Sally Rand was playing the Lyric Theatre, next door to ours. The stage doors faced each other in the alley. Joe Flynn and Sally's press agent had been busy working up a feud between us. I would have liked to oblige Joe, but I had never met Sally Rand. I hadn't even caught her act, and I couldn't think of a reason why I should feud with her. One of the newspapermen tried to supply the reason. Shoving a copy of his paper under my nose he said, "What do you think of that?"

To his disappointment I thought it was very good publicity. The story was a triple column on the front page. There were two pictures, one of Sally peeking out from behind her fan, and one of me peeking out from behind a parasol. The headline read: "Barely a Strip Separates Gypsy and Sally. What Will Happen if They Meet?"

Sally must have taken an earlier train than mine because there was a quote from her. When asked by the reporter what she thought was the secret of my success, Sally was alleged to have tapped her forehead and said, "Brains."

"And," I added, "a little something below."

The scheduled fued between us never came off. Sally was playing four shows a day and her press agent and Joe couldn't get together on the time. Besides, their idea for a picture of us wearing bathing suits in a boxing pose appealed as little to Sally as it did to me. Neither of us looked well in a bathing suit and we both knew it.

We met briefly, by mistake, and with no photographers around, in the stage alley. Then, on the closing night of the *Follies,* Sally came to visit me. She sneaked in through the stage door, a shawl over her head, a fur coat covering her to the ankles. Fanny had been dying to meet her, so when the doorman told me she was on her way to my dressing room, I hurried to tell Fanny. We were both there, waiting, when Sally tapped on the door. I suddenly remembered

the ad Mother sent me. Was Sally the replacement the Shuberts
had in mind? I tried to dismiss the thought, but it was in my mind
and I found it difficult to be as cordial as Sally was.

"I just caught part of the show," she said breathlessly, shedding
the coat and scarf. "It was lovely—really lovely." Her eyes traveled,
rather wistfully, I thought, to my costumes hanging on the wall.
"I loved your clothes. It must be interesting to wear so many. I get
awfully bored with nothing but fans and balloons."

Fanny introduced herself, while I cleared off a chair; then we all
sat and looked at one another. Sally's hair, now that the shawl was
removed, fell over her shoulders in golden ringlets. No one, un-
acquainted with false hair, would have known where the added
curls began. Her make-up was dead white with heavy blue eyeshadow and dark red lipstick. Her fingernails, as she snapped them
nervously, were dry looking with no polish. Flecks of white body
paint were buried under the cuticles.

"I had to give it up," she said.

"The balloons?" Fanny asked. "Or the fans?"

"No, Honey. The body paint. I really had to. It's so drying. Just
look what it's done to my hands. I'm like that all over."

There was a pause while Fanny and I considered this, then Sally
went on. "It wasn't easy giving it up. They tell me you can't tell
the difference from the front, with the dark blue spotlight and all,
but the first time I went on without it I just wanted to die. I never
felt so naked in all my life. Really, I'd rather be caught without my
fans. But if the Government needs it—"

"Needs what?" Fanny asked, leaning forward in her chair.

"The body paint," Sally explained. "There's something in it
they need to paint battleship bottoms."

The talk drifted back to balloons. I discovered one thing about
Sally Rand in those few minutes she was visiting; somehow, the
conversation gets around to Sally and her career and stays there.
"I have my balloons made to order," she said. "Heavy-duty rubber.
They cost me seventeen dollars and sixty-eight cents wholesale,
then I play a date like New Haven and those college boys sit in
the front rows and flick bent pins at them. Honest to God, someday

I'm going to have a baby and give it all up!"

"Where are you playing after Indianapolis?" I asked as offhand as I could.

"Paris," Sally replied, scrambling into her coat and scarf. "Paris, France. They want me to open a new fair there, a Congress of Fraternity or Equality or something."

That took a load off my mind, so our good-bys were friendlier.

"We're doing five shows today," Sally said while she disguised herself for the leap across the alley. "I guess all this publicity helped—both of us, that is."

Fanny was thoughtful after the door closed. She looked over at me, a peculiar expression on her face. "I don't get it," she said. "Of all the things you two dames might have done in the theatre, whatever started you taking off your clothes?"

"It's a long story," I replied a bit stiffly.

My replacement joined us in Columbus. She was tall, blonde and as beautiful as a bisque doll. Her name was Marion Martin. For seven years she had been a featured show girl at Joe Moss's Hollywood Night Club in New York. Mr. Moss, I'd heard, let her go with reservations. "Silly girl," Louis Sobel reported him as saying. "This could have been a life-time job."

Then, before I knew it, it was June 10 and my closing night with the *Follies* in Detroit. My train tickets to Hollywood were in my purse. The dogs waited patiently beside their carrying cases for the show to end. My luggage, all but my finale gown and make-up box, was packed. Fanny and I had adjoining dressing rooms at the Cass Theatre. Through my mirror I watched her rummaging around in the pharmaceutical trunk for a box of pills she assured me would ward off train sickness. "Lee Shubert gave them to me when I went to Europe," she was saying. Her voice, coming from the depths of the trunk had a muffled sound. "I took two of them when I got on the boat and went out like a light for five days."

It had been six years, I knew, since Fanny's last trip to Europe, but I swallowed the pills anyway. I wanted to go out like a light, too. I had hated saying good-by many times before in my life, but never as much as I hated saying good-by to Fanny and the Ziegfeld *Follies.* I felt as though I were saying good-by to an era. Everything

I knew and understood and loved seemed to be bound up in that dressing room. This place I was leaving was a theatre, a place where I belonged. My mother was there, June was there, Gordon, too, and the little boys in the act and all the countless chameleons and white mice and guinea pigs. I could close my eyes and see the gilded guns, and the patent-leather dancing shoes. I could hear the dogs barking and the baby pig squealing and Gussie honking, and over it all I could hear Mother telling me to be careful when I crossed the street and to pin my money to my underwear.

I remember vaguely doing the finale and saying good-by to everyone, my baggage being piled into a cab and the stage door closing behind me. Fanny went with me to the train. I was sitting at the window and looking out at her waving to me from the platform. I tried to wave back but my arm was too heavy, Fanny's face blurred and I felt myself falling, falling . . . and the pillow was cold and hard and damp with my tears. When I looked up again the lights of the station had gone. The sky, with its stars like flitter on a back drop seemed stagy and unreal.

I closed my eyes and along with the familiar noise of the train Mother seemed to be telling me again how lucky I was. "What a wonderful life you've had—the music, lights, applause—everything in the world a girl could ask for. . . ."

AFTERWORD

I'll never forget the day Mother began writing *Gypsy*: it was November 8th, 1952. I was seven, and Mother was thirty-eight, more or less. We were in Europe. Mother had come over to do her striptease/comedy act at the Palladium in London, and I had come along, as I always did, because she believed a child belonged with its mother. It was our first time abroad. When she closed at the Palladium, she decided to do some sightseeing. One year later, we had covered all Europe and most of North Africa. Along the way, Mother played twenty-five weeks in England, Germany and Scandinavia, and made a movie in Spain. She had also traded in her Cadillac for a Rolls Royce and picked up a Siamese cat in Barcelona. We had named him Gaudi, after the surrealist Spanish architect who had designed the building in which the cat was born.

We were on our way from Rome to Paris. Mother had chosen the alpine route because the weather reports were predicting dense fog along the Riviera.

We left Torino early in the morning for the Simplon pass into Switzerland. It was a beautiful fall day, mild enough for my kilt. Mother bought the national outfit for me in every country we visited, but few of them were comfortable. The lederhosen from Germany chafed, the wooden shoes from the Netherlands were actually medieval torture devices, the sequins kept falling off my bullfighter outfit, which was too tight in the crotch anyway, and my Norwegian sailor suit picked up all of Gaudi's hair. As long as it wasn't too cold, however, the kilt was great, especially for long drives. I've never understood, given their anatomical differences, why men wear pants and women skirts; logically it should be the other way around.

But I digress. The point is that when we began our day in Torino, it was sunny and mild; five hours later and six thousand feet higher, we were in the middle of a blizzard. The snow was falling so thickly I could barely see the front of the car. Mother was a great driver. She had driven everywhere and in every imaginable condition, and she almost got us through that pass. It might have been the new car, but I think it was really just a matter of the snow. There was so much of it. Finally, we just couldn't go any farther. Nothing dramatic happened. One moment we were creeping ahead, the next the car just stopped. Mother tried backing up and rocking the car back and forth, but nothing helped. We had already passed the summit, and during lulls in the storm we could actually see a village way down in the valley below us.

We got out to survey the damage. The wheels were sunk in deep, ice-lined ruts. Mother thought for a second.

"Get me Gaudi's bidet," she directed me sharply.

Only Mother could have a cat that trouped a bidet. It was, however, much less outrageous than it sounds. Every hotel room in Europe is furnished with a bidet. In better hotels, it's usually porcelain and equipped with running water. Mother, however, hated spending money on ephemeral luxuries like first-, or even second-class hotels, so we often stayed in *pensions* where the bidet was simply a small enamel basin on a stand. "The perfect size," Mother noticed when we got Gaudi, "for behind the front seat of the Rolls." So she "liberated" one to use as his traveling sand box.

I got the bidet out of the car and started to empty it. "Oh my God, no!" Mother shouted, stopping me just in time. "Just give it to me, darling."

Carefully, she emptied it in front of the rear wheels and tried to drive out of the ruts, but they were too deep and too slick. Then she tried using the bidet as a shovel, but the ice was too hard. As a last resort, she tried to break up the ice with my toy pistol, but it was useless.

We got back in the car, shivering from the cold. "They're bound to check the pass before nightfall," she said confidently, "especially in this kind of weather. Why, people must get stuck in this pass all the time. We'll just have to wait for them to find us. God only knows how long that may take, so we'd better conserve our gas. We're almost down to a quarter of a tank as it is. As soon as we're warm, we'll bundle up and turn off the engine. Then when it gets too cold, we'll start it up again." She opened her window a crack. "And be sure there's a window open all the time."

"Why?" I asked, horrified at the idea of letting cold air in the car.

"Because we'll asphyxiate ourselves if we don't." I didn't know what the word meant, but clearly we didn't want it happening to us.

Mother had picked up a couple of car blankets in Scotland, and a few minutes later we wrapped them around us and turned the engine off. The silence was total, except for an occasional creak from the car's engine as it cooled. It was eerie, watching the snow fall around us.

Mother broke the silence. "I was stuck in a blizzard like this many years ago, when I was just a little bit older than you. Mother and I..."

"How old were you?"

"Twelve...fourteen. It's not important. Now, where was I? I do wish you wouldn't interrupt; it makes me lose my whole train of thought. Oh, yes. Mother and I were headed home for Seattle. June had just run away, and all the little boys in the act had followed her. Except for Henry, bless his heart. He knew that neither Mother nor I could drive, and he wouldn't leave us stranded. What a sweet oaf he was. Huge, and even clumsier than me, but he was determined to be a dancer.

"At any rate, we were in Kansas, as I remember, when it started to snow. It was already dark, and Henry wanted to stop for the night, but Mother wouldn't let him. She said we didn't have enough money for a hotel room.

"It was a horrible night. Gradually the snow tapered off, and then it got bitter, bitter cold. And we didn't have any heater in the car."

"You didn't? How come?"

"Heaters were very expensive in those days. So there we were, out in the middle of nowhere, when suddenly there's this snap from under the car." Mother clapped her hands together for emphasis. "And the next thing I know we're sliding sideways down the road, right into a snow drift that was ten feet high if it was an inch.

"It was only by the grace of God that no one was hurt. Poor Henry. He couldn't believe he'd had an accident. Later we found out that the steering knuckle had cracked, or something like that, so it really wasn't his fault, but at the time he felt terrible."

"What did you do?"

"Well, we had a shovel in the car, and Henry and I took turns trying to dig us out, but it was no use. The snow was so heavy I could barely lift the shovel, and we were leaning so precariously against the snow bank that we weren't even sure digging was such a good idea. So after a while, Henry decided to go for help.

"You can't imagine how courageous that was. It was pitch black out, we were in the middle of nowhere, the cold was beyond belief, and all he had was this threadbare old overcoat. Mother tried to get him to wrap up in the blanket he wore in the car, but he wouldn't take it. He told her that the walking would keep him warm and that we'd need it more, sitting in the car."

It occurred to me that in telling me this Mother was also giving me a lesson in my responsibilities as a man. I looked out of my window, over the edge of the road, at the village far below. Lights were coming on in the deepening dusk. Walking down to it didn't seem an impossible or especially dangerous task. Cold, yes, especially in my kilt. But not impossible.

"Would you like me to go down to the town and bring back help?" I asked.

"No, darling." Mother smiled. "I don't think that will be necessary. Somebody's bound to be through before long."

Relieved that I was spared having to go out into the cold, I pulled my blanket around me. "What happened next?"

"We watched Henry trudge off until he disappeared in the night, then we turned off our headlights and waited. I remember feeling frightened and alone, even though Mother was sitting in the front seat with the dogs." I wanted to ask about the dogs, but there was something in her tone that stopped me from interrupting.

"That's when I first heard them, sniffing around the car. The dogs heard them, too, and growled, but Mother held them tight and they stopped..."

She was so engrossed in telling me the story, and I in hearing it, that neither of us were aware of the monster outside the car until he knocked on Mother's window. I call him a monster because he looked like one, covered from head to toe in arctic gear, complete with goggles and some kind of breathing apparatus that made him look like an anteater with a short snout.

"Oh, thank God you're here!" Mother exclaimed, rolling down the window. "We're stuck. We can't move. Here. I'll show you." She started to get out of the car, but he motioned her to stay put. Then, without so much as a word, he turned and headed down the mountain on his snowshoes.

"Well, it's only a question of time now," Mother said, starting the car. "Let's treat ourselves to some heat."

I wondered how she *knew* that he would come back, but only for a moment. I was far more curious about Henry and the sniffing. "What happened?" I asked. "And what was sniffing outside the car?"

"They were wolves," she said dramatically, "and the more they sniffed, the bolder they got. Soon they were standing up against the car, sniffing and scratching at the windows and talking to each other with these little cries. Mother and I didn't say a word, and all I could think about was poor Henry, out there all alone."

"Would the wolves have eaten him?"

She nodded. "But they didn't, thank God, and a little while later he was back with help."

"What about the wolves?"

"The men with Henry had a gun, and they used it to frighten them away."

"What if wolves eat that man before he tells people we're here?"

"That won't happen," she said, smiling. "There are no wolves around here."

I guess she was right because an hour or so later, a black Renault with four men in it arrived from the village and rescued us.

• • •

That was the first story from her childhood that I remember Mother telling me, but it certainly wasn't the last. We spent most of the next four years trouping around the country with Mother's act or in summer stock. Mother preferred traveling by car, so we drove virtually everywhere, often in long two- and three-day stretches that would take us from one part of the country to another. But short trip or long, Mother always entertained me with the stories of her childhood, the stories that eventually became *Gypsy*.

They were the fairy tales of my childhood. I heard them over and over again, and I hung on every word. So I noticed, of course, every time Mother changed them. At first I corrected her "mistakes," but she quickly put an end to that. Historical accuracy was much less important to her than a good punch line. She was, after all, an entertainer first and a writer second.

Given her lack of a formal education, it's amazing that she was a writer at all. She always credited George Davis with getting her started. Few today would recognize Davis's name, but for many years he played an important offstage role in the New York literary scene. Mother never told me much about him, but Janet Flanner, who wrote *The New Yorker*'s "Letter from Paris" for over forty years and knew Davis well, describes him in her introduction to *Paris Was Yesterday* as "...a sulky, ultrasensitive, brilliant character and a deadly wit who developed into the...fiction editor of *Harper's Bazaar*...where he was the first to put serious fiction into a fashion magazine and helped develop two new, amazing young American writers, Carson McCullers and Truman Capote."

He was also, I gather, an eccentric, antiques-loving spendthrift who was always struggling to make his financial ends meet. Thus in 1940, when he was evicted from his Manhattan apartment, he rented a magnificent, turn-of-the-century house on Middagh Street in Brooklyn. Because it was even more expensive than the apartment, he took in boarders. What boarders! At one time or another W. H. Auden, Benjamin Britten, Oliver Smith, Paul and Jane Bowles, and Gypsy Rose Lee lived in the house. All that talent under one roof—and all that temperament. Everyone credits Auden for making it work. He collected the rent and food money, sat at the head of the long table where dinner was served every night by an underpaid but adequate cook, and insisted on rules that were conducive to work. When company was invited to dinner, for example, they were told ahead of time that they were expected to leave promptly at 11:00 p.m. Auden's rules and Davis's prompting clearly worked for Mother. She wrote her first book, *The G-String Murders*, while living on Middagh Street, and went on to write another book, two plays, and over a dozen articles before starting *Gypsy*.

She began the actual writing of *Gypsy* in February 1956, during a four-week layoff between closing *Twentieth Century* at the Palm Beach Playhouse and opening her act at the Sans Souci Hotel in Miami Beach. Rather than drive to New York and back for a few weeks at home, she checked us into a cheap efficiency motel, rented a typewriter, and went to work. For the entire month our routine never varied. She'd get us up at the shriek of dawn, we'd have breakfast, and then she'd send me off with my lunch to spend the day at the local fishing pier while she worked. Late in the afternoon I'd come home, she'd let me read her day's output and we'd discuss it while she made dinner, then we'd watch a little TV and go to bed. It was a great month. I liked my days on the pier, even though I didn't catch one lousy fish, and Mother was very productive. On the day we left for Miami Beach she wrote in her date book, "Well, I have over 200 pages. They're overwritten and repetitious, but I'm on my way…"

When we returned home from Miami Beach, Mother devoted herself to the book with the kind of obsessive intensity that marked everything that she did. She set up a work area in her bedroom that she nicknamed, most appropriately, the "snake pit" and began work at dawn, every day. She never took any phone calls, and she rarely ate lunch, subsisting on a diet of cigarettes and tea, which she drank with cream and sugar. Aside from a short break around midday to return any phone calls that might have come in, she worked straight through until five o'clock or so. Then she'd buzz the cook on the intercom to start dinner and buzz me to come up to her room for our evening visit. If she had finished a scene, she'd give it to me to read; otherwise we'd discuss my day at school or other trivia until 5:30 when the maid would serve dinner on a tray. After dinner, she'd watch a couple of hours of television to unwind, and she'd be asleep by nine.

Except for a one week interruption to do the "U.S. Steel Hour" on television and a five-week summer stock tour with *Fancy Meeting You Again*, she sustained this schedule without a break until December 26th, when she finished the book. She used to say *Gypsy* took her nine months and was a much more difficult pregnancy than having me.

Mother's powers of concentration were phenomenal. Nothing interfered with her work. That is until it began getting warm, when she opened her windows and discovered that a singer had moved into the neighborhood. She practiced her scales all day long, and it drove Mother crazy. "Do-re-mi-fa-sol-la-ti-do. Do-re-mi-fa-sol-la-ti-do." Over and over again. She called the police, but they couldn't do anything. Or wouldn't. So Mother and her secretary made a tape recording of them both singing scales together. Thirty minutes of a very off-key duet. And from then on whenever the woman began practicing, Mother put the tape recorder on the windowsill and let it rip. Full blast. It wasn't long before the police were knocking on our door. Mother's response was classic: She looked the cop right in the eye, said "You found me, now find her!" And slammed the door in his face. Either he did or the singer moved, because the neighborhood was blissfully quiet for the rest of the summer.

Gypsy was first published in May 1957, and it was an immediate success. The critics liked it, it was reprinted in England and Italy, excerpts appeared in *Harper's* and *Town & Country*, Mother got a lot of publicity, and it made *The New York Times* best-seller list.

Gypsy's major success, however, came when it was translated into one of Broadway's greatest musicals by Arthur Laurents, Jule Styne, and Stephen Sondheim. It opened at the Broadway Theatre on May 21, 1959, starring Ethel Merman as my grandmother, Rose. I was Mother's escort that night, and I tell what it was like in my book *Gypsy & Me: At Home and on the Road with Gypsy Rose Lee.*

When we arrived at the theater, the excitement in the air was palpable. The audience was buzzing with anticipation, as though it knew that the show would be a smash. It was infectious, and Mother glowed as we walked down the aisle to our seats. She looked wonderful that night. She was wearing a long black silk taffeta skirt belted at the waist, a white silk blouse, her sable jacket, and antique diamond pendant earrings. It was a simple outfit, but stunning, and she was far more elegant than the overdressed and overjeweled matrons who stared at us as we passed.

While waiting for the house lights to dim, I noticed that people all over the theater were looking in our direction, and I realized that Mother was the most important person in the theater that night. She was the reason that everyone else was there. She was the show.

During the overture, which is a powerful and stirring piece of music, tiny lights above the stage flashed "Gypsy Rose Lee." I had often seen Mother's name in lights, but never like this. I got chills and thought, "All this is about my mother." I felt so proud. I grabbed her hand and squeezed it. She squeezed back, and we sat holding hands for much of the first act.

In the middle of the first act, Louise sits alone in a tight spotlight at the corner of the otherwise darkened stage and sings a song to a baby lamb she has just received for her birthday. It is a beautiful but melancholy song, filled with the loneliness of an adolescent girl. As I watched and listened, I remembered the many stories that Mother used to tell me to help her stay awake as we drove through the night from date to date. She had always tried to keep the stories light and funny, but her unhappiness as a young girl came through nonetheless, and occasionally we had even discussed how difficult it had been. I looked up at her and saw a tear rolling down her cheek. She, too, was remembering.

At intermission, Mother and I went into the lobby so she could have a cigarette. People kept congratulating her, and while she modestly directed their praise to the creators of the show, her eyes sparkled, and I knew how proud she felt.

When the play was over, the audience gave the cast a standing ovation and then began calling "Author, Author!" I thought they wanted Mother and nudged her, but she knew better.

She didn't need to take a bow. She had walked into the theater a famous personality; she was going to leave it a legend.

—Erik Lee Preminger